MW00426884

PRAISE FOR *UNCONFORMED TO THE AGE*

"For Tracey Rowland, the real 'clericalism' enervating the Church is a bureaucratic pseudo-Christianity characterized by endless meetings, documents, and discussions—what she calls 'Catholic Inc.' Dedicating this book to 'the young priests and religious who have offered their lives in the service of something other than a multinational bureaucracy,' Rowland takes Catholics stuck in the malaise of Catholic Inc. by the scruff of the neck and sets them before their forgotten true love: Jesus Christ. *Unconformed to the Age* reminds us that the Church is Christ's bride and not an NGO, something we are given rather than something we create, a theological reality before a sociological one. These essays will enlighten minds, stimulate contemplation, and revitalize vocations. Seldom are prophetic voices so theologically informed."

Fr. Vincent L. Strand, S.J.
Catholic University of America

———————•———————

"The Apostle Paul tells us, 'Do not be conformed to this age, but be transformed by the renewal of your mind' (Rom 12:2). In this volume of essays, Tracey Rowland provides a clarion call for the renewal of our mind to know and love the Church—and not try to conform the Church to the dictates of the present *Zeitgeist*."

Fr. Andrew Hofer, O.P.
Dominican House of Studies

———————•———————

"As one may expect of a Ratzinger Prize awardee, with unequalled precision Tracey Rowland shares with the reader critical ecclesiological fault lines as they have developed over the past seventy years. Rowland points to the real danger of the Church mutating into a faceless bureaucracy. Catholics must master the transition from a pre-Vatican II view of the Church as hierarchy, to understanding her foremost as the Church from the Cross and the side of Jesus Christ. From the Eucharist and from the altar she must be the Church ever afresh—as *Communio* with the Lord and the Saints. Rowland ably demonstrates that while the human lens may change, the Church remains actually selfsame. *Unconformed to the Age* is theological mystagogy! This is a most necessary, healing, and uplifting book!"

Fr. Emery de Gaál
Mundelein Seminary

"In this book, the eminent Ratzingerian scholar Tracey Rowland addresses central topics related to ecclesiology, old and new. She demonstrates that Tradition is in our Catholic DNA, and she does it with both erudition and elegant simplicity, which makes her a disciple of Joseph Ratzinger, in content and even in style. This is a rich and keenly insightful book that will gain the attention of faraway readers, like me, a Byzantine Catholic delighted to read such a necessary mysteric Theology."

Alin Tat
Babeș-Bolyai University

———————●———————

"With her new book, Tracey Rowland confirms her position as one of the first-ranking Catholic theologians in the world. As with her previous publications, she demonstrates an impeccable ear for hearing which theological issues are central to our current debates. This book is grounded in the conviction that the Catholic Church is the salt and light of the world; everything that happens in the Church has a direct impact on the course of human history. Rowland emphasizes that the Church is always called to respond to human history and culture with the transforming light of the Gospel and the supernatural power of Christ's saving grace. The reader can recognize in this book familiar traits of Rowland's writing: fidelity to the Magisterium of the Church combined with the courage to ask difficult questions, impeccable theological scholarship combined with a broad cultural erudition, historical analysis of discussed issues combined with the proper judgment. This book should become an obligatory reading for students of ecclesiology."

Fr. Jarosław Kupczak, O.P.
Pontifical University of John Paul II

RENEWAL WITHIN TRADITION

SERIES EDITOR: MATTHEW LEVERING

Matthew Levering is the James N. and Mary D. Perry Jr. Chair of Theology at Mundelein Seminary. Levering is the author or editor of over thirty books. He serves as coeditor of the journals *Nova et Vetera* and the *International Journal of Systematic Theology*.

ABOUT THE SERIES

Catholic theology reflects upon the content of divine revelation as interpreted and handed down in the Church, but today Catholic theologians often find the scriptural and dogmatic past to be alien territory. The Renewal within Tradition Series undertakes to reform and reinvigorate contemporary theology from within the tradition, with St. Thomas Aquinas as a central exemplar. As part of its purpose, the series reunites the streams of Catholic theology that, prior to the Council, separated into neo-scholastic and *nouvelle theologie* modes. The biblical, historical-critical, patristic, liturgical, and ecumenical emphases of the Ressourcement movement need the dogmatic, philosophical, scientific, and traditioned enquiries of Thomism, and vice versa. Renewal within Tradition challenges the regnant forms of theological liberalism that, by dissolving the cognitive content of the gospel, impede believers from knowing the love of Christ.

PUBLISHED OR FORTHCOMING

Reading the Sermons of Thomas Aquinas: A Beginner's Guide
Randall B. Smith

The Culture of the Incarnation: Essays in Catholic Theology
Tracey Rowland

Self-Gift: Humanae Vitae *and the Thought of John Paul II*
Janet E. Smith

On Love and Virtue: Theological Essays
Michael S. Sherwin, O.P.

UNCONFORMED TO THE AGE

Unconformed to the Age

Essays in Catholic Ecclesiology

Tracey Rowland

EMMAUS
ACADEMIC

Steubenville, Ohio
www.emmausacademic.com

EMMAUS
A C A D E M I C

Steubenville, Ohio
www.emmausacademic.com
A Division of The St. Paul Center for Biblical Theology
Editor-in-Chief: Scott Hahn
1380 University Blvd.
Steubenville, Ohio 43952

Library of Congress Cataloging-in-Publication Data applied for.
ISBNs: 978-1-64585-398-5 hc | 978-1-64585-399-2 pb | 978-1-64585-400-5 eb

Cover design and layout by Allison Merrick.
Cover image from Matthias Church in Budapest, Hungary

For the young priests and religious who have offered their lives in the service of something other than a multinational bureaucracy.

Table of Contents

Acknowledgments

My thanks are due to Matthew Levering, Chris Erickson, and the other members of the Emmaus Academic team for making this collection possible. I am also grateful to the editor of *The Thomist*, Rev. Andrew Hofer, O.P., for his permission to republish the essay from the April 2023 special edition of *The Thomist* on the concept of synodality, as well as to the authorities at Wipf and Stock for their permission to republish the essays on "Ecclesiology in the Third Millennium" and "Pneumatology in the Third Millennium," already published in their *Theology in the Third Millennium* series.

As a member of the editorial board of *Communio: International Catholic Review* (the English language edition), I am delighted to place a couple of my *Communio* articles touching on the field of ecclesiology into this collection. And finally, I wish to acknowledge that the essay on "Febronianism" was first published by *Catholic World Report*, and an earlier version of the "Catholic Education and the Bureaucratic Usurpation of Grace" essay was first published in the journal *Solidarity* of the University of Notre Dame (Australia). The essay on the theology of the Cross was composed as a contribution to a conference celebrating the 300th anniversary of the foundation of the Passionist Order of St. Paul of the Cross (1694–1775).

The collection is dedicated to the young priests and religious who understand that the Church is the Body of Christ, a sacramental communion, and who often find themselves on the front lines in the battles against the darkness of the powers and the principalities, the spiritual wickedness in heavenly realms, as St. Paul well understood.

TRACEY ROWLAND
Feast of St. Margaret of Hungary 2024

Preface

This collection of essays is a kind of sinfonietta on the theme of ecclesiology. Recurring melodies concern treating the Church as a secular corporation, applying business management and other social theories to the governance of the Church, separating the work of the Holy Spirit from the revelation of Christ, confusing the discernment of spirits with a debate about feelings, and the occlusion of the Cross from its central position in the life of the Church. There is something of an antithetical juxtaposition of the Church understood as the Body and Bride of Christ, and the Church understood as Catholic Inc. dispensing philanthropy.

The Cambridge historian Richard Rex noted the first great crisis in Christianity was over the nature of the Trinity, especially over the nature of Christ, hence the early Christological heresies. The second great crisis, associated with the Reformation, was over the nature of the Church. This entailed the Protestant attack on sacramentality and the sacred hierarchy. The third great crisis, the one we are enduring today, is over the nature of the human person. Here the concrete issues revolve around sexual difference: does the difference between masculinity and femininity have any theological significance?

This overview of the history of ecclesial crises is very perceptive but one might add that within the Catholic Church today the crisis is not confined to matters of anthropology. Rather, a perfect storm has been building across the various branches of theology. In some cases, the crisis has been created because elements of Catholic intellectual tradition that should exist in a symbiotic relationship have been de-coupled from one another and left in a kind of free-floating state. For example, moral theology has been de-coupled from dogmatic theology. Quite simply, the field of fundamental theology that undergirds all other branches of Catholic theology has been an intellectual battle zone for the past half century. There is no common agreement within the Catholic theological academies over such "building blocks" as the relationship between nature and grace, faith and reason, history and ontology, or Scripture and Tradition and the principles that ought to govern scriptural exegesis. Not only are the relationships a subject of academic debate but the individual concepts themselves are not understood in the same way across Catholic scholarship. There is, for example, no common agreement about key concepts like "grace," "sacrament," "tradition" and even "priesthood." Notions like understanding a priest as "*alter Christus*" (another Christ) are accepted by some but rejected by others. Some scholars believe that priesthood entails an ontological change in the recipient of the sacrament, while others believe this idea is medieval nonsense. Some scholars read the Scriptures through the lens of contemporary social theories, such as Critical Theory or a wide variety of feminist theories, while others accept the teaching in *The Interpretation of the Bible in the Church* (1993), a publication of the Pontifical Biblical Commission, that is expressly critical of the employment of Marxist and feminist social theories.

Amidst so much dissension, Pope Francis has fostered a series of synods where proponents of alternative theological visions and fundamental principles can present their case. These meetings, badged an exercise in "synodality," are unprecedented in the life of the Church. While many synods occurred over the centuries, only bishops, scholars, and some academic authorities in the field under discussion were invited to attend. The contemporary form of synods, however, includes lay members who are hostile to magisterial teachings. For some, simply being on the Church's payroll is a sufficient criterion for inclusion in the meetings. This is unprecedented and it has occurred notwithstanding that two documents of the International Theological Commission (ITC)—Sensus Fidei *in the Life of the Church* (2014) and *Synodality in the Life and Mission of the Church* (2018)—offered criteria that needed to be satisfied before any lay person could be thought to possess the *sensus fidei* (sense of the faith). (See appendix 1 in this collection.) In both documents, fidelity to magisterial teaching is necessary because the Church is completely different from a debating society. In the words of Hans Maier, there is an analogy between what constitutional lawyers call a *bloc incontestables* (a block of incontestable ideas or propositions), which set the boundaries for any debate about constitutional law, and what theologians call the deposit of faith or teachings of Jesus Christ, which set the boundaries for theological discussions. Never before in ecclesial history have individuals been invited to offer their opinions based on nothing more reliable than their feelings and never before have mere feelings (marketed as the promptings of the Holy Spirit) been allowed to trump Scripture and Tradition.

A significant sociological development over the past half century has been employing lay Catholics in Church agencies, schools, universities, and hospitals. As vocations to religious life plummeted after the 1960s, a new generation of lay Catholics replaced religious in managing ecclesial institutions. Simultaneously, many such institutions began to receive funding from secular governments. This development is most pronounced is Germany. Statistics from 2022 show the Catholic Church in Germany employs approximately six hundred and fifty thousand people. One hundred and fifty thousand work directly in the Church in pastoral positions and administration, and this includes clergy. Five hundred thousand work in other ecclesial institutions, such as schools and hospitals. The Catholic Church in Germany has approximately twenty-two million believers, of which approximately 1.2 million attend services on Sundays (sometimes in the form of a prayer service when there is no priest). The *Frankfurter Allgemeine Zeitung* recently reported a survey conducted among Catholics and Evangelical Protestants. In both denominations, the percentage of people who believe that "God revealed himself in the person of Jesus of Nazareth" is approximately 30 percent. However, in both denominations, the blessing of homosexual couples is accepted or supported by approximately 85 percent. Furthermore, in 2022 a record 522,821 Catholics formally left the Church in Germany.

The German *Synodale Weg* (Synodal Path) was an epiphenomenal manifestation of this situation. While hundreds of thousands of people are employed by the Church in Germany because of government funding through the *Kirchensteuer* system of taxation, their employment is not synonymous with Catholic belief and practice. A significant number of Germans identifying as "Catholics" have trouble affirming a belief in Christ's divinity, let alone the many other less central elements in Catholic intellectual tradition. It is difficult to understand how inviting such people to national talkfests will resolve this crisis in faith and belief.

One explanation for the spiritual disaster that is Catholic Germany is that the immediate post World War II generation needed a narrative to explain how the Nazi regime could have survived for over a decade and how the holocaust could have occurred at the hands of German officers. The narrative that many accepted, especially in the immediate post-war generation, was provided by the Critical Theory of the Frankfurt School that was hostile to concepts like objective truth and social hierarchy. When Critical Theory is applied to an analysis of ecclesial governance it fosters the deconstruction of the sacred hierarchy. It "de-mythologizes" the papacy, the priesthood, and the episcopacy, and it promotes a democratization of the Church in the direction of congregationalism. These ideas were not only popular in Germany but in the Netherlands and Belgium as well. They have also spread to other countries through graduates of theology academies in Germany, the Netherlands, and Belgium, especially Germany and Belgium. It is a historical fact that every single intellectual leader of the liberation theology movement (regarded as a quintessentially Latin American movement) obtained his doctorate from European (mostly German and Belgium) universities. Quite simply, liberation theology was "made in Germany!"

Another German phenomenon is the influence of Immanuel Kant. Kant wanted to separate theology from philosophy, marginalize the theology thus separated, and then defend the Christian moral tradition by reference to reason alone uncontaminated by theological principles. This led to what German-speaking theologians call "moralism"—a presentation of the Christian faith as a moral code. While Catholic faith includes moral theology, moral theology is not the end or purpose of the Christian life. The end or purpose of Christian life is participation in the life and love of the Holy Trinity. The Catholic "moral code," so to speak, is one element in the means to achieve this—it is a means, not an end.

The research of the sociologist Julie Pagis on the leaders of the student protest movements in 1968 concludes that many of the students who became Marxists were brought up in Christian families. Significantly, the hallmark of such families was that Christianity was presented to the children as a moral code. One might say that the student rebels were brought up on a Kantian kind of Christianity, even if they were baptized Catholics. Once they arrived at university, they retained the desire to be moral people but preferred the morality of Marxism with its emphasis on liberating "victims of social oppression" to the morality of the Church. The availability of the contraceptive pill lured the generation of 1968 away from Christian moral theology.

One result was that many middle-class Catholics absorbed elements of Marxist social theory into their intellectual frameworks, while ignoring the teaching of the Church on matters pertaining to sexual morality. This development was a central theme in the Italian philosopher Augusto del Noce's works. Del Noce understood that the Marxism of the "New Left," typified by people like Antonio Gramsci and the social theorists of the Frankfurt school, "reaches a much deeper form of irreligiosity than [a simple] atheistic negation, and in this form it allies itself with the bourgeois-secular spirit pushed to its final conclusion."[1] In short, del Noce's insight was that contemporary liberal Catholicism is built upon an alliance of the bourgeois-secular

---

[1] Augusto del Noce, *The Age of Secularization* (Montreal: McGill-Queen's University Press, 2017), 242.

spirit, especially the interest in upward social mobility, with forms of "New Left" Marxism. It is logical, therefore, that attacks on the tradition of moral theology, and especially the moral theology of St. John Paul II, from scholars (predominately clerics) who identify as "Catholic" almost always appeals to social sciences and a corresponding diminution of the authority of Sacred Scripture.

This influence of the alliance of the bourgeois-secular spirit with currents of New Left Marxism within Catholic academies and within Catholic families and Catholic agencies has led African Catholic leaders to lament that first-world Catholics (Catholics in Western Europe and the Anglosphere) have become syncretists. In other words, legitimate elements of the Catholic faith have become entangled with a cocktail of intellectual ideas absorbed from hostile traditions. This syncretism, which represents a form of idolatry, is a significant cause for the dismally low rates of participation in the sacramental life of the Church and the equally dismal numbers of youth entering the priesthood and religious life in first-world countries. The general African attitude is "by their fruits you shall know them," and the crops, so to speak, in places like Germany and Belgium are almost complete failures. There is something sterile about liberal, German Catholicism.

Another way to look at the problem is to say that the archetypically German syncretism aligns itself, consciously or unconsciously, to a form of humanism described by Gottlieb Söhngen as a *humanism contra crucem*:[2] a humanism that avoids asceticism and is wary of self-sacrificial love; a humanism that wants to steer clear of the Cross. The essay in this collection that was delivered to celebrate the anniversary of the foundation of the Passionist Order addresses this issue.

Lest I stand accused of being unfair to German Catholics, many essays in this collection show that I regard Joseph Ratzinger and other Germans in his intellectual circle, such as the above-mentioned Gottlieb Söhngen, as Church doctors who offered an accurate diagnosis of the spiritual pathologies underlying the contemporary crisis. In so many ways Ratzinger found himself in the epicenter of the storm of contemporary fundamental theology. His occasional addresses, homilies, and essays can be pieced together to create both a pathology report on the implosion of the Catholic faith in Europe and a road map out of the labyrinth created by a couple centuries of German attempts to improve human life without recourse to God.

In a homily delivered in 1959, a young Fr. Joseph Ratzinger described

---

2   Gottlieb Söhngen, *Humanität und Christentum* (Essen: Verlagsgesellschaft Augustin Wibbelt, 1946), 48.

the first Christmas Day as the "winter solstice of world history." Christ is something more than another moral teacher or celebrity philanthropist, and his Church—including the priesthood, the Petrine office, and the episcopacy—is a sacred institution, not another multinational welfare agency. As the Catechism says, echoing *Lumen Gentium* §3,

> The Church is born primarily of Christ's total self-giving for our salvation, anticipated in the institution of the Eucharist and fulfilled on the Cross. "The origin and growth of the Church are symbolized by the blood and water which flowed form the open side of the crucified Jesus." "For it was from the side of Christ as he slept the sleep of death upon the cross that there came forth the 'wondrous sacrament of the whole Church.'" As Eve was formed from the sleeping Adam's side, so the Church was born from the pierced heart of Christ hanging dead on the cross. (CCC, §766)

The essays in this collection seek to affirm this teaching.

TRACEY ROWLAND

CHAPTER 1

Ecclesiology at the Beginning of the Third Millennium[1]

Since its foundation in 1817, the Faculty of Roman-Catholic Theology of the University of Tübingen has given rise to a number of important Catholic theologians. Among these were Johann Sebastian von Drey and Johann Adam Möhler in the nineteenth century, and more recently Cardinal Walter Kasper and to some degree his nemesis Joseph Ratzinger (Benedict XVI). So much that has happened in Catholic ecclesiology over the past two centuries can be traced back to Tübingen scholarship. Even scholars prominent in ecclesiology, who were never students or professors in Swabia, are cited as heirs to the Tübingen legacy or described as people running on parallel lines. Most notable among these are St. John Henry Newman, Henri de Lubac, S.J., Yves Congar, O.P., Louis Bouyer, and Hans Urs von Balthasar. Newman reached similar conclusions to Möhler about the role of tradition in the life of the Church, de Lubac[2] received the Tübingen patrimony via Maurice Blondel and Georges Goyau, and Congar credited Möhler with placing an accent on the primacy of the Church's supernatural ontology, and with understanding that the whole ecclesial community is an organ of tradition. Bouyer directly engaged the ideas of Tübingen scholars in his ecclesiological work *The Church of God: Body of Christ and Temple of the Spirit*, and Balthasar was influenced by Möhler's ecclesiological masterpiece

---

[1] This essay was first published in Kevin Wagner, et. al. (eds); *Ecclesiology at the Beginning of the Third Millennium* (Eugene, OR: Pickwick Publications, 2019). Used with permission.

[2] Author of three ecclesiological works: *Catholicisme* (1938), *Méditation sur l'Église* (1953), and *Les églises particulières dans l'Église universelle, suive de La maternité de l'église* (1971).

published in English as *Unity in the Church, or, the Principle of Catholicism*.[3] In short, most roads in Catholic ecclesiology at the beginning of the third millennium start either in Swabia or in Newman's study in Oxfordshire.

In a "state of the question" style chapter, there are at least three possible ways of proceeding: first, one can trawl through the magisterial documents; second, one can trawl through the publications of the big names; and third, one can examine the concrete issues that arose. This chapter will ambitiously attempt all three, although priority will be given to the magisterial teaching as a foundation for understanding the contemporary issues.

In the twilight years of the second millennium, the most significant of the magisterial documents for the field of ecclesiology was Pope Pius XII's encyclical *Mystici Corporis Christi* (1943). This document affirmed the Pauline teaching that the Church is the mystical body of Christ. In its introduction, Pius XII stated there were three wrong approaches to ecclesiology: 1) A false rationalism which ridicules anything which transcends human genius. According to this mentality the Church is merely a human institution; there is nothing supernatural about it. Its ecclesial offices, including the papacy and the college of bishops, are mere human artifacts. 2) Popular naturalism, which views the Church as nothing but a juridical and social union. Its conclusions are almost identical to those of the rationalists, and likewise occludes the supernatural dimension of the Church. 3) A "false mysticism" that "attempts to eliminate the immovable frontier that separates creatures from their creator."[4]

In emphasizing that the Church is the mystical body of Christ, Pius XII affirmed the accent on the supernatural which was strong in Tübingen ecclesiology and in the works of St. John Henry Newman. Pius XII also sought to affirm the principle argued by St. Robert Bellarmine, a Church Doctor of the Counter-Reformation era, that the Church is a visible reality notwithstanding the importance of her mystical or invisible dimension. *Mystici Corporis Christi* §65 claims that there can be no real opposition or conflict between the invisible mission of the Holy Spirit and the juridical commission of Ruler and Teacher received from Christ (which is associated with the more visible dimensional of the Church) since they mutually complement and perfect each other—as do the body and soul in the human person. Arguably this is the ideal situation while in practice the exercise of juridical authority by the organs of the visible Church can sometimes fall far

---

[3] James Ambrose Lee II, "Shaping Reception: Yves Congar's Reception of Johann Adam Möhler" (*New Blackfriars* 92 (2016): 693–72.

[4] Pius XII, *Mystici Corporis Christi* (1943), §9.

short of this ideal. This is a major reason why the sixteenth century schisms occurred, and why the Church in first-world countries is currently under scrutiny for its handling or mishandling of the child abuse crisis, and why the visible Church has lost so much of her moral authority. Paragraph 66 concedes that at times there will appear to be imperfections in the Body of Christ, but that such weakness should not be attributed to the Church's juridical constitution, to her structure as such, but to the regrettable inclination to evil found in each individual.

This tension between the visible and the invisible, the mystical and the all too fleshly human, will no doubt form a common topic of ecclesiological scholarship at the beginning of the third millennium. Not only is there the fall-out from the sex abuse crisis but serious sexual and financial corruption exists within the Curia, manifested in tens of millions of "missing" euros and the operation of a "lavender mafia" network. When reports appear in the mainstream press of a cocaine fueled gay orgy involving curial officials being closed down by police inside the Vatican, one is reminded of Dorothy Day's comment that though the Church does sometimes play the harlot she will always be her mother.[5] The metaphors of "mother" and "harlot" stand in stark juxtaposition and the task of untangling that relationship will no doubt concern Catholic scholars in the years that lie ahead.[6]

Mystici Corporis Christi was followed in 1964 by the Second Vatican Council's dogmatic constitution on the Church *Lumen Gentium*, which is a reference to Christ (not the Church herself) as the Light of the Nations. Chapter 1 took up *Mystici Corporis Christi*'s emphasis on the mystery of the Church. Paragraph 6 noted that just as the revelation of the Kingdom is often conveyed by means of metaphors in the Old Testament, today the inner nature of the Church is made known in different images taken either from tending sheep or cultivating land, from building, or even from family life and betrothals.

The second chapter is titled "The People of God" and presents the members of the Church as a new spiritual community analogous to the chosen people of the Old Testament. Paragraph 10 holds that the baptized, by regeneration and the anointing of the Holy Spirit, are consecrated as a

---

[5] Dorothy Day, "In Peace Is My Bitterness Most Bitter," *Catholic Worker* 33, no. 4 (January 1967): 2. The exact quotation is "As to the Church, where else shall we go, except to the Bride of Christ, one flesh with Christ? Though she is a harlot at times, she is our Mother."

[6] For a history of the "harlot" metaphor, see Aidan Nichols, *Figuring out the Church: Her Marks, and Her Masters* (San Francisco: Ignatius Press, 2013). See also Balthasar, *Spouse of the Word: Volume II*, and Giacomo. Biffi, *Casta Meretrix, "The Chaste Whore": An Essay on the Ecclesiology of St. Ambrose* (Farnborough, England: St. Austin Press, 2000).

spiritual house and a holy priesthood. The common priesthood of all the faithful, otherwise known as the Royal Priesthood, is said to be distinguished from the ministerial and hierarchical priesthood in essence, not only in degree. The organic structure of the priestly community both royal and sacerdotal is brought into operation by the sacraments. Both the members of the Royal Priesthood and those of the ministerial priesthood participate in the prophetic, priestly, and kingly ministry of Christ, though they do this differently since the two priesthoods are essentially different. However, the precise nature of this difference is not explained in any depth.

It is acknowledged that the individual people of God have been blessed with different gifts to serve the ecclesial body, the English translation "particular churches" will retain their own traditions, and these "legitimate differences" will be protected by the Petrine office. However, there is almost no analysis of what constitutes a legitimate difference of a particular church. The reference to lower case 't' traditions implies that the Council fathers had in mind things like different liturgical languages and devotional practices. Today, however, some theologians, including Cardinal Kasper, would extend the ambit of "legitimate differences" to a far broader range of issues.

Paragraph 15 offers an olive branch to Christians who remain outside the Church by acknowledging that they share a Christian baptism, belief in the Trinity, and respect for the Sacred Scriptures, while §16 addresses those of other faiths in very irenic phrases. Jews are told that they remain most dear to God, Muslims are affirmed for professing to follow the faith of Abraham, and those who, through no fault of their own, do not know the Gospel of Christ but sincerely try to do God's will as it is known to them through the dictates of conscience are said to be capable of attaining salvation. Nonetheless the Council fathers affirm Christ's great commission to preach the Gospel to every creature and state that the Church is compelled by the Holy Spirit to do her part so God's plan may be fully realized, whereby the Father constituted Christ as the source of salvation for the whole world. The obligation of spreading the faith is imposed on all the faithful, not exclusively upon members of the ministerial priesthood.

The third chapter of *Lumen Gentium* is entitled "On the Hierarchical Structure of the Church and in particular on the Episcopate." Here bishops are described as the successors of the apostles whom Christ willed to be shepherds in his Church, while the Petrine office is said to have been established by Christ so the episcopate itself might be one and undivided. The relationship between the Petrine office and the college of bishops is addressed in §22: "Just as in the Gospel, St. Peter and the other apostles constitute one apostolic college, so in a similar way the Roman Pontiff, the successor of Peter, and the bishops, the successors of the apostles, are joined together."[7] Moreover, the pope is said to have "full, supreme and universal power over the Church,"[8] while the order of bishops is said to have full, supreme power but only when acting with the consent of the pope. This paragraph has been criticized for offering little practical guidance about the relationship between what today is commonly called, in the parlance of liberation theology, the center and the periphery, or the Roman Curia and the local church.

This chapter also describes papal infallibility as limited to matters of faith and morals, and this jurisdiction extends only "as far as the deposit of Revelation extends, which must be religiously guarded and faithfully expounded."[9] In other words, the power of the pope and the college of bishops is circumscribed by revelation itself, as written in the gospels or orally handed down.[10] This principle was recently emphasized by Cardinal Gerhard Müller:

> In the exercise of its teaching ministry, it is not enough for the Church's Magisterium simply to appeal to its judicial or disciplinary power as if its teachings were nothing but a matter of legal and doctrinal positivism. Rather, the Magisterium must seek to present a convincing case, showing how its presentation of the faith is in itself coherent and in continuity with the rest of Tradition. The authority of the papal Magisterium rests on its continuity with the teachings of previous popes. In fact, if a pope had the power to abolish the binding teachings of his predecessors, or if he had the authority even to reinterpret Holy Scripture against its evident meaning, then all his doctrinal decisions could in turn be abolished by his successor, whose successor in turn could undo or redo everything as he pleased. In this case we would not be witnessing a development of doctrine, but the dire spectacle of the Barque of Peter stranded on a sandbank.[11]

---

[7] Second Vatican Council, *Lumen Gentium* (1964).

[8] *Lumen Gentium*, §22.

[9] *Lumen Gentium*, §25.

[10] For those with artistic interests, a representation of this principle is in a fresco by Fra Angelico in the Niccoline Chapel inside the Vatican Museum. Kevin Salatino, "The Frescoes of Fra Angelico for the Chapel of Nicholas V: Art and Ideology in Renaissance Rome" (PhD diss., University of Pennsylvania, 1992).

[11] Gerhard Müller, "Development, or Corruption?," *First Things*, February 20, 2018, https://www.firstthings.com/web-exclusives/2018/02/development-or-corruption.

The fourth chapter of *Lumen Gentium* is simply entitled "The Laity" and is unremarkable except that it emphasizes that lay people are also called to participate in the mission of the Church, and thus they are not simply sheep to be protected or, to quote Monsignor Talbot, one of Cardinal Newman's sparring partners, people whose sole responsibility is to "hunt, to shoot and to entertain."[12] Calling the lay faithful to evangelize is a good segue to chapter five, which promotes the universal call to holiness.

The sixth chapter is addressed to religious and affirms the evangelical counsels of poverty, chastity, and obedience as a particularly fruitful path to holiness, but this chapter is often criticized for not offering anything particularly new or creative. Chapter seven is similarly without novelty and addresses eschatology, reiterating the Church teaching that all will be judged by Christ and the possibility of eternal damnation.

The final chapter deals with the relationship between Mariology and ecclesiology. Here the teaching of St. Ambrose is positively endorsed, according to which Mary is a type of the Church in the order of faith, charity, and perfect union with Christ. It is said that the Church is rightly called mother and virgin, and that Mary stands out in eminent and singular fashion as exemplar both of virgin and of mother.[13]

Lumen Gentium concludes with an appendix Pope Paul VI requested to be inserted. At the theoretical level, the appendix is about the meaning of the word "college" as used in the phrase "the college of bishops." Practically, the appendix underscores that bishops are not to act independently of the pope. In theological language, the principle is that "without hierarchical communion the ontologico-sacramental function [of the bishops] which is to be distinguished from the juridio-canonical aspect, cannot be exercised."[14]

These themes were later amplified in the 1998 by the Congregation for the Doctrine of the Faith (CDF): the purpose of the Petrine office is "the unity of faith and communion."[15] The ministry of St. Peter's successor

---

[12] George Talbot, "Letter to the Archbishop of Westminster," cited in *Life of Cardinal Manning: Archbishop of Westminster*, vol. 2, by Edmund Sheridan Purcell (London: Forgotten Books, 2018).

[13] Quoting from the Mozarabic Rite, "The one gave salvation to the nations, the other gives the nations to the Saviour. The one carried life to her womb, the other carries it in the sacramental font. What was once accorded to Mary in the carnal order is now accorded spiritually to the Church She conceives the Word in her unfailing faith, she gives birth to it in a spirit freed from all corruption, she holds it in a soul covered with the Virtue of the Most High."

[14] Appendix to *Lumen Gentium*, §4.

[15] Congregation for the Doctrine of the Faith, *The Primacy of the Successor of Peter in the*

is inscribed in the heart of each particular Church and thus does not reach it from the outside. Rather, this interiority of the bishop of Rome's ministry to each particular Church is an expression of the mutual interiority between the universal Church and particular Church. Against what Pius XII would identify as rationalist or naturalist readings of the Petrine primacy, the CDF document states that "the primacy differs in its essence and in its exercise from the offices of governance found in human societies . . . it is not an office of co-ordination or management, nor can it be reduced to a *primacy of honor*, or be conceived as a political monarchy."[16] Moreover, like the faithful, the pope is subject to the word of God, as presented in Scriptures and interpreted by Tradition. His power is circumscribed by divine law itself and thus he is "the rock which guarantees a rigorous fidelity to the Word of God against arbitrariness and conformism."[17] This CDF document, which bears more than a few Ratzinger watermarks, includes the clause "hence the martyrological nature of his primacy."[18] It has been argued by Bishop Voderholzer of Regensburg that Ratzinger's view of the papacy was strongly martyrological, and that Ratzinger regarded Cardinal Reginald Pole's essay *De summo pontifice Christi in terris vicario eiusque officio potestate liber vere* (cited in its short form as *De summo pontifice*) as "one of the most profound theologies of papal primacy."[19]

The Second Vatican Council also passed the decree *Christus Dominus* on the Pastoral Duties of Bishops and *Presbyterorum ordinis*, a decree on the ministry and life of priests. In 1967 Pope Paul VI released an encyclical entitled *Sacerdotalis Caelibatus* in which he described priestly celibacy as a brilliant jewel, and he defended the practice theologically by referencing the intensely Christological nature of the priesthood. St. John Paul II and Benedict XVI also strongly supported maintaining celibacy.[20] In his interview with Peter Seewald, Benedict XVI stated that celibacy has a Christological

---

Mystery of the Church (1998), §4.

[16] CDF, *Successor of Peter*, §7 (emphasis original).

[17] CDF, *Successor of Peter*, §7.

[18] CDF, *Successor of Peter*, §7.

[19] Rudolf Voderholzer, "Joseph Ratzinger's Martyrological Understanding of Papal Primacy," a paper delivered at Mundelein Seminary, October 19, 2017. Cf. "Joseph Ratzinger's Martyrological Understanding of Papal Primacy: A Key for Unresolved Ecumenical Problems," in *Joseph Ratzinger and the Healing of the Reformation-Era Divisions*, ed. Emery de Gaál and Matthew Levering (Steubenville, OH: Emmaus Academic, 2019), 1–17. Pole (1500–1558) was the last Catholic Archbishop of Canterbury. He composed *De summo pontifice* during the conclave of 1555.

[20] This is made explicit in John Paul II's post-synodal apostolic exhortation *Pastores Dabo Vobis* (1992), §29, on the formation of priests in the circumstances of the present day.

and an apostolic meaning: "The point is not simply to save time—so I then have a little bit more time at my disposal because I am not a father of a family. That would be too primitive and pragmatic a way to see things. The point is really an existence that stakes everything on God and leaves out precisely the one thing that normally makes a human existence fulfilled with a promising future."[21] As pope, Benedict XVI made some off-the-cuff statements about celibacy in a Q and A session with priests in June 2010, adding that there is an eschatological dimension to priestly celibacy: celibacy is an anticipation of the world of the resurrection. "Celibacy and priesthood" was also the theme of an address delivered by Cardinal William Levada in the Archdiocese of Belo Horizonte in 2011 when he was prefect for the CDF. Following John Paul II and Benedict XVI, Levada also referenced the Christological character of the priesthood in defense of celibacy.[22']

At the beginning of the third millennium there is a tendency among scholars to accept that celibacy will continue to be the norm for Latin Rite Clergy but to ask questions about how to better prepare seminarians for a celibate life, which is perceived as something good, as a spiritual gift no less, rather than simply as a cross one stoically learns to carry. Among clergy, the issue has resurfaced in rumors that Pope Francis favors a liberalization of canon law to allow for married clergy in some select regions of the world, such as Brazil, while Cardinal Marx of Munich-Freising encourages reopening the debate about clerical celibacy in situations where the number of those entering seminaries in particular dioceses in Europe, such as his own, is beyond a crisis. In 2016 the great Bavarian Catholic Archdiocese of Munich-Freising received only one new seminarian.

Returning to the magisterial teaching, in 1985 John Paul II called an extraordinary synod to reflect on the reception of the teaching of the Second Vatican Council. A central theme emerged—one of the most significant conciliar achievements was the ecclesiology of *Lumen Gentium*, by this time labeled "Communio ecclesiology." This ecclesiology emphasized the relationships of communion within the Church. In another CDF document entitled *Letter to the Bishops of the Catholic Church on Some Aspects of the*

---

[21] Joseph Ratzinger, *Salt of the Earth: The Church at the End of the Millennium. Interview with Peter Seewald* (San Francisco: Ignatius Press, 1997), 195.

[22] Significant academic publications treating this issue include Dietrich von Hildebrand, *Celibacy and the Crisis of Faith* (Chicago: Franciscan Herald, 1971); Stanley Jaki, *Theology of Priestly Celibacy* (West Chester, PA: Christendom, 1997); and Alfons Stickler, *The Case for Clerical Celibacy: Its Historical Development and Theological Foundations* (San Francisco: Ignatius Press, 1995). For a more ambivalent perspective, see Edward Schillebeeckx, *Clerical Celibacy Under Fire* (London: Sheed and Ward, 1968; London: Macmillan, 1895).

Church Understood as Communion (1992), the concept of *communion* is described as a "key for the renewal of Catholic ecclesiology."[23]

> If the concept of *communion*, which is not a univocal concept, is to serve as a key to ecclesiology, it has to be understood within the teaching of the Bible and the patristic tradition, in which *communion* always involves a double dimension: the *vertical* (communion with God) and the *horizontal* (communion among men). It is essential to the Christian understanding of *communion* that it be recognised above all as a gift from God, as a fruit of God's initiative carried out in the paschal mystery. The new relationship between man and God, that has been established in Christ and is communicated through the sacraments, also extends to a new relationship among human beings.[24]

However, §8 says that some approaches to ecclesiology "suffer from a clearly inadequate awareness of the Church as a *mystery of communion*, especially insofar as they have not sufficiently integrated the concept of *communion* with the concepts of *People of God* and of the *Body of Christ*, and have not given due importance to the relationship between the Church as *communion* and the Church as *sacrament*."

> Sometimes, however, the idea of a "communion of particular Churches" is presented in such a way as to weaken the concept of the unity of the Church at the visible and institutional level. Thus it is asserted that every particular Church is a subject complete in itself, and that the universal Church is the result of a *reciprocal recognition* on the part of the particular Churches. This ecclesiological unilateralism, which impoverishes not only the concept of the universal Church but also that of the particular Church, betrays an insufficient understanding of the concept of communion."[25]

Prescriptively, §9 declares that "the universal Church cannot be conceived as the sum of the particular Churches, or as a federation of particular Churches." It is not the result of the communion of the churches but, in its

---

[23] Congregation for the Doctrine of the Faith, *Letter to the Bishops of the Catholic Church on Some Aspects of the Church Understood as Communion* (1992), §1.

[24] CDF, *Letter to Bishops*, §3.

[25] CDF, *Letter to Bishops*, §8.

essential mystery, it is a reality *ontologically and temporally* prior to every *individual* particular Church.[26]

According to the early church fathers, ontologically speaking, the Church precedes creation and gives birth to particular churches as her daughters. Thus, there is the tradition of referring to France as "the eldest daughter of the Church."[27] The long-standing teaching that the Church was first manifested, *temporally*, on the day of Pentecost in the community of the one hundred twenty gathered around Mary and the twelve apostles. This one hundred twenty are described as representatives of the one unique Church and the founders-to-be of the local churches, who have a mission directed to the world: from the first the Church *speaks all languages.*[28]

Much of the theological analysis offered in this CDF document can be found in Henri de Lubac's work *The Motherhood of the Church.* Speaking of what he called the "problem of ecclesial nationalism," de Lubac remarked that bishops must resist such psychological action—from voodoo worship to the profession of an Aryan Christianity.[29]

What might be called the Lubac-Ratzinger interpretation of *Communio* ecclesiology did not received a sympathetic reception from Cardinal Kasper. In the first decade of the third millennium, the hottest topic in ecclesiology was the so-called Ratzinger-Kasper debate, an exchange between two German cardinals initially appearing in the German journal *Stimmen der Zeit* and then in *America: The Jesuit Review* and the London *Tablet.* Kasper rejects that the universal Church was first made manifest at Pentecost. He follows

---

[26] Cf. Henri de Lubac, *The Motherhood of the Church* (San Francisco: Ignatius Press, 1982), 199–200: "The particular church is not merely an administrative division of the total Church, she does not result from a partition which would fragment the expanse of the universal Church, but from a concentration of Church exercising her own capacity for fulfilment. She is not a section of a vaster administrative body, one part fitted to other parts in order to form a larger whole, each of these parts remaining exterior to the others, in the way the French provinces, for example, are fitted to each other in order to form the administrative body of the State. It is for this reason that some would even have wished to proscribe from ecclesiastical language the word 'diocese' which can by its origin evoke the idea of a circumscription analogous to the ancient dioceses of the Roman Empire."

[27] This point was made by de Lubac in his work *The Splendor of the Church* (San Francisco: Ignatius Press, 1999). De Lubac argued that prior to the Incarnation, the Church was betrothed to Christ and that this betrothal will to a "certain extent" remain in place until the end of time, when the Church will finally be united with the Lord in the bridal chamber of the heavenly kingdom.

[28] This phrase, that the Church speaks all languages, echoes St. Augustine who said of the Church: I am in all languages. Greek is mine, Syrian is mine, Hebrew is mine, [the languages] of all peoples are mine, for I am the unity of all peoples.

[29] De Lubac, *Motherhood of the Church*, 228–29.

the judgment of Michael Theobald who claims that at Pentecost the focus was not on the nascent universal Church but upon the Jewish diaspora. Kasper was critical of Ratzinger for approaching issues intellectually from the perspective of systematic theology and not from a pastoral perspective. Kasper even offered a psychological explanation for Ratzinger's stance saying that Ratzinger thinks in a platonic world of ideas rather than in an Aristotelian world of facts.[30] At the outbreak of the debate, Cardinal Avery Dulles, author of the very popular *Models of the Church*, weighed in with Ratzinger.[31]

Notwithstanding this debate, throughout the pontificates of John Paul II and Benedict XVI, the reigning ecclesiology was very much *Communio* ecclesiology with intellectual debts to Newman, Möhler, and de Lubac for the understanding of the Church's supernatural nature. Likewise, there are debts to Yves Congar for the understanding of tradition and its mediation in history, debts to Louis Bouyer for the understanding of foundational principles for ecumenism, and a debt to Balthasar for his creative defense of the Petrine office, which suffered a high level of flak from Hans Küng.[32]

Balthasar's defense of the papacy was presented in his *Der antirömische Affekt* (1974)[33] as a foil to Küng's best-seller *Infallible? An Inquiry* (1971). It began with a few missile shots declaring the recent attacks on the papacy as a peasant rebellion driven by Germanic guilt over the obedience given to Adolf Hitler. In the 1960s and 70s not only Hans Küng but members of the Frankfurt School of Social Theory were busy attacking the whole idea of hierarchies and authority figures as a symptom of "false consciousness." Some people were said to suffer from this condition because they were being

---

[30] For an extensive analysis of Kasper's "Platonic criticism," see Tracey Rowland, "The Reception of *Einführung in das Christentum* among the Reviewers," forthcoming in the University of Notre Dame's Proceedings on the Conference to mark the 50th anniversary of Joseph Ratzinger's publication of *Introduction to Christianity*.

[31] Walter Kasper, "On the Church: A Friendly Reply to Cardinal Ratzinger" *The Tablet* 255 (June 23, 2001): 927–30; Joesph Ratzinger, "The Local Church and the Universal Church: A Response to Walter Kasper," *America: The Jesuit Review* 185, no. 16 (November 19, 2001): 7–11; Avery Dulles, *Models of the Church* (New York: Doubleday, 1978). Dulles's famous five models were (1) institution, (2) mystical communion, (3) sacrament, (4) herald, and (5) servant.

[32] A synthesis of these contributions can be found in Benoît-Dominique de la Soujeole, *Introduction to the Mystery of the Church* (Washington, DC: Catholic University of America Press, 2014). This work is likely to be used as an ecclesiological "primer" in many Catholic academies since it brings together numerous elements of *Communio* ecclesiology.

[33] The English translation is *The Office of Peter and the Structure of the Church* (San Francisco: Ignatius Press, 1986).

unwittingly coerced by cultural leaders, others suffered because they were the agents of coercion. Either way, authority figures and hierarchies have been regarded with suspicion by intellectual elites imbued with various forms of Marxist ideology of which the Frankfurt School of Social Theory represents the most sophisticated and influential example.

Balthasar was not moved by any of these elements in the Zeitgeist of the 1960s and 70s. He regarded leadership and thus hierarchies as a necessary part of the human condition. The Church, he said, was not a pure spirit nor an angelic idea. This would not be appropriate for an institution of the Incarnation. Creatively, Balthasar argued that ecclesial leaders were of four basic types, representing four particular charisms or missions. In some places he called them the four pillars of the Church, in other places he referred to a Christological constellation or network of figures surrounding Christ who were prototypical of future ecclesial leaders. Specifically, he spoke of the pillars of Sts. Peter, John, James, and Paul: the first becomes the Petrine ministry focused on ecclesial governance; the second, or the Johannine ministry, is linked to the Church's contemplative life; the third guards tradition; and the fourth, the Pauline pillar, is associated with the newness of grace and perpetual ecclesial renewal. Balthasar also spoke of the Marian archetype of the Church and used nuptial imagery to affirm both the femininity of the Church and the masculinity of the priesthood.[34]

According to Balthasar, these four pillars represent ecclesial missions that are always held in tension. The good of the Church depends upon their harmonious interaction; if one or other gains the upper hand to such a degree that the other three are suppressed or marginalized, the Body of Christ suffers. For example, Balthasar suggested that Johannine love can "degenerate into orthopraxis or a universal humanitarian benevolence that takes its values from a 'change in social structures' which would redistribute goods more

---

[34] In language that has ruffled the fur of some feminists, Balthasar observed, "Woman must conceive from man if she is effectively to bear and develop what she has received. It follows that the all-inclusive feminine *ecclesia*, like the masculine ministry that is rooted in her, is obviously dependent upon something beyond her, on the grace given by Jesus Christ, through whom the trinitarian life is mediated to the Church and to her children. If the Church as a whole is characterised as feminine, and if the masculine ministry is funda-mentally anchored in this sphere, a twofold danger is avoided at a single stroke: first, that the Church might become a self-sufficient entity, interposing herself as an 'intermediary' between the believer and Christ, whereas she is primarily an open womb and reaches mankind, in her and with her, to be similarly open; and secondly, that the clergy might equate their paternal role with the divine, paternal authority of God instead of recognising that their exercise of authority is pure service." Balthasar, *Office of Peter*, 185.

equitably."[35] Although he did not use the words "liberation theology," this is what he seems to gesture toward. Broadly, it is the mentality that all we need is love and social justice and that orthodoxy should be subordinated to orthopraxy. More specifically, Balthasar spoke of the problem of theologians who want to break up the concrete unity of the *Catholica* into an abstract unity of *humanitas*.[36] By this he meant that some theologians are tempted to give priority to the so-called brotherhood of man rather than the community of those bound together by the one baptism and one faith. As a caricature, one might say that such types are often more excited by realizing the dreams of the French Revolution than carrying out the Great Commission, and indeed that their mistake is precisely to conflate the two.

While the Johannine section of the ecclesial orchestra needs to guard against the temptation to chant the Beatles' "All we need is Love" mantra, the pillar of St. James, responsible for maintaining the integrity of tradition, needs to guard against what Balthasar called a "reactionary clinging to obsolete forms."[37] This problem is often associated with traditionalist movements, where people will go to war over cultural practices, like whether or not to wear a mantilla. Traditionalists are correct when they say that cultural practices are not theologically neutral—that different practices convey different meanings, including different theological meanings and accents—but this valid insight can become problematic if, for example, communities end up divided on issues, like whether Gothic vestments are preferrable to baroque or vice versa. Meanwhile the Pauline charism to be "all things to all men" can become, in Balthasar's words, "a diplomatic *aggiornamento* to all that is popular and fashionable."[38] This is the mentality of those who want to accommodate the practices and culture of the Church to whatever is fashionable in the world at large. Ratzinger referenced this problem when he said the Church is not a haberdashery shop that updates its windows for each new fashion season. Balthasar diplomatically refrained from defining the pathological operation of the Petrine pillar, saying that the "Petrine distortions have been too often exposed to need further mention."[39] As a general principle, Balthasar argued for an "eschatological center of gravity" provided by the Gospel of Christ which holds together these pillars or tensions within the Body of Christ.

Balthasar died in 1998 and thus did not live to read the CDF declaration

---

[35] Balthasar, *Office of Peter*, 328.
[36] Balthasar, *Office of Peter*, 43.
[37] Balthasar, *Office of Peter*, 329.
[38] Balthasar, *Office of Peter*, 329.
[39] Balthasar, *Office of Peter*, 329.

Dominus Iesus—On the Unicity and Salvific Universality of Jesus Christ and the Church—promulgated in 2000. Nonetheless, given all the above, especially his warnings about watering down the *Catholica* in favor of the abstract unity of the *humanitas*, it is safe to say that Balthasar would have concurred with the central teachings of *Dominus Iesus*. These include the declarations in §§6, 12, and 16: the theory of the limited, incomplete, or imperfect character of the revelation of Jesus Christ, which would be complementary to that found in other religions, is contrary to the Church's faith (§6); the action of the Spirit is not outside or parallel to the action of Christ (§12); and the Catholic faithful *are required to profess* that there is a historical continuity—rooted in the apostolic succession—between the Church founded by Christ and the Catholic Church. Paragraph 16 also states that when *Lumen Gentium* held that the fullness of revelation subsists in the Catholic Church, governed by the successor of Peter and by the bishops in communion with him, the expression *subsistit in* was used to harmonize two doctrinal statements: 1) the Church of Christ, despite the divisions among Christians, continues to exist fully only in the Catholic Church, and 2) that "outside of her structure, many elements can be found of sanctification and truth,"[40] that is, in those Churches and ecclesial communities which are not yet in full communion with the Catholic Church. But with respect to these, it needs to be stated that "they derive their efficacy from the very fullness of grace and truth entrusted to the Catholic Church."[41] A concrete example of ecumenism conducted with respect for these principles was the establishment of the Anglican Ordinariate under the apostolic constitution *Anglicanorum Coetibus* during the pontificate of Benedict XVI.

Before leaving the Wojtyła-Ratzinger era, it should also be mentioned that in 1994 John Paul II promulgated the apostolic letter *Ordinatio Sacerdotalis* wherein he declared that the Church had no authority whatsoever to confer priestly ordination on women. This followed upon the 1976 CDF declaration *Inter Insigniores*—On the Question of the Admission of Women to the Ministerial Priesthood. Both documents emphasize that Christ did not include any women among his chosen twelve apostles, not even his mother. *Inter Insigniores* adds that since the "whole sacramental economy is based upon natural signs or symbols imprinted on the human psychology," and since Christ's role in the Eucharist is to be expressed sacramentally, the "natural resemblance," which must exist between Christ and his minister, would not

---

[40] Congregation for the Doctrine of the Faith, *Dominus Iesus* (2000), §16; cf. *Lumen Gentium*, §8.

[41] *Dominus Iesus*, §16; cf. Second Vatican Council, *Unitatis Redintegratio* (1964), §3.

be present if the place of Christ were to be taken by a woman.[42] This is often referred to in theological literature as the anthropological argument, while the fact that the twelve apostles were all male and did not choose to ordain women is the argument from tradition. Speaking as a private theologian, Joseph Ratzinger also remarked that for him it was theologically significant that priestesses were highly popular in Old Testament times. They abounded in many ancient religions but not in the religious practices of the Jews, who were the people to whom God first chose to reveal himself. A further argument one often finds in the academic literature is that the use of masculine "Father" language for God and the masculinity of God the Son is appropriate since it points to the transcendent nature of God in relation to the world. The world is willed by God, but it is not an emanation of God. As Aidan Nichols, O.P., expresses the idea, "A mother goddess is too continuous with the world, too much like the womb from which we came, to stand for the divine reality revealed in the Old Testament, a reality that is decisively other than the world, different from the world, discontinuous with the world."[43]

Nonetheless, notwithstanding the arguments from tradition and from anthropology, the whole subfield of theology known as feminist theology opposes the restriction of priesthood to men. There is not space in this chapter to offer a profile of every subspecies of feminist theologian, even though, like Australian parrots, they do come in an interesting array of colors.[44] There are, for example, the differences between first, second, third, and fourth wave feminism, and between essentialist feminists and constructivist feminists, and between structuralist and post-structuralist feminists, to name but a few of the most common intellectual species. Suffice to say that the differences between feminist theologians (regardless of which particular philosophy or social theory drives their theological analysis) and magisterial teaching usually lie deep in the territory of fundamental theology.

Feminists come with their own feminist scriptural hermeneutics, their own feminist social theories, and sometimes even their own linguistic philosophies. Since Catholic theology is not a fideism but rather a partnership of faith and reason, what happens in the realm of reason, more specifically today in the realm of social theory, has huge repercussions for theology.

---

[42] Congregation for the Doctrine of Faith, *Inter Insigniores* (1976), §5.

[43] Aidan Nichols, *Holy Order: Apostolic Priesthood from the New Testament to the Second Vatican Council* (Dublin: Veritas, 1990), 149–50.

[44] See, for example, Susan Frank Parsons, ed., *The Cambridge Companion to Feminist Theology* (Cambridge: Cambridge University Press, 2002), and Mary McClintock Fulkerson and Sheila Briggs, eds., *The Oxford Handbook of Feminist Theology* (Oxford: Oxford University Press, 2014).

The debates between feminist theologians and non-feminist theologians concerning ecclesiology are the epiphenomena of debates thrown up by different approaches to fundamental theology. Concretely, the argument from anthropology makes no sense if one believes that femininity and masculinity are mere social constructs that have no ontological foundations. Conversely, if one reads the words in Genesis, "male and female he created them," as positing that humanity is divided into two distinct forms, a male form and a female form, and holds this as theologically significant, as part of the data of revelation no less, then this also has huge implications for one's understanding of sacramental theology and ultimately ecclesiology. Also, logically, if one starts from a theological baseline of believing that a priest is primarily the minister and sacramental representative of Christ, that he celebrates the sacraments *in persona Christi*, then the anthropological argument is much more important than if one holds to a different understanding of the nature of the priesthood. Advocates for the ordination of women often argue that a priest also represents the Holy Spirit, or alternatively for a change to the understanding of Eucharistic theology so the sacrificial dimension is muted, which makes a sacerdotal priesthood less necessary.

As we move from the era of Wojtyła-Ratzinger to that of Bergoglio-Kasper there is a definite change in ecclesial metaphors. There is far less talk about the mystical body of Christ and sacramental relationships and much more talk about the field hospital and diplomatic relationships. The new buzz word in ecclesiology is not "Communio" but "Synodality," not sacramentality but dialogue. "People's Theology" (in Spanish *Teologia del Pueblo*)—which is the Argentinian strain of liberation theology—embodies what might be called a "preferential option for the view from the periphery." *Teologia del Pueblo* has been described in both the academic and popular press as a form of liberation theology, which is Peronist not Marxist. The adjective Peronist is derived from the political platform of the Argentinian general Juan Perón, who was elected president of Argentina three times between 1946–1955 and 1973–1974. Peronism as a political agenda was both intensely nationalist and intensely anti-intellectual. The nationalist elements within the *Teologia del Pueblo* dovetail well with Cardinal Walter Kasper's desire to give ontological priority to the local church over the universal Church. This means, in turn, that a contemporary "hot area" in ecclesiology is that of the powers of synods and national and regional bishops' conferences.[45]

For those who seek to give ontological priority to the local church—and

---

[45] For a history of the issues in this context, see Francis A. Sullivan, "The Teaching Authority of Episcopal Offices," *Theological Studies* 63 (2002): 472–93.

here the big names are Walter Kasper and the late Jean-Marie Tillard, O.P.—
national or regional bishops' conferences are held in very high regard.[46] Vatican
II's decree on the pastoral office of bishops in the Church, *Christus Dominus*,
§§37–38, described an episcopal conference as "a kind of assembly (*coetus*)
in which the bishops of some nation or region discharge their pastoral office
in collaboration, the better to promote the good which the church offers to
people, and especially through forms and methods of apostolate carefully
designed to meet contemporary conditions." In 1966, in the decree *Ecclesiae
Sanctae*, St. Paul VI mandated the establishment of episcopal conferences
wherever they did not already exist. In 1988 St. John Paul II issued the *motu
Apostolos Suos* in which §22 declared that bishop's' conferences could only
make statements about matters of faith and morals if they were unanimous
in their decision or otherwise had the approval of the Holy See.

In *The Ratzinger Report* interview of 1985, Cardinal Ratzinger was not
very complimentary about bishops' conferences. His basic argument was a
point about group dynamics. Whenever there is a document put together
by a committee, it inevitably becomes a flattened kind of document representing the lowest common denominator of agreement. He observed that
during the Nazi era, the best documents were produced by individual heroic
bishops not by the German bishops as a collective. In *The Motherhood of
the Church*, de Lubac was less than enthusiastic about national bishops'
conferences and downplayed its theological status. He drew a distinction
between a collective act of bishops and a collegial act of bishops with the
former not having the same weight as the latter.[47]

> The primary objective of episcopal conferences is an immediately
> practical one; and their efficacy is connected to this limited char-
> acter. Their most usual activity, devoted to local affairs, does not
> in itself constitute an exercise in collegiality. All the more reason
> that this must be said of the activity of the commissions and the
> various bureaus of secretariats they assign to themselves.[48]

Episcopal synods clearly have more theological status than episcopal
conferences, but even here their precise powers vis-à-vis the papacy remains
a subject of ongoing theological reflection. Joseph Ratzinger argued, for

---

[46] For a bibliography of Tillard's works, see Christopher Ruddy, *The Local Church: Tillard
and the Future of Catholic Ecclesiology* (New York: Herder and Herder, 2006), 235–39.

[47] De Lubac, *Motherhood of the Church*, 259–60.

[48] De Lubac, *Motherhood of the Church*, 259–60.

example, that it is in governing the particular churches that bishops share in the governance of the universal church and not the other way around:

> The idea that it is only by being represented at the centre that they will have significance for the whole represents a fundamental misjudgement of the nature of the Church; it is the expression of a centralism which the Second Vatican Council in fact wanted to overcome. If one wanted to pursue this idea in order to overcome papal centralism, then all that would be introduced would be a new and much coarser centralism which would bring the Church's real nature to disappearing-point and subordinate it to the logic of contemporary political theories of the state.[49]

Ratzinger further argued that synods require time to responsibly deal with issues. Where Church teaching is at stake, complex theological problems should not be discussed in soundbites like a high school debate or a current affairs Q and A program on television. However, the longer the duration of synods the less time bishops can spend in their own diocese. If a permanent synod were to be established, it would take bishops away from their dioceses and in effect create a second tier of curial government, which would increase centralization and lead to a neglect of dioceses. Paradoxically, Ratzinger's argument is that the enthusiasm for synods leads to centralism even though it is a form of governance promoted to give greater voice to the non-curial bishops.

Not all synods are, however, comprised entirely of bishops. When lay people are invited to participate, this raises another contemporary "hot topic"—that of how to understand the *sensus fidelium* of the laity.[50]

Sensus Fidei linked the *sense of faith* to the prophetic mission of the laity. This concept does not appear in scripture but was developed by John Henry Newman in his essay *On Consulting the Faithful in Matters of Doctrine* (1859). Newman sought to demonstrate that the faithful have an active role in conserving and transmitting the faith, an idea developed by Yves Congar in his account of the Holy Spirit's role in the life of the faithful, and it found its magisterial endorsement in *Lumen Gentium*. In *Sensus Fidei*, the *sensus fidei fidelis* is defined as a spiritual instinct that enables the believer

---

[49] Joseph Ratzinger, *Church, Ecumenism, and Politics: New Essays in Ecclesiology* (New York: St. Paul Publications, 1988), 52.

[50] See International Theological Commission, *Sensus Fidei* (2014); and *Synodality in the Life and Mission of the Church* (2018).

to judge spontaneously whether a particular teaching or practice is or is not in conformity with the Gospel and with apostolic faith.[51] This "spiritual instinct" is linked to grace and the theological virtues and is proportional to the holiness of one's life.[52] "In the actual mental universe of the believer, the correct intuitions of the *sensus fidei* can be mixed up with various purely human opinions, or even with errors linked to the narrow confines of a particular pastoral context. . . . Not all the ideas which circulate among the People of God are compatible with the faith."[53] Thus, it is the magisterium's responsibility to judge "whether opinions which are present among the People of God, and which may seem to be the *sensus fidelium*, actually correspond to the truth of the Tradition received from the Apostles."[54] Chapter 4 of *Sensus Fidei* therefore concludes with a list of dispositions needed for an authentic participation in the *sensus fidei*: active participation in the life of the Church, listening to the word of God, openness to reason, adherence to the magisterium, holiness, and seeking the edification of the Church. It is also noted that throughout the Church's history, the minority and not the majority of the baptized have witnessed to the faith.

In *The Office of Peter and the Structure of the Church*, Balthasar believed the trend toward "provincialization" would simply lead to a multiplication of bureaucratic structures to such a degree that the "church militant" would become the "photocopying church."[55] He suggested that individual bishops swamped with paper—reports from this and that subcommittee—may find themselves calling upon the pope "as a defender of freedom against a more or less anonymous bureaucratic machine."[56] The sociological fact that Church councils, synods, conferences, and the like are never peaceful events. They are intensely confrontational with different theological factions and different personalities trying to politically out-maneuver one another.

> Ecumenical councils have had a lively history. At some, people were bribed; at others, they were beaten up; at others, shots were fired. Political pressures of all kinds were the order of the day. Nevertheless—*Dei providentia et hominum confusione*—some gains were made for Christianity. On the other hand, the immense expenditures in time, health, money and materials on the part of national

---

51 *Sensus Fidei*, §48.
52 *Sensus Fidei*, §57.
53 *Sensus Fidei*, §55.
54 *Sensus Fidei*, §77.
55 Balthasar, *Office of Peter*, 40.
56 Balthasar, *Office of Peter*, 39–47, at 40.

synods have not yet been justified. In all the bustle one thing stands out: as never before, the Church is preoccupied with herself, and, in particular, the clergy are preoccupied with themselves. They struggle for identity (which is a clinical problem), they practice individual and collective "navel-gazing," and the greater the confusion of voices, the less the national church knows who she really is.[57]

The great reform movements in the Church have never been initiated by boards and panels but by saints, and thus, Balthasar suggested that the question our ecclesial leaders should be asking is how does a people produce a saint? One might add, if we are to have more lay participation in ecclesial decision-making, how do we structure things so that the holiest people are those consulted and not those who are the noisiest self-promoters or most highly efficient bureaucratic paper shufflers? How do we make sure that ecclesial governance does not become a parody of the British comedy *Yes, Minister*, where the common solution to problems is to call a meeting of all the protagonists, issue a report which shows the problems are intractable, and then set up a quango to study the report and appoint leading protagonists to the quango? The protagonists do often feel happy about this outcome. Their appointments give them another line on their *curriculum vitae*, and the more boards they sit on, the higher their chances of receiving a civil honor. The problems, however, remain unresolved.

The Church mimicking contemporary bureaucratic ways of managing conflict relates to another ecclesial hot issue: the excessive corporatization of Church agencies, and the attempt to run Church agencies according to the most fashionable business management theories, as if the Church has no ideas about management.[58] In sociological terms, corporatization of the Church's pastoral work means the demise of charismatic authority and its replacement with rational-bureaucratic authority. In practice it also often means turning dioceses into miniature corporations, delegating legitimate episcopal authority to people with degrees in accounting and business management, who confuse evangelization and the salvation of souls with strategic plans and key performance indicators.

Real Catholic pastoral work, educational formation, and evangelization can only take place when there is a personal encounter with Christ mediated by one faithful Catholic to another person, either to someone who

---

[57] Balthasar, *Office of Peter*, 41–42.

[58] Lyndon Shakespeare offers an extensive analysis of this problem in *Being the Body of Christ in the Age of Management* (Eugene, OR: Cascade, 2016).

has the faith but needs the maternal care of the Church in some way, or to someone who is beginning the journey of faith. People can only encounter Christ's love through others who act as completely whole, integrated persons with intellects and wills, indeed with their whole hearts, engaged with the encounter with that other person. The corporatization of the Church's agencies plants roadblocks in the path of such real heart-to-heart encounters because risk-management theory identifies personal encounters as danger zones, as situations which might give rise to litigation. Every effort is therefore taken to minimize the possibility that any one person can take personal responsibility for any "delivery of a service." Service has to be "depersonalized" and decision-making relegated to committees so no individual exercises prudential judgment. No individual, as an individual, can be called to account for any practice, policy, or program. In this system, responsibility is so diffused that there is no opportunity for real leadership, real heroism, and real charismatic office bearing. The grace of the Incarnation is thwarted, the Holy Spirit has no room to breathe.

Interestingly, the apostle who betrayed Christ was the one responsible for the money, and unsurprisingly there is no place in Balthasar's "four pillars" for someone whose primary job description is accountant or business manager or diplomat. The gospels do not mention an apostle being given responsibility for negotiations with the Sanhedrin or the court of the Roman governor. This raises the question about the place of the Vatican Diplomatic Corps. Arguably, it is *not* one of those parts of the ecclesial structure that was established by Christ and foreshadowed in the Old Testament. There was no sacred league of diplomats traveling the roads of the ancient biblical world paying court to the powerful.

At present, one of the most serious issues in ecclesiology, real and practical, not merely theoretical, is the fate of Catholics in China who worship in the underground Church. Vatican diplomats are bending over backward to obtain diplomatic recognition from the Chinese government, which is demanding, as a condition, significant influence over the appointment of bishops. Cardinal Zen Ze-kiun has said that for the Vatican to accede to the Communist Party's demands would be to condemn faithful Chinese Catholics to life in a "Communist cage."[59] It is also a breathtaking disregard for the "white martyrdom" of the late bishop Kung of Shanghai, the Servant

---

[59] Venus Wu, "Cardinal Says Vatican-China Deal Would Put Catholics in Communist Cage," *Reuters World News*, February 10, 2018, https://www.reuters.com/article/idUSKBN1FT283/. See also Joseph Zen, *For Love of My People I Will Not Remain Silent: On the Situation of the Church in China* (San Francisco: Ignatius Press, 2019).

of God, who was sentenced to life imprisonment because he opposed the Communist Party's demand to control episcopal appointments. It has been further argued that the whole idea of ceding episcopal appointment authority to the Chinese government is contrary to *Christus Dominus*:[60] "In order to safeguard the liberty of the Church and more effectively to promote the good of the faithful, it is the desire of the sacred Council that for the future no rights or privileges be conceded to the civil authorities in regard to the election, nomination, or presentation to bishoprics."[61]

That conciliar desire was then given legislative effect in the 1983 Code of Canon Law. One of Cardinal Newman's arguments in favor of the superiority of the Catholic Church over the Church of England was precisely that the Petrine office served to protect Catholics from being governed by local civil authorities.[62] However, in the last century, time and again the members of the Vatican Diplomatic Corps have capitulated to tyrannical governments with the effect that the Catholic martyrs and other heroes living under the tyranny are sold out by the very institution which is most able to help them and to which they have offered their own lives in humble service. The Vatican's *Ostpolitik* strategy for dealing with Communist leaders in Central and Eastern Europe, especially in Czechoslovakia and Hungary, provides

---

[60] George Weigel, "Pope Francis is Playacting Realpolitik," *Foreign Policy*, February 15, 2018, https://foreignpolicy.com/2018/02/15/pope-francis-is-playacting-realpolitik/.

[61] Second Vatican Council, *Christus Dominus* (1965), §20.

[62] John Henry Newman, *Certain Difficulties Felt by Anglicans in Catholic Teaching Considered* (London: Longmans, Green & Co, 1894), 184–86: "Our ears ring with the oft-told tale, how the temporal sovereign persecuted, or attempted, or gained, the local Episcopate, and how the many or the few faithful fell back on Rome. So it was with the Arians in the East and St. Athanasius; so with the Byzantine Empress and St. Chrysostom; so with the Vandal Hunneric and the Africans; so with the 130 Monophysite Bishops at Ephesus and St. Flavian; so was it in the instance of the 50 Bishops, who, by the influence of Basilicus, signed a declaration against the Tome of St. Leo; so in the instance of the Henoticon of Zeno; and so in the controversies both of the Monothelites and the Inconoclasts. . . . In later and modern times we see the same truth irresistibly brought out; not only, for instance, in St. Thomas's history, but in St. Anselm's, nay, in the whole course of English ecclesiastical affairs, from the Conquest to the sixteenth century, and, not with least significancy, in the primacy of Cranmer. Moreover, we see it in the tendency of the Gallicanism of Louis XIV, and the Josephism of Austria. Such, too, is the lesson taught us in the recent policy of the Czar towards the United Greeks, and in the present bearing of the English Government towards the Church of Ireland. In all of these instances, it is a struggle between the Holy See and some local, perhaps distant, government, the liberty and orthodoxy of its faithful people being the matter in dispute; and while the temporal power is on the spot, and eager, and cogent, and persuasive, and dangerous, the strength of the assailed party lies in its fidelity to the rest of Christendom and to the Holy See."

a case study of how to undermine the morale of an oppressed people and destroy their faith in the visible Church.[63]

In summary, one might say that a contemporary issue in ecclesiology is how to distinguish a Christian form of governance from popular bureaucratic, corporate and, in the context of the Diplomatic Corps, pragmatic ends-justify-the-means models? A related issue is the operation of the Petrine office itself.

The papacies of Karol Wojtyła and Joseph Ratzinger have been criticized on the grounds that during these years we had professor popes who were great scholars but not very good at the day-to-day management of the Curia. More positively, academic literature states these two men exercised the Petrine ministry in a very Pauline way, in the sense that St. Paul is associated with theological leadership. With reference to Balthasar's four pillars, the two papacies showed a Jacobite interest in the defense of tradition, especially the papacy of Benedict XVI.

However, with the papacy of Francis we move away from professor popes to something more like a general pope. Instead of Balthasar's "four pillars" of ecclesial governance, Francis offers four "principles for building a people": 1) time is greater than space, 2) unity prevails over conflict, 3) reality is more important than ideas, and 4) the whole is greater than the sum of its parts.[64] It is said that he extracted these principles from a letter written by the nineteenth century Argentinian dictator Juan Manuel de Rosas (1793–1877) to the caudillo Facundo Quiroga (1788–1835) in 1834.[65] One gets a sense from these principles and from the history of the Bergoglio papacy to date, that Pope Francis does not regard conflict as necessarily a bad thing. One also gets a sense that he is much more inclined to look at issues in ecclesiology from the position of Walter Kasper than from the position of Joseph Ratzinger. We do not know what he thinks of the historical fact that his apostolic exhortation *Amoris Laetitia* is interpreted in different ways in different dioceses throughout the world. That a practice can be a mortal sin in one country and a mere irregular situation in another may or may not be of concern to him. He may find it stressful, or he may see it as a problem to which one can simply apply the principles—time is greater than space, reality is more important than ideas, unity will prevail over conflict,

---

[63] See, for example, Desmond O'Grady, *The Turned Card: Christianity Before and After the Wall* (Chicago: Loyola, 1997).

[64] Francis, *Evangelii Gaudium* (Roma: Libreria Editrice Vaticana, 2013), §§221–37.

[65] Juan Carlos Scannone, "El papa Francisco y la teología del pueblo," *Razón y Fe* 217 (2015): 31–50.

and the whole is greater than the parts. It does, however, cause significant stress for those in the Church who see this sociological fact as evidence for a breakdown in the unity of the Church—an attack on the Church's Catholicity no less. Cardinal Kasper would argue that there is no such attack because the disputed issues are mere matters of Church discipline, not matters of faith and morals. However, this is hotly disputed, which raises the issue of the relationship between ecclesiology and sacramental theology, especially Eucharistic theology, and then the relationship between Eucharistic theology and moral theology. When members of the faithful, professional theologians, and bishops speak about these relationships and seek to explain how a decision in one field of theology has repercussions in others, the advocates for Cardinal Kasper's position usually reply that people are being too logical, too systematic, and not pastoral. The word pastoral seems to be code for not rational. As Fr. Antonio Spadaro famously tweeted, "2 plus 2 in theology can make 5."[66] This proposition, however, is hard for many Catholics to swallow when they have been taught to believe that Catholicism is built on *both* reason and revelation, and that love and reason are the "twin pillars" of all reality, no less. Love without reason is blind, reason without love is cold. The Catholic preference is always for an integration of love and reason, and of reason and revelation, not a choice for one rather than the other. What is reasonable is never contrary to what is pastorally appropriate.

One of Pope Francis's favorite metaphors to describe the Church is the field hospital. Field hospital work is certainly something that the Church provides, but like so many appropriate metaphors, the Church as a field hospital highlights only one aspect of her reality.[67] Field hospitals can only do so much. Catholics certainly want to bandage the broken hearted, the spiritually wounded, and provide consolation to the sick and the dying and the unemployed, and to those in any dysfunctional family situation. However, one cannot think of ecclesiology without considering eschatology and here part of the Church's mission is to restore all things in Christ, which means the mission is not limited to pouring ointment on wounds but includes a thorough-going impregnation of every human act and every social practice with the grace of the Incarnation. This is the task of both priests and laity. As

---

[66] Antonio Spadaro (@antoniospadaro), "Theology is not #Mathematics," Twitter, January 5, 2017, 6:04 p.m., https://twitter.com/antoniospadaro/status/817144723093733377?lang=en.

[67] For a work on this concept, see William. Cavanaugh, *Field Hospital: The Church's Engagement with a Wounded World* (Grand Rapids, MI: Eerdmans, 2016).

St. John Paul II wrote, "The lay faithful are called to restore to creation all its original value. In ordering creation to the authentic well-being of humanity in an activity governed by the life of grace, they share in the exercise of the power whereby the Risen Christ draws all things to himself and subjects them along with himself to the Father, so that God may be everything to everyone."[68] If this eschatological reading of the Church's mission is correct then the Church cannot be a "mere booth in the fairground of postmodernity" (to use Robert Spaemann's expression) or just another institution trying to provide social welfare.[69]

If the Church were to present herself to the world as a mere booth, just another philanthropic association with Jesus Christ as her inspirational founder, then few would have any objections. However, she faces great hostility because she claims to have an eschatological mission. Therefore, the Church often finds herself out of favor with governments and, in particular, out of favor with contemporary Western governments and institutions like the European Union that see themselves, not the Church, fulfilling a salvific function. As William Cavanaugh has argued, the modern liberal state operates as a parody of the Body of Christ.[70] Thus, yet another contemporary "hot issue" in ecclesiology is the relationship between the Church and the modern liberal state, and in particular the state's claims to occupy a "neutral" stance toward all moral and theological principles.[71]

This chapter began by referencing the influence of the Tübingen theologians. Certainly it would seem, if one trawls though the magisterial documents and the academic debates, that the ideas at issue often have a

---

68 John Paul II, *Christifideles Laici* (1988), §14.

69 In relation to the topic of the laity as a royal priesthood, de Lubac quotes Hugh of St. Victor: "The incarnate Word is our king: now, He came into this world to give battle to the devil, and all the saints who lived before his coming are, as it were, soldiers who form the advance guard of the royal army; those who have come since then, and are to come up to the end of the world, are the soldiers who march behind their king. The king Himself takes His place at the center of His army, and he advances surrounded by the defensive wall which His troops form around Him. And although all sorts of different arms can be seen in so great a multitude—for the sacraments and observances of the ancient peoples are not the same as those of the new—still, all are fighting for the same king and under the same standard, pursue the same enemy and are crowned by the same victory." Lubac, *Splendor of the Church*, 185.

70 W. Cavanaugh, "The City Beyond Secular Parodies," in *Radical Orthodoxy*, ed. John Milbank, Catherine Pickstock, and Graham Ward (Oxford: Blackwell, 1999), 182–201.

71 The ITC's declaration on religious freedom addresses this topic. International Theological Commission, *Religious Freedom for the Good of All: Theological Approaches and Contemporary Challenges* (2019).

Swabian pedigree. However, just as we speak of left-wing Hegelians and right-wing Hegelians, a division is developing within ecclesiology between what might be called a Lubacian appropriation of Tübingen ecclesiology and a Kasperian appropriation. The papacies of John Paul II and Benedict XVI fostered the first; the papacy of Francis is fostering the second. There are some points of overlap but also elements of difference. Whether the universal Church has ontological priority over the local church, whether bishop's' conferences and lay assemblies are an affirmation of diversity or an exercise in increased bureaucratization and centralization, and whether we should mute the eschatological button for the sake of social peace are all hot topics in ecclesiology beginning the third millennium. Joining the conversation are whether bishops should be gentlemen bureaucrats who do paper work or social leaders who do people work, whether the powers of the Petrine office trump everything, or whether the Petrine office is itself subject to revelation and to the judgments of the Jacobite pillar, to use Balthasar's idiom. Another issue is the corporatization of the Church's pastoral mission and the principles by which the Vatican Diplomatic Corps operates. Indeed, some commentators have called for total reconsideration of the Diplomatic Corps' structure and the education of its members. Until these many and varied issues are resolved, "the Barque of Peter" may very well find herself "stranded on a sandbank."[72]

---

[72] Müller, "Development, or Corruption?," para. 16.

CHAPTER 2

The Operations of the Trinity Are Indivisible

Milestones in Pneumatology from Divinum Illud Munus *to* Dominum et Vivificantem[1]

Between 1897 and 1986 only two papal encyclicals directly addressed the subject of pneumatology. Almost one century of theological scholarship is bookended by Leo XIII's *Divinum Illud Munus* (*On the Holy Spirit*) and John Paul II's *Dominum et Vivificantem* (*The Lord, the Giver of Life*).

Divinum Illud Munus emphasized the unity of the persons of the Trinity. In §3, the heart of the encyclical, Leo XIII declared the persons of the Trinity are not to be honored separately in divine worship, nor are they considered as acting separately in the work of sanctification. Even if the three persons are mentioned separately in prayers such as litanies, such prayers should always end with an invocation to the Blessed Trinity. Leo XIII also referenced St. Augustine's comment in *De Trinitate*, that the words "of Him, and by Him, and in Him" are not to be taken indiscriminately; but rather, "of Him refers to the Father, by Him to the Son, and in Him to the Holy Ghost."[2] Pope Leo then affirmed the Church's custom of attributing to the Father those works of the divinity in which power excels, to the Son those in which wisdom excels, and to the Holy Spirit those in which love

---

[1] This essay was first published in Kevin Wagner, Peter John McGregor, and M. Isabell Naumann, eds., *Pneumatology at the Beginning of the Third Millennium* (Eugene, OR: Pickwick Publications, 2023), chap. 15. Used with permission.

[2] Augustine, *De Trinitate*, 1, i, c. 6.

excels. Notwithstanding this appropriation, he quickly added the caveat that all perfections and external operations are common to the divine persons because the "operations of the Trinity are indivisible."[3]

The sequel to this 1897 encyclical is Pius XII's 1943 encyclical *Mystici Corporis Christi* (*The Mystical Body of Christ*), which refers back to *Divinum Illud Munus* to the effect that while Christ is the head of the Church, the Holy Spirit is her soul.[4] This principle is defended in §§56–57 where the various works of the Holy Spirit in the life of Christ and in the Church are enumerated: it is the Holy Spirit, "the principle of every supernatural act in all parts of the Body [of Christ],"[5] who makes the members of the Church adopted sons of God, and who assists them in proportion to their various duties and offices and in proportion to the greater or lesser degree of spiritual health which they enjoy.

In both encyclicals, the Holy Spirit is treated primarily in the context of the Spirit's relationship to the other two persons of the Trinity; second, in the context of the Spirit's work in the life of the Church; and third, in the context of the Spirit's work in the souls of individual members of the Body of Christ. These contexts correspond to the fields of Trinitarian theology, and what Yves Congar calls *ecclésiologie pneumatologique* and *anthropologie pneumatologique* (pneumatological ecclesiology and pneumatological anthropology).

In Catholic Trinitarian theology, arguably the most seminal work of the twentieth century was Karl Rahner's 1967 publication in the *Mysterium Salutis* series, and its reprint three years later as a stand-alone volume simply titled *The Trinity*. This publication is famous for Rahner's criticism that Catholics had become "almost mere monotheists" and for his axiom "The economic Trinity is the immanent Trinity and the immanent Trinity is the economic Trinity."[6] This axiom spawned so many publications that it could have opened up its own subfield of Trinitarian theology. Although the axiom first appears in the 1967 publication, it was foreshadowed in Rahner's earlier works, including his 1939 article published in *Zeitschrift für katholische Theologie*.[7] While various authors criticized the second half of the axiom, that the immanent Trinity is the economic Trinity, something like universal agreement developed regarding Rahner's general judgment

---

[3] Augustine, *De Trinitate* I. 1, cc. 4–5; cf. Leo XII, *Divinum Illud Munus* (1897), §3.

[4] Pius XII, *Mystici Corporis Christi* (1943), §57; cf. *Divinum Illud Munus*, §6.

[5] *Mystici Corporis Christi*, §57.

[6] Karl Rahner, *The Trinity* (New York: Herder & Herder, 1970), 5.

[7] Karl Rahner, "Zur scholastiischen Begrifflichkeit der ungeschaffenen Gnade," *Zeitschrift für katholische Theologie* 63 (1939):137–57.

about a constructive, unwitting, monotheism existing in much pre-conciliar Catholic theology.

Consistent with Rahner's concern about an unintentional monotheism throughout the decades of the second half of the twentieth century, many scholarly monographs examined the salvific work of one particular person of the Trinity. Most notable in this genre is Louis Bouyer's trilogy *The Eternal Son*, *The Invisible Father*, and *The Consoler*, first published in their French versions between 1973 and 1980.

In pneumatological ecclesiology and pneumatological anthropology, the "lion" was Yves Congar with his *I Believe in the Holy Spirit* trilogy and the later short monograph *The Word and the Spirit*, which included material on the Holy Spirit as "co-instituting the Church" and the charisms as structuring principles of the Church. One of Congar's recurring themes was that institution and charism were not opposed to one another, notwithstanding the tension between the two. Congar's work was a milestone because it sought to unify pneumatological ecclesiology with pneumatological anthropology. Cornelis van Vliet argued in his summary that Congar examined the relationship between the ecclesiological and anthropological work of the Holy Spirit through the lens of three biblical motifs: the mystical body of Christ, the people of God, and the temple of the Holy Spirit. The mystical body motif dominated Congar's ecclesiology between 1931 and 1944; the theology of the people of God dominated between 1959 and 1968; and the theology of the temple of the Holy Spirit came to the fore between 1969 and 1991.[8] All three motifs are given extensive treatment by Benoît-Dominique de La Soujeole in his *Introduction to the Mystery of the Church*.[9] They also appear in *Lumen Gentium*. The ecclesiology of Vatican II is both Christological and pneumatological, and speaking of the pneumatological dimension, Aloys Grillmeier wrote,

> The Church is a unity of communion in the holy Eucharist, in the Holy Spirit, in the (visible) hierarchical government and in the various forms of service. It is an animated bodily unity in the variety of its members and their functions. And the hierarchical order is a self-communication of the Spirit just as are charismatic

---

[8] Cornelis Th. M. van Vliet, *Communio sacramentalis*: *Das Kirchenverständnis von Yves Congar—genetisch und systematisch betrachtet* (Mainz: Matthias-Grünewald, 1995), 83–87, 200–208, and 244–46. See also Elizabeth Teresa Groppe, *Yves Congar's Theology of the Holy Spirit* (Oxford University Press, 2004), chap. 4.

[9] Benoît-Dominique de La Soujeole, *Introduction to the Mystery of the Church* (Washington, DC: Catholic University of America Press, 2014).

endowments. Thus the Spirit is embodied in the Church, where he produces a mystical person from many persons.[10]

In his treatment of the conciliar understanding of the Church as the temple of the Holy Spirit, Benoît-Dominique de La Soujeole emphasizes that "unity among Christians is received from the Holy Spirit in Person; it is not 'produced' by human initiative. . . . The pastors do not bring about the deepest unity of the Church as a colonel brings about the unity of a regiment—in other words, principally by commanding and by being obeyed."[11] Unity is, rather, the fruit of the gifts of the Holy Spirit, the "hierarchy is not 'productive' of the fundamental unity (as in a socio-juridical scheme), but rather the servant of the gift of unity."[12] In short, unity cannot be coerced by Petrine or episcopal decree.

Discerning the will of the Holy Spirit is not, however, an easy task, and Congar observed that "revelation and knowledge of the Spirit are affected by a certain lack of conceptual mediation."[13] While the idea of a Father and Son are easy to understand, the "Spirit" is much less accessible. "The Holy Spirit empties himself, in a kind of kenosis of his own personality, in order to be in a relationship, on the one hand, with 'God' and Christ and, on the other, with men, who are called to realise the image of God and his Son."[14] The Holy Spirit is therefore revealed to us and known to us not in himself but through what he brings about in us.[15] This makes sense of Christ's principle that "by their fruits you shall know them" (Matt 7:15–20). A key element of any pneumatological anthropology is therefore a person's receptivity to the gifts of the Holy Spirit.

In the context of his pneumatogical anthropology, Congar, following St. Thomas Aquinas, affirmed the importance of the seven gifts of the Holy Spirit for moral theology. He described the gifts as "dispositions" that make the Christian ready to grasp and follow and inspirations of the Holy Spirit "beyond the power of the virtues, beyond his reason as animated by faith, beyond his supernatural prudence, by another who is infinitely superior

---

[10] Aloys Grillmeier, "The Mystery of the Church," in *Commentary on the Documents of Vatican II*, ed. Herbert Vorgrimler (New York: Herder & Herder, 1969), 1:142.

[11] La Soujeole, *Mystery of the Church*, 189.

[12] La Soujeole, *Mystery of the Church*, 189.

[13] Yves Congar, *I Believe in the Holy Spirit*, vol. 1, *The Experience of the Spirit* (London: Geoffrey Chapman, 1983), vii.

[14] Congar, *Experience of the Spirit*, 1:vii.

[15] Congar, *Experience of the Spirit*, 1:viii.

and has sovereign freedom."[16] The "another" here is the Holy Spirit. For Congar, the gifts are not superior to the theological virtues of faith, hope, and love, but are at the service of the virtues, "enabling them to be practiced perfectly."[17] "This is a position far removed from a purely rational moral attitude, or from an attitude often imputed to Thomas, that is, a morality based on models derived from a nature of things that is established outside time."[18] On the contrary, "Thomas allows for the *event* of the Spirit; for him, morality is based on the saving and sanctifying will of God, according to norms which go beyond human and even supernatural reason."[19] While reason and a conception of natural law both have their place in Thomistic moral teaching, such teaching cannot be reduced to arguments based upon reason and natural law alone.[20]

In addition to building bridges between pneumatological ecclesiology and pneumatological anthropology, Congar criticized Joachimism: the idea that there can be a relatively autonomous and new time of the Holy Spirit, transcending the time of Christ, as put forward by Joachim of Fiore (ca. 1135–1202), the founder of the monastic order of San Giovanni in Fiore. According to Congar, Thomas Aquinas was "resolutely, severely and radically critical of Joachim's teaching. He regarded Joachim as a lout playing with theology; 'in *subtilibus fidei dogmatibus rudis*,' and his theology of the Trinity in particular as wrong."[21]

> Joachim introduced into the history of this world, which was for
> him, of course, the history of the Church, an eschatology that was
> characterized by the great novelty of a rule of the inner life and
> of freedom. Joachim in his way opened the flood-gates to admit
> what could well become the torrent of human hopes. This could
> at any time result in social protest, a polarized attempt to reform
> the Church, or many different searches for freedom and novelty. It
> could take the form of philosophies of reason, of progress, of the
> "spirit." . . . There have been, parallel to what Etienne Gilson called

---

[16] Congar, *Experience of the Spirit*, 1:119–20.

[17] Congar, *Experience of the Spirit*, 1:120.

[18] Congar, *Experience of the Spirit*, 1:120.

[19] Congar, *Experience of the Spirit*, 1:120.

[20] For a treatment of these issues see Livio Melina, *Sharing in Christ's Virtues: For the Renewal of Moral Theology in the Light of Veritatis Splendor*, trans. William E. May (Washington, DC: Catholic University of America Press, 2001).

[21] Congar, *Experience of the Spirit*, 1:127. See also, for a criticism of Joachimism, La Soujeole, *Mystery of the Church*, 143–44.

"metamorphoses of the City of God," a series of metamorphoses of Joachimism which have often been forms of secularization of the Spirit. I summarise the most important.[22]

Congar's summary ran for two pages and included Kant, Hegel, Schelling, and Adolf Hitler as examples of those infected with the spirit of Joachimism before he ended with a quotation from the Episcopalian theologian Thomas Altizer as an example of where the dangerous trajectory of Joachmite ideas can end. Altizer was associated with the "death of God" movement.

> The radical Christian also inherits both the ancient prophetic belief that revelation continues in history and the eschatological belief of the tradition following Joachim of Floris. This tradition maintains that we are now living in the third and final age of the Spirit, that a new revelation is breaking into this age and that this revelation will differ as much from the New Testament as the New Testament itself does from its Old Testament counterpart. . . . We can learn from earlier radical Christians the root radical principle that the movement of the Spirit has passed beyond the revelation of the canonical Bible and is now revealing itself in such a way as to demand a whole new form of faith. To refuse such a new revelation of the Spirit would be to repudiate the activity of the Word which is present and to bind oneself to a now empty and lifeless form of the Word. Nor can we expect the new revelation to be in apparent continuity with the old. . . . Yet this should by no means persuade us that no new revelation has occurred. We can only judge by the fruits of the Spirit and if a new vision has arisen recoding a universal and eschatological form of the Word, a form of the Word pointing to a total redemption of history and the cosmos, then we should be prepared to greet it with the full acceptance of faith.[23]

Congar was strongly critical of such thinking, which in Catholic circles often arose in discussions about reading the signs of the times:

> However useful and indeed necessary the work of sociologists may be, these indications should not be interpreted purely sociologically, but rather in the light of the gospel, inspired by faith and led

---

[22] Congar, *Experience of the Spirit*, 1:129.
[23] Congar, *Experience of the Spirit*, 1:133.

by the Holy Spirit. . . . I do not deny that God acts in the history of the secular world or that historical events and movements can tell us something of what God wants for us and therefore of what he is. What is difficult, however, is the interpretation of those events. Interpretation is able to go further than mere conjecture and personal conviction only if the meaning of the facts is tied to and illuminated by the positive revelation of God's plan with Jesus Christ at its centre. And here we need to bear in mind that the salvation and the kingdom that God's plan envisages include the world of creation and are God's response to creation's groaning and its hope (see Romans 8: 20–24).[24] . . .

The Spirit, however, is the Spirit of Jesus Christ. He does no other work but that of Jesus Christ. There is no time of the Paraclete that is not the time of Jesus Christ, contrary to what Joachim of Fiore, who misinterpreted the original and correct idea that he had of history as open to hope and newness, seemed to believe. The catholicity of the Church is the catholicity of Christ. The soundness of any pneumatology is its reference to Christ.[25]

Congar thus insisted that the Spirit does not invent or introduce a new and different economy. Rather, he gives life to the flesh and words of Jesus (John 6:63). He recalls those words to mind and penetrates the whole truth: "He will not speak on his own account, but whatever he hears he will speak. . . . He will glorify me."[26]

Congar also concurred with St. Augustine's idea that the Church exists in two orbs or circles. The first is the *communio sacramentorum*, which is the work of Christ, and the second is the *societas sanctorum*, which is the work of the Holy Spirit.[27] Following the line of argumentation in the magisterial documents, Congar also noted that for Augustine, the Holy Spirit performs that function in the Church that is carried out in the body by the soul.[28]

Hans Urs von Balthasar also strongly opposed Joachimism. While Rahner, Bouyer, Congar, and others contributed to pneumatology by exploring the economic Trinity, Balthasar and the mystic Adrienne von Speyr went exploring in the opposite direction with their speculations on the work of

---

[24] Yves Congar, *I Believe in the Holy Spirit*, vol. 2, *Lord and Giver of Life* (London: Geoffrey Chapman, 1983), 32.

[25] Congar, *Lord and Giver*, 2:35.

[26] Congar, *Experience of the Spirit*, 1:56–57.

[27] Congar, *Experience of the Spirit*, 1:80.

[28] Congar, *Experience of the Spirit*, 1:80.

kenosis within the immanent Trinity. One of the best examinations of this aspect of Balthasarian thought is Michele M. Schumacher's *A Trinitarian Anthropology*.[29] In this work, Schumacher seeks to promote dialogue between disciples of Balthasar (d. 1988) and those of Aquinas (d. 1274) on the critical theological question of how analogies and metaphors drawn from the philosophy and theology of the person (that is, from anthropology) may rightly be used to address the mystery of the Trinity.[30] In *Creator Spirit*, Balthasar offered his analysis of the problems with Joachimism:

> The only thing that must be set down as certain for the moment is that the trinitarian Spirit will never let his divine freedom blow elsewhere than in the sphere of the love between Father and Son, and that he will not encounter and direct the human spirit in any other way than by judging it and redeeming it and giving it admittance to this love of which he is the fruit and the witness.[31]

Brendan McInerny argues that Balthasar's description of the immanent Trinity provides a way to speak of how "God is love" in himself, beyond his relationship to creatures.[32] He then shows how Balthasar's speculation into the immanent Trinity serves as the substructure of his theology of deification. One might say that pneumatology is the bridge between spirituality and dogmatic theology for Balthasar.

A work that drills deep into the relationship between Balthasar's Trinitarian theology and his theology of deification is Sigurd Lefsrud's *Kenosis in Theosis*. Lefsrud argues that in Balthasar's theology, "becoming like God" goes beyond simply being "like Christ" to participating in the kenotic relations of the three persons of the Trinity.[33] In other words, there is a movement from describing humanity as the *imago Dei* to characterizing

---

[29] Michele M. Schumacher, *A Trinitarian Anthropology: Adrienne von Speyr and Hans Urs von Balthasar in Dialogue with Thomas Aquinas* (Washington, DC: Catholic University of America Press, 2014).

[30] For those seeking to understand Balthasar's pneumatology, see Hans Urs von Balthasar, *Theo-Logic*, vol. 3, *The Spirit of Truth*, trans. Adrian J. Walker (San Francisco: Ignatius Press, 2005); and Balthasar, *Explorations in Theology*, vol. 3, *Creator Spirit* (San Francisco: Ignatius Press, 1993).

[31] Balthasar, *Creator Spirit*, 3:156.

[32] Brendan McInerny, *The Trinitarian Theology of Hans Urs von Balthasar* (Notre Dame, IN: University of Notre Dame Press, 2020).

[33] Sigurd Lefsrud, *Kenosis in Theosis: An Exploration of Balthasar's Theology of Deification* (Eugene, OR: Pickwick Publications, 2020), 141.

this image as the *imago Christi*, and finally to considering humanity as the *imago trinitatis*.[34]

Running parallel with Balthasar was Jean Daniélou's *La Trinité et la Mystère de l'existence* (1968), published in English as *God's Life in Us*. Marc Nicholas described it as offering a doxological humanism, highlighting the place of pneumatology in theological anthropology. The book offers a theological reflection upon the words "Through Him, with Him, in Him, in the unity of the Holy Spirit, all glory and honor is yours, almighty Father, for ever and ever." Daniélou (1905–1974) concurred with Léonce de Grandmaison's statement that the continuing work of the Word and the Spirit in the world aims at "all men becoming Christians and all Christians becoming saints."[35] In other words, "the primary goal of missionary activity is the expansion of Trinitarian life through the believer's sharing in the divine life of the triune God."[36]

While Daniélou represented the Jesuit tradition, his fellow country-man Marie-Joseph le Guillou (1920–1990) represented the Dominican tradition and followed Congar in producing works on the Holy Trinity.[37] He also followed Bouyer and Congar in working in ecumenism, especially Catholic-Orthodox ecumenism, where pneumatology is the axial issue.

Arriving now at the papacy of St. John Paul II (1978–2005), just one decade after the publication of Rahner's *The Trinity*, St. John Paul II began

---

[34] Lefsrud, *Kenosis in Theosis*, 141.

[35] Quoted in Jean Daniélou, "Missionary Nature of the Church," in *The Word in the Third World*, ed. James P. Cotter (Washington, DC: Corpus Books, 1968), 11–43, at 14.

[36] Marc Nicholas, *Jean Daniélou's Doxological Humanism: Trinitarian Contemplation and Humanity's True Vocation* (Eugene, OR: Pickwick Publications, 2012), 89.

[37] Marie-Joseph le Guillou, *Les Témoins sont parmi nous. L'expérience de Dieu dans l'Esprit Saint* (Paris: Fayard, 1976); Guillou, *L'expérience de l'Esprit-Saint en Orient et en Occident* (Saint-Maur, France: Parole et Silence, 2000); and Guillou, "Le développement de la doctrine sur l'Esprit Saint dans les écrits du Nouveau Testament," in *Credo in Spiritum Sanctum. Atti del Congresso teologico internazionale pneumatologia*, ed. J. Saraiva Martins, Roma, 22–26 marzo 1982 (Libreria Editrice Vaticana, Città del Vaticano, 1983), 729–39.

The latter is an essay contribution on the development of the doctrine of the Holy Spirit in the books of the New Testament at the congress *Credo in Spiritum Sanctum*, held in Rome in 1982 to celebrate the 1600th anniversary of the Council of Constantinople and the 1550th anniversary of the Council of Ephesus. The Congress brought together the leading scholars in pneumatology from around the world, including Yves Congar, who passionately affirmed the reality of the Holy Spirit's work in the contemporary world, Ignace de La Potterie, and John Zizioulas. See Congar, "Actualité de la Pneumatologie," in *Credo*, 15–28; La Potterie, "L'Esprit Saint et l'Église," in *Credo*, 791–808; and Zizioulas, "The Teaching of the Second Ecumenical Council on the Holy Spirit in Historical and Ecumenical Perspective," in *Credo*, 29–53.

his quarter-century teaching pontificate with a suite of encyclicals on each of the divine persons: *Redemptor Hominis* (1979) was on God the Son, *Dives in Misericordia* (1980) was on God the Father, and *Dominum et Vivificantem* (1986) was on God the Holy Spirit. John Paul II followed this pattern in the second decade of his Wojtylian pontificate, declaring 1997 as the Year of God the Son, 1998 as the Year of the Holy Spirit, and 1999 as the Year of God the Father. These years of reflection on the divine persons prepared for the celebration of the second millennium of Christianity.

Dominum et Vivificantem (1986) begins with references to the inseparable relationship between Christ and the Holy Spirit, echoing Leo XIII, Congar, Balthasar, and many others concerned about Joachimist tendencies to separate the two:[38] "Between the Holy Spirit and Christ there thus subsists, in the economy of salvation, an intimate bond, whereby the Spirit works in human history as 'another Counsellor,' permanently ensuring the transmission and spreading of the Good News revealed by Jesus of Nazareth."[39]

The emphasis on the Holy Spirit as both love and gift, which is also strong in the theology of Balthasar, appears in §41:

> The Holy Spirit as Love and Gift comes down, in a certain sense, into the very heart of the sacrifice which is offered on the Cross. Referring here to the biblical tradition, we can say: He consumes this sacrifice with the fire of the love which unites the Son with the Father in the Trinitarian communion. And since the sacrifice of the Cross is an act proper to Christ, also in this sacrifice he "receives" the Holy Spirit. He receives the Holy Spirit in such a way that afterwards—and he alone with God the Father—can "give him" to the Apostles, to the Church, to humanity. He alone "sends" the Spirit from the Father. He alone presents himself before the Apostles in the Upper Room, "breathes upon them" and says: "Receive the Holy Spirit; if you forgive the sins of any, they are forgiven," as John the Baptist had foretold: "He will baptize you with the Holy Spirit and with fire." With those words of Jesus, the Holy Spirit is revealed and at the same time made present as the Love that works in the depths of the Paschal Mystery, as the source of the salvific power of the Cross of Christ, and as the gift of new and eternal life.

---

[38] For an overview of the Trinitarian theology of St. John Paul II, see Antoine E. Nachef, *The Mystery of the Trinity in the Theological Thought of Pope John Paul II* (New York: Peter Lang, 1999).

[39] John Paul II, *Dominum et Vivificantem* (1986), §7.

Another strong motif is that the Holy Spirit will convince the world concerning sin. St. John Paul II links this concept to theological anthropology so it becomes an exercise in pneumatological anthropology.

> The Gospel's "convincing concerning sin" under the influence of the Spirit of truth can be accomplished in man in no other way except through the conscience. If the conscience is upright, it serves "to resolve according to truth the moral problems which arise both in the life of individuals and from social relationships"; then "persons and groups turn aside from blind choice and try to be guided by the objective standards of moral conduct."[40]

The Holy Spirit being both gift and love is repeated in §52 where reference is made to the human person becoming a partaker in the divine nature through the Holy Spirit who grants him access to God the Father, as grace bears within itself both a Christological and a pneumatological aspect (§53). These principles of a pneumatological anthropology are then drawn together in §55:

> In the texts of St. Paul there is a superimposing—and a mutual compenetration—of the ontological dimension (the flesh and the spirit), the ethical (moral good and evil), and the pneumatological (the action of the Holy Spirit in the order of grace). His words (especially in the *Letters to the Romans* and *Galatians*) enable us to know and feel vividly the strength of the tension and struggle going on in man between openness to the action of the Holy Spirit and resistance and opposition to him, to his saving gift.

Returning then to the mission of the Holy Spirit to convince the world concerning sin, §56 concludes,

> The resistance to the Holy Spirit which St. Paul emphasizes in the interior and subjective dimension as tension, struggle and rebellion taking place in the human heart, finds in every period of history and especially in the modern era, its external dimension, which takes concrete form as the content of culture and civilization, as a philosophical system, an ideology, a program for action and for the shaping of human behaviour.

---

[40] *Dominum et Vivificantem*, §43.

Concretely, St. John Paul II identified materialism, including its manifestation in varieties of Marxism, as the dominant ideology of the late twentieth century resistant to the work of the Holy Spirit. This materialism underpins what the philosopher Rémi Brague calls an exclusive humanism, a humanism that excludes Christ.[41]

From this brief review of the milestones in pneumatology between the two encyclicals, a common theme cascading down the decades is the inseparable relationship between Christology and pneumatology and the importance of understanding the bridges between pneumatology and ecclesiology and pneumatology and theological anthropology. Included is recognizing the recurring attraction for new forms of Joachimism, which may be yet another manifestation of resistance to the Holy Spirit taking concrete form in both the culture of the world and the culture of the Church.

---

[41] Rémi Brague, *The Kingdom of Man: Genesis and Failure of the Modern Project* (Notre Dame, IN: University of Notre Dame Press, 2018).

CHAPTER 3

Joseph Ratzinger on Democracy within the Church[1]

Since the 1960s, activist groups demanding a democratization of ecclesial structures have operated on the margins of ecclesial life in most parts of the Anglosphere, but this has not been the case in Germany, Austria, and Switzerland. In these German-speaking regions, together with Belgium and the Netherlands, debates about the nature of the priesthood, the episcopacy, and the Petrine office have been percolating for half a century. Today these debates have become a matter of global interest. This is partly due to the failure of two or three generations of bishops to act as responsible shepherds when confronted by sexual scandals. Both presbyterate and episcopacy are now subjected to intense theological and sociological analyses, generating calls for desacralizing both and promoting democracy and bureaucracy as substitutes for sacred offices and sacred institutions. Ratzinger, however, to take a cue from Fr. Martin Onuoha, author of two academic works on the Mariology of Joseph Ratzinger, fought "tooth and nail" against a view of the Church as a bureaucratic structure administering social welfare services and programs for political action.[2]

---

[1] This essay was written for publication in *Communio: International Catholic Review*—the special commemorative edition celebrating the intellectual legacy of Benedict XVI. Used with permission.

[2] Martin Onuoha, Actio Divina: *The Marian Mystery of the Church in the Theology of Joseph Ratzinger* (New York: Peter Lang, 2021), 60.

The Church as "Catholic Inc." or the Church as the Mystical Body of Christ

For one party of protagonists, let us call them the democratization activists, the Church is predominately a bureaucratic structure comprised of agencies offering social welfare and educational and medical services inspired by Gospel parables like the Good Samaritan. The leadership of such agencies has commonly passed from members of religious orders (nuns, brothers, and priests) to professional lay Catholics. The qualifications required for senior positions in these institutions are scarcely different from those required for a CEO, though a unit or two of theology on the curriculum vitae is useful.

Women in these positions often find they are more highly educated than the priests with whom they work and, even more importantly, they are often more highly educated than the bishops to whom they report. They see the Church as a vast bureaucracy; they look at the power structures within the bureaucracy and are often frustrated to find their ideas thwarted by some male whose only qualification is having been to the same school as the bishop. The so-called "sacramental" life of the Church is not of much interest to such as these. They tend to see sacraments as social milestones and opportunities for the Church to administer pastoral care. Sacraments become something like another service provided by a utilitarian Church. Priests and bishops (in the case of Confirmation) are responsible for this and they are all males. Those who understand the Church as something like Catholic Inc. find the idea that these "sacrament providers" have to be male incomprehensible. They break down the "job description" of the priest to the delivery of liturgical services, a bit of scriptural exegesis, the provision of pastoral care and spiritual encouragement, and keeping the parish administration running. They ask why a woman could not perform these jobs as equally well as any male. They determine they are working for an organization about a century behind the corporate world. Sometimes such women also experience a form of male chauvinism. Given their negative experiences in ecclesial bureaucracies, they start to see themselves as oppressed by those in Holy Orders. To deal with this problem, they look to the source of priestly and episcopal authority (the very notion of Holy Orders) and begin chipping away at it. They conclude that they must demythologize or desacralize the episcopacy and priesthood, and they find intellectual support in the works of theologians, predominately those from German-speaking countries.

Quite another understanding of the Church is that of the mystical body of Christ and indeed the "Bride of Christ." This non-bureaucratic view sees the Church as a sacred institution, established by Christ to carry on his mission to lead all humanity into a relationship with the Holy Trinity. The language of "sanctification," "redemption," the "deposit of faith," "grace," and "vocation" predominate with this group. They regard social welfare, medical, and educational services provided by the Church as a subordinate part of the mission to bring people into a relationship with the Holy Trinity, not a "stand alone" community service. They do not really care who governs such institutions, male or female, religious or lay, provided they are governed according to the faith and teachings of the Church. Accordingly, they expect Catholic schools to teach the Catholic faith, Catholic social welfare institutions to not hand out contraceptives in care packages, and Catholic medical institutions to not foster practices like in vitro fertilization, euthanasia, or gender reassignment surgery.

Discerning the ethos of ostensibly Catholic institutions matters to this group: is this ethos determined by Catholic teaching or by something else, such as business management theory? They have no interest in what arithmetical proportion of minority groups are in leadership positions within the institution. Those who think this way are also often unhappy about the behavior of bishops. They find some of them to be "mere bureaucrats" presiding over the corporate governance of Catholic Inc. and offering little or nothing by way of leadership, spiritual or otherwise. They are disappointed when bishops do not bear witness as "shepherds" or "confessors of the faith" but come across as mere "company men" stamping their names to the bottom of policy documents and the decisions of their business managers, who often have no interest in the pastoral care of the faithful Catholics, either on the payroll or in the pews.

This group also includes many highly educated women who accept the magisterial teaching that ordination must be reserved to men—not because women lack the intellectual capacity to perform aspects of the "job"—but because of the reasons given in ecclesial documents like *Inter Insigniores* regarding the Christological nature of the priesthood. Not only do the women in this group not want women priests but many say that were the Catholic Church to start ordaining women, they would leave and become Greek or Russian Orthodox. They also point out that Protestant denominations that ordain women have fractured and their participants have plummeted.

While this is merely a thumbnail sketch of sociological generalizations, it highlights two different understandings of the Church in play. Further, those in the first group tend to see the solution to the recent failures of priests and bishops in the imposition of greater corporate and legal practices to circumscribe and sanction their behavior. They would replace charismatic authority and exercising prudential judgment with bureaucratic authority, establishing committees to monitor the decisions of priests and bishops and radically diminish the possibilities for prudential judgment.

On the contrary, for those who view the Church as a sacred institution, as the mystical body of Christ, the proliferation of consultative committees only exacerbate the failures of bishops to take personal responsibility for the mismanagement of the abuse crisis. In diocese after diocese, bishops have relegated the problem to committees of "experts" comprising lawyers, accountants, and psychologists. The lawyers acted to reduce the liabilities of "Catholic Inc.," the accountants acted to protect the assets of "Catholic Inc.," and the psychologists acted to defuse the moral culpability of Church functionaries and their superiors by prescribing a variety of courses to treat the psychological flaws that lay at the base of the sinful behavior. For those who want to affirm the theology of the Church as the mystical body of Christ, the solution to the current crises is neither more bureaucracy, nor more committees of experts exercising de facto episcopal authority, but more episcopal holiness and heroism.

It is clear from Ratzinger's many statements in his pre-papal and papal publications that he was inclined toward the second position. For Ratzinger, the Church is the mystical body of Christ, and the ecclesial structure that embraces the office of priest, bishop, and pope is divinely ordained, not some obsolete administrative hangover from the period of the Roman empire.

DEMOCRACY ACCORDING TO CRITICAL THEORY

From the days of his childhood experience of fascism, Joseph Ratzinger understood that popular democracy was not in itself a sufficient foil against totalitarian ideologies and other forms of oppressive behavior: "If the moral principles underpinning the democratic process are themselves determined by nothing more solid that social consensus, then the fragility of the process becomes all too evident."[3] Only a belief in a truth that transcends all forms of tribalism and of mob opinion can be a sufficient foil to totalitarian ideologies and practices. Democracy as a concept and as a political practice is much more ambivalent in its relationship to human freedom. In particular, the nexus between truth and democratic practice becomes particularly problematic in the account of democracy offered by the Critical Theory of the Frankfurt School of Social Research that became fashionable after the Second World War.

---

[3] Benedict XVI, Address to the Representatives of British Society, Westminster Hall, Westminster, September 17, 2010.

Some of Ratzinger's strongest statements against the recourse to "democracy" as a solution to current problems within the Church appear in the work *Demokratie in der Kirche*,[4] which contains essays by Ratzinger and by Hans Maier, a West German politician.[5] Ratzinger approaches the issues theologically, while Maier offers insights from his own experience of democratic processes as a politician. The book was republished in 2000 with additional essays in which Ratzinger and Maier reflected upon the events of the intervening three decades. Ratzinger began his new essay by saying,

> When, at the publisher's invitation, I took my almost forgotten article on the democratization of the church off the bookshelf and read it again, I was surprised to find that I still agree with everything that was said then. I myself was amazed at how constant my views have remained in these eventful thirty years, which have also brought about serious upheavals in my own life.[6]

Ratzinger observed that post-World War II, democracy had morphed from a theory about forms of government into a doctrine of politically administered salvation: "'Democracy' is primarily, and not only in the area of student movements, the code for a doctrine of salvation, which Karl Rahner recently adopted in an astonishingly undifferentiated manner in his lecture on 'Freedom and Manipulation in the Church.'"[7] According to this view, "freedom is equated with the complete unrestrictedness of the ego, which is not subject to any social limitations; the institution [including the Church] as such therefore becomes synonymous with manipulation."[8]

The word "manipulation" was fashionable in the 1960s due to the

---

4   Joseph Ratzinger and Hans Maier, *Demokratie in der Kirche: Möglichkeiten und Grenzen* (Limburg: Lahn-Verlag, 2000).

5   The collection was published in Spanish as *Democracia en la Iglesia?* (1971; 2005), in French as *Démocratisation dans l'Église? possibilités, limites, risques* (1972), in Portuguese as *Democracia na igreja: possibilidade limites perigos* (1976), in Polish as *Demokracja w Kościele. Możliwości i ograniczenia* (2005), and in Italian as *Democrazia nella Chiesa. Possibilità e limiti* (2005). As far as we have been able to discern, there is no published version of the collection in English and the quotations in this article are our' own translations.

6   Joseph Ratzinger, "Demokratisierung der Kirche—Dreissig Jahre Danach," in *Demokratie in der Kirche: Möglichkeiten und Grenzen*, by Joseph Ratzinger and Hans Maier (Limburg: Lahn-Verlag, 2000), 78.

7   Joseph Ratzinger, "Der Ausgangspunkt vom Begriff der Demokratie," in Ratzinger and Maier, *Demokratie in der Kirche*, 12. Ratzinger is referencing Karl Rahner, *Freiheit und Manipulation in Gesellschaft und Kirche* (München: Kösel Verlag, 1970).

8   Ratzinger, "Begriff der Demokratie," 12.

influence of Critical Theory. Manipulation and "false consciousness" (thinking you are free when you are being manipulated) were key concepts in Critical Theory, which was the worldview driving the generation of 1968 student rebels.[9] When Karl Rahner called his lecture "Freedom and Manipulation in the Church," he was calling on the idiom of Critical Theory. Critical Theory merged a central plank of liberal political tradition, the concept of democracy, with utopian dreams of Marxism. Democracy had been assimilated to eschatology via a notion of a god-like freedom common to Kantian or Marxist philosophies. As Paul Henry described it, "Marxism represented the materialistic messianism of a laicized Christian hope, for whom Christ is only a stopover from which to pass beyond, a dialectical moment of the historical becoming."[10] Similarly, Ratzinger noted that "the view that the Bible speaks exclusively in terms of salvation history (and thus, anti-metaphysically) facilitated the fusing of the biblical horizon with the Marxist idea of history."[11] In effect, "it [history] swallows up the concepts of God and Revelation and takes over the role of God."[12] The concepts of freedom and democracy are conflated with the notion of salvation. Ratzinger argued that the logic of this new conception of democracy was that "democracy would therefore no longer be a form of rule but a lack of rule, anarchy alone would be true democracy because it alone would mean the end of manipulation."[13] The "decisive error of the whole conception lies in the misunderstanding of man that prevails here: in this vision man is confused with God, in that he is regarded as the essence of absolute freedom."[14]

Ratzinger offered a student protest at a German university in the late 1960s as a concrete example of this. He did not say at which university, but it was probably Tübingen. A group of students disrupted a lecture as a political act to oppose what they called the "authoritarian transfer of knowledge from one teacher to many students." According to such an interpretation of democracy, those who hold doctorates should not be treated as members of a higher academic class than undergraduates. The lecturer responded to the

---

[9] See Herbert Marcuse, *One Dimensional Man: Studies in the Ideology of Advanced Industrial Society* (London: Taylor and Francis, 2013); Raymond Geuss, *The Idea of a Critical Theory: Habermas and the Frankfurt School* (Cambridge University Press, 1981); and Dino Franco Felluga, *Critical Theory: The Key Concepts* (London: Routledge, 2002).

[10] Paul Henry, "Christian Philosophy of History," *Theological Studies* 13, no. 1 (March 1952): 419–32, at 430.

[11] Joseph Ratzinger, *The Ratzinger Report* (San Francisco: Ignatius Press, 1985), 182.

[12] Ratzinger, *Ratzinger Report*, 182.

[13] Ratzinger, "Begriff der Demokratie," 12.

[14] Ratzinger, "Begriff der Demokratie," 13.

invasion of his class by inviting his students to vote on whether they wanted to leave. The entire cohort, several hundred in number, voted to remain. The protesters deemed they "had just voted in accordance with the system," and this behavior "confirmed that they were subject to the system and were not at all able to express themselves freely."[15] Those who wished to remain in class were suffering from false consciousness. Ratzinger concluded that "now we are being told that what the average person considers his freedom is only the systemic constraint that has become immanent to his consciousness and is therefore no longer transparent to him. The actual abyss of his slavery is that he regards the coercion of the system itself as his freedom."[16] He deemed this mentality "cynical."

A more recent illustration of such cynicism, this time in an ecclesial context, appeared in a report on the Australian Plenary Council, an event sponsored by the Australian Catholic Bishops' Conference as a synodal-style exercise. It was said that those women who have no desire to change Church teaching in the fields of moral theology or ecclesiology, were "crumb maidens," a term coined by *Guardian* journalist Amy Remeikis.[17] Rather than acknowledging the Catholic women who have perfectly sound theological reasons for supporting magisterial teaching, it alleged that such women suffer from a form of false consciousness. They falsely believe they are better off receiving the "crumbs" that might fall their way from episcopal tables than being a part of a protest movement that wins the war for female ordination.

Against accusations of "false consciousness" or "fake freedom," Ratzinger suggests to ask this question: "Who decides what is a constraint that has become immanent to consciousness and what is real freedom?"[18] In other words, why should we put our faith in the judgment of Marxist students or, we might add, *Guardian* journalists? Why are their views superior to the teaching of Christ?

A *"Bloc des Idées Incontestables"*

In his contribution to *Demokratie in der Kirche*, Maier noted that the "churches are helpless in the face of the tendency to expand and ideologically intensify the concept of democracy, which is expressed in the catchphrase

---

[15] Ratzinger, "Begriff der Demokratie," 14.

[16] Ratzinger, "Begriff der Demokratie," 14.

[17] Monica Doumit, "The Day I became a 'Crumb Maiden,'" *The Catholic Weekly*, Archdiocese of Sydney, July 14, 2022, https://www.catholicweekly.com.au/monica-doumit-the-day-i-became-a-crumb-maiden/.

[18] Ratzinger, "Begriff der Demokratie," 15.

'democratisation.'"[19] He suggested that the demand for the democratization of all areas of society, including the Church, was "essentially a totalitarian concept" but Catholic leaders often failed to see this because they had little experience of democratic processes and little understanding of the varieties of democratic theory.[20] Moreover, some German theologians, principally Jürgen Moltmann and Johann Baptist Metz, bought into the new conceptions of freedom and democracy. They argued that a new relationship between theory and practice, knowledge and morality, reflection and revolution must also determine theological work. In other words, "political reason must be involved in all critical reflections on theology."[21] Maier remarked that "the reader has to engage in a quasi-Hegelian historical construction in order to be able to discuss freedom and democracy with these theologians at all" and such academic projects are devotions "to history disguised as revolutionary theology."[22] As a politician engaged in the real world of democratic processes, Maier concluded,

> The theological reception of democracy, at least in the German-speaking world, is still almost entirely limited to historical-philosophical preludes and vague attempts at a theory of ideas of democracy. It does not reach or does not want to come close to the reality of existing democracy.... [Real, existing democracy] is a complicated composite of many formal elements that can only be explained historically and sociologically, and many other influences and building principles are at work in it than simply those of popular sovereignty, emancipation, equality and direct egalitarian participation, concepts that are constantly mentioned in theological discussion.[23]

Nonetheless, Maier did acknowledge that several positive analogies could be drawn between how the Church is structured and how real, existing democracies operate: a relationship of trust exists between those who govern and those governed; the exercise of power is bound to constitutional procedures or conventions; and the decision-making process is shaped by the rule of law for the state or the deposit of faith for the Church, and

---

[19] Maier, *Demokratie in der Kirche*, 53.
[20] Maier, *Demokratie in der Kirche*, 53.
[21] Maier, *Demokratie in der Kirche*, 55.
[22] Maier, *Demokratie in der Kirche*, 56–57.
[23] Maier, *Demokratie in der Kirche*, 59–60.

this concept—the deposit of faith—itself includes the notion of a *bloc des idées incontestables*.[24] Maier observes that "faith and dogma are, analogously speaking, the constitutional substance of the church. They belong to the 'unchangeable constitutional law.'"[25] While doctrine can develop per constitutional amendments, some constitutional elements can never change: for example, no constitutional convention could ever simply recreate "France."[26]

Ratzinger made a similar point in his essay on liturgical developments in which he rejected the idea that a pope is an absolute monarch because papal judgments are circumscribed by Scripture and Tradition. This circumscription makes the papacy more of a constitutional monarchy than an absolute monarchy: "Even the supreme authority in the Church may not change the liturgy arbitrarily, but only in the obedience of faith and with religious respect for the mystery of the liturgy" (CCC, §1125). Referencing this passage, Ratzinger declared that "the Pope is not an absolute monarch whose will is law, but the guardian of an authentic Tradition." He cannot do whatever he likes with the liturgy, and he is duty-bound to oppose the initiatives of those who believe that they can do whatever "comes into their head." He has "the task of a gardener, not that of a technician who builds new machines and throws the old ones on the junk-pile." The various liturgical Rites of the Church are nothing less than a "living form of *paradosis*—the handing-on of tradition."[27] While these statements were made concerning liturgical theology, for Ratzinger they would apply to ecclesiology as well.

For those who accept the powers of the Petrine and episcopal offices being circumscribed by Scripture and Tradition—the *bloc des idées incontestables* (the constitution of the Church, as it were)—the crucial issue becomes the bond of trust between clerical leaders and the laity, not the democratization of the Church. Each sphere or dimension of the Church has duties and responsibilities in relation to the other and the system only works if the trust is not broken.

Speaking of those who in the late 1960s showed little interest in the discussions leading up to the Synod of Würzburg (1971–1975), Ratzinger remarked,

> There are complaints that the majority of believers generally show little interest in dealing with the Synod. I have to admit that this

---

[24] Maier, *Demokratie in der Kirche*, 71.
[25] Maier, *Demokratie in der Kirche*, 71.
[26] Maier, *Demokratie in der Kirche*, 72.
[27] Joseph Ratzinger, preface to *The Organic Development of the Liturgy*, by Alcuin Reid (Farnborough: St. Michael's Abbey Press, 2004), 3.

reluctance seems to me to be more of a sign of health. From a Christian point of view, i.e. for what is actually meant by the New Testament, little is gained by people passionately grappling with synodal problems—just as little does anyone become a sportsman as a result of his being deeply involved in the structure of the Olympic Committee.[28] . . .

The fact that people are gradually becoming indifferent to the busyness of the ecclesiastical apparatus, making people talk about themselves and to bring themselves to mind, is not only under-standable, but also correct from an objective ecclesiastical point of view. They don't always want to know how bishops, priests and full-time Catholics can balance their offices, but rather what God wants from them in life and in death and what He doesn't want.[29]

Three Key Theological Concepts

Having thus affirmed the attitudes of Catholics who are more interested in the sacramental life of the Church than with those who sit on committees, Ratzinger then offers an analysis of the theological scaffolding underpinning calls for the democratization of ecclesial governance. He suggests there are three key theological concepts, each capable of theologically sound inter-pretation but misconstrued in practice and applied to the democratization of the Church: (1) charisma, (2) people of God, and (3) synodality as an extension of collegiality.

Charisma, he notes, has been "associated with the concept of democracy through the idea of the 'charismatic constitution' of the church, which in turn is a variation on the idea of a society free of domination with purely func-tional tasks."[30] Nonetheless, this association has no foundation in the sources of the concept since "charisma is, historically speaking, not a democratic but a pneumatic principle, that is, a concept referring to a non-disposable authority from above, not a joint disposition from below."[31] A decade later, Ratzinger described the emphasis on charismatic authority as an effect of the Reformation "to make the individual person's orientation determinative,

---

[28] Ratzinger, "Begriff der Demokratie," 15.

[29] Ratzinger, "Begriff der Demokratie," 21.

[30] Joseph Ratzinger, "Demokratische Auslegung der Grundelement des Kirchen-Begriffs," in Ratzinger and Maier, *Demokratie in der Kirche*, 26.

[31] Ratzinger, "Demokratische Auslegung," 26.

and responsibility for the Christian order was deliberately referred to the world, to the princes, in order, precisely in this way, to expose the lack of historical actuality in the Church that was herself unable to form her own history or communicate salvation by her continuity."[32] In place of succession, charismatic authority of the Holy Spirit was emphasized, and in place of typology, which pointed to the continuity of history in promise and fulfillment, there appeared the appeal to what was in the beginning.[33] Since ontology is the basic philosophical expression of the concept of continuity, Ratzinger noted that it was initially rejected as a Scholastic and later as a Hellenistic perversion of Christianity and contrasted with the idea of history.[34] Moreover, "since the concept of the Incarnation is the real anchor-point of ontology in theology, it is opposed antithetically by emphasis on the Cross as the real axis of the Christ-event." The Cross itself is construed as "the expression of radical discontinuity, as the permanent escape from organised historical forms (even if they are Christian) into the *extra partam* of a faith that is ultimately not to be institutionalized."[35]

The Church again appears to be in this cultural position. The failure of those in Holy Orders has led to a questioning of the belief in the ontological change effected by the Sacrament of Orders and to a questioning of the typological association of the episcopacy with the twelve apostles and the twelve tribes of Israel. During the Reformation period, history replaced ontology in the theology of the Reformers, and in our current era ontology is being replaced by social theories with a Marxian pedigree that link freedom to the historical unfolding of democratic forces. As the Reformation gave rise to many disparate self-governing ecclesial communities with a tendency to splinter into smaller groups, so too, the contemporary calls for the democratization of the Church have strong centrifugal tendencies. National do-it-yourself committees and bureaucracies are promoted as the progressive alternative to a static hierarchical structure of offices centered in Rome. It is as if we are back at the beginning of the sixteenth century with some 1789 and 1968 elements thrown into the cultural mix.

With respect to the concept of the "people of God," Ratzinger declared that a "resolute protest" must be made against a "purely sociological understanding of the concept," and that "to use the term 'God's people' on a level

---

[32] Joseph Ratzinger, *Principles of Catholic Theology: Building Stones for a Fundamental Theology* (San Francisco: Ignatius Press, 1987), 157.

[33] Ratzinger, *Principles of Catholic Theology*, 157.

[34] Ratzinger, *Principles of Catholic Theology*, 158.

[35] Ratzinger, *Principles of Catholic Theology*, 158.

with terms like 'French people' or 'German people' is not only wrong, but fundamentally presumptuous."[36]

> The idea of the people of God is initially only adopted in the New Testament in the form of the word "ἐκκλησία" (assembly). "Assembly" is, so to speak, the active form of the root word "people." This again has to do with the fact that Jesus appeared among the people of Israel to proclaim the kingdom of God. In the prophetic tradition of Israel, however, the proclamation of the kingdom of God is never just a word event, but takes place as the gathering and purification of the people for the kingdom. This process decisively determined the self-understanding of the developing church. It is not simply a new people alongside an old one, but it exists only as the constant process of gathering and purifying the people for the kingdom, which now of course goes beyond Israel. It consists in the active, as the process of assembly, and it is therefore not called λαός but ἐκκλησία," not people, but assembly.[37]

In an article published in *Communio* in 1986 Ratzinger made the point even more bluntly:

> The Old Testament scholar Norbert Lohfink has shown that even in the Old Testament the term "People of God" does not simply designate Israel in its empirical facticity. Seen purely empirically, no people is the "people of God." To present God as a sign of descent or as a sociological mark of identification could never be more than an insufferable presumption and ultimately a blasphemy. Israel is designated by the concept of the people of God insofar as it is turned toward the Lord, not simply in itself but in the act of relationship and of self-transcendence which alone makes it what it is not of itself.[38]

For Ratzinger, it is axiomatic that the section of *Lumen Gentium* dealing with the concept of the "people of God" needs to be read in the context of the

---

[36] Ratzinger, "Demokratische Auslegung," 28.

[37] Ratzinger, "Demokratische Auslegung," 28.

[38] Joseph Ratzinger, "The Ecclesiology of the Second Vatican Council," in *Joseph Ratzinger in Communio*, vol. 1, *The Unity of the Church* (Grand Rapids, MI: Eerdmans, 2010), 76. See also the same article in *Communio: International Catholic Review* 13, no. 3 (Fall 1986): 239–52.

entire document, and this includes the notion of the Church as a sacrament. He believed that "one remains true to the Council only if one always reads and thinks these two central terms of its ecclesiology together, sacrament and People of God."[39] It would be "absurd . . . if one wished to deduce a changed conception of the hierarchy and the laity from the fact that the chapter on the people of God comes before the chapter on the hierarchy, as if really all the baptised already bore all the powers of orders in themselves and the hierarchy was only a matter of good order."[40]

Ratzinger's doctoral dissertation "The People and the House of God in the Doctrine of St. Augustine on the Church" concerned the correct understanding of the people of God This particular subject was suggested by his *Doktorvater* Gottlieb Söhngen, who was aware that *Ekklesiologie im Werden* (1940), by Mannes D. Koster, O.P., promoted the concept.[41] Rather than concluding, as Söhngen initially imagined, that "the people of God" was the central concept of St. Augustine's ecclesiology, Ratzinger concluded that St. Augustine wanted to show that people can only become "God's people" through their communion with Christ as members of the "Body of Christ."[42] To be a member of the "Body of Christ" is, in turn, a sacramental concept. To be a part of the Body of Christ means to exist in a network of sacramental relationships. This is a very different concept from something like an "employee" of the Catholic Church, or a chief executive officer of an institution funded by the Catholic Church, or persons who in some sense identify as believers in Jesus Christ, or a generic, no brand, theist.

This distinction between membership construed from above and one construed from below is highly important regarding synodality, especially the participation of lay Catholics in synods. St. John Henry Newman's concept of the *sensus fidelium* theologically defends the inclusion of lay members in synodal discussions, and the legitimacy of any "input" from lay Catholics presupposes that they are members of the Body of Christ who possess this *sensus fidelium*. This was emphasized in *Sensus Fidei* and reiterated in *Synodality in the Life of the Church*, §108.[43] If they are merely people "on the payroll" with little theological or spiritual formation or participation in

---

[39] Ratzinger, "Ecclesiology," 76.

[40] Ratzinger, "Ecclesiology," 77.

[41] Mannes D. Koster, *Ekklesiologie im Werden* (Paderborn: Bonifatius-Druckerei, 1940).

[42] For a more comprehensive treatment of Ratzinger's engagement with the "people of God" concept, see Santiago Madrigal Terrazas in the forthcoming *Ratzinger Lexikon* to be published by Ignatius Press.

[43] International Theological Commission, *Sensus Fidei* (2014); and *Synodality in the Life of the Church* (2018).

the sacramental life of the Church, then their theological opinions are no better, no sounder, than those of someone randomly opinion-polled—the kind of person British legal theorists describe as the "man on the Clapham Omnibus." An element of *sensus fidelium* is the will to follow the magisterium in its teachings on faith and morals, also mentioned in both ITC documents.

Regarding synodality, under the heading "The Question of the Synodal Structure," Ratzinger wrote,

> The assertion that the early church councils were made up of lay people and bishops and that only Trent or even Vatican I completed the transition to a pure bishop's council is, from a historical perspective, quite simply wrong. It also does not apply to the Acts 15 concept according to which the assembly in Jerusalem was drawn, which decided on the question of the relationship between Jewish and Gentile Christians. Rather, Luke-Acts represents this meeting according to the model of the ancient ἐκκλησία (people's assembly). The property of the ancient assemblies consisted (sounding quite modern) in their fundamentally public nature, which of course presupposes the distinction between the decision-making body and the public present. The public is by no means condemned to passivity: through its (positive and negative) "acclamations" it has often decisively influenced events without directly taking part in the *suffragium* (vote). According to Acts 15, the Council of the Apostles met according to this model: It took place in front of the public of the whole "ekklesia," but only "apostles and presbyters" are designated as its decision-makers (15.6 and 15.22). The early church adhered to this form in its councils from beginning to end, and any assertion to the contrary is simply without historical basis. . . .
>
> The idea of the mixed synod as a permanent supreme governing body of the national churches is a chimerical idea in terms of the tradition of the church as well as its sacramental structure and its specific goal. Such a synod would lack any legitimacy and therefore obedience has to be decisively and unequivocally denied.[44]

This position is consistent with the theology of St. John Henry Newman, according to whom the tradition of the apostles manifests itself in many different ways, through many different agencies, including the beliefs of the lay faithful, while the "the gift of discerning, discriminating, defining,

---

44 Ratzinger, "Demokratische Auslegung," 30–31.

promulgating and enforcing any portion of that tradition resides solely in the *Ecclesia docens*."[45] This position distinguishes between the teaching authority of the magisterium and the witness to the truth of faithful laity and is directly opposed to Karl Rahner's call for a national synod of bishops, priests, and lay people operating as the supreme governing body of the individual national churches, to which the bishops as individuals should be subject.[46] According to the Rahnerian model, the laity also enjoy a share of the magisterial authority.

Fifteen years after the publication of *Demokratie in der Kirche*, Ratzinger remarked, "The Church of Christ is not a party, not an association, not a club. Her deep and permanent structure is not democratic but sacramental, consequently hierarchical."[47] In *Images of Hope* he added,

> The Church cannot conceptualize for herself how she wants to be ordered. She can only try to understand ever more clearly the inner call of faith, and to live from faith. She does not need the majority principle, which always has something atrocious about it: the subordinated part must bend to the decision of the majority for the sake of peace even when this decision is perhaps misguided or even destructive. In human arrangements, there is perhaps no alternative. But in the Church the binding to the faith protects all of us: each is bound to faith, and in this respect the sacramental order guarantees more freedom than could be given by those who would subject the Church to the majority principle.[48]

---

[45] John Henry Newman, "On Consulting the Faithful in Matters of Doctrine," *The Rambler* (July 1859): §2. For a more extensive analysis of the author's treatment of Newman's concept of the *sensus fidelium*, see Tracey Rowland, "On the Development of Doctrine: A Via Media between Intellectualism and Historicism," in *A Guide to John Henry Newman: His Life and Thought*, ed. Juan R. Vélez (Washington, DC: Catholic University of America Press, 2022), 352–72. For a more extensive analysis of the author's treatment of the synodality concept, see Tracey Rowland, "Between the Theory and the Praxis of the Synodal Process," *The Thomist* 87, no. 2 (April 2023): 233–54.

[46] Rahner, *Freiheit und Manipulation*, 54. For an express rejection of Rahner's position, see Ratzinger, *Demokratie in der Kirche*, 29.

[47] Ratzinger, *Ratzinger Report*, 49.

[48] Benedict XVI, *Images of Hope: Meditations on Major Feasts* (San Francisco: Ignatius Press, 2006), 33–34.

Affirmation of Paternity
and Cultural Diversity

While Ratzinger firmly believed democratization of the Church "cannot consist in setting up even more voting bodies," it was possible to give "more space to life and its diversity."[49] This, however, is not assisted by the creation of bureaucracies. Bureaucracies do not like exceptions and so they discourage diversity and encourage uniformity. There is a sociological phenomenon that the philosopher Alasdair MacIntyre is famous for highlighting, and while the Marxist tradition purports to foster human freedom, in every real (not merely imagined) Marxist state, human freedom has been suffocated by the apparatus of the state, that is, by bureaucracies. Bureaucracies and human freedom do not fit well together. In *Salt of the Earth*, Ratzinger declared, "I have said very often that I think we have too much bureaucracy. . . . Everything should not take place by way of committees; there must also be the personal encounter."[50] In other words, each "sheep" needs personal care. "The more administrative machinery we construct, be it the most modern, the less place there is for the Spirit, the less place there is for the Lord, and the less freedom there is."[51]

These statements highlight another intellectual cleavage between the proponents of Catholic Inc. and those who espouse the theology of the mystical body of Christ. According to the first corporate model, there is no distinction between sheep and shepherd. Everyone is simply a shareholder in the company and legally eligible to apply for executive positions. In the second model, some are deemed to be ontologically different from others, having received Holy Orders. Those in Holy Orders are expected to be the shepherds who lay down their lives for those in their care and treat every member personally: every individual has particular strengths and weaknesses, gifts to be encouraged and pastoral needs to be addressed. Since those in Holy Orders are male, the priests and bishops exist in a paternal relationship to those under their care.

Robert Sarah argued that Ratzinger's spirituality was deeply imbued with an understanding of the fatherhood of God, and this influenced Ratzinger's understanding of the priesthood.[52] For Ratzinger, the priesthood and paternity go together. However, in "Freedom and Manipulation," Karl Rahner spoke

---

[49] Ratzinger, "Demokratisierung der Kirche," 92.

[50] Joseph Ratzinger, *Salt of the Earth: The Church at the End of the Millennium. Interview with Peter Seewald* (San Francisco: Ignatius Press, 1996), 266.

[51] Joseph Ratzinger, *Called to Communion: Understanding the Church Today* (San Francisco: Ignatius Press, 1996), 90.

[52] Robert Sarah, *He Gave Us So Much* (San Francisco: Ignatius Press, 2023).

of dismantling "feudalistic and paternalistic models of [ecclesial] office" in the direction of "a functional understanding of the office."[53] The image of the father should no longer inform the understanding of the priestly office since "in today's 'fatherless society' the concept can no longer be normative."[54]

These two starkly alternative positions highlight that fatherhood is an iceberg lying beneath contemporary debates in ecclesiology. That feminists want to replace the notion of God the Father with God the creator is further evidence that fatherhood is the pivotal issue around which these alternative understandings of the Church revolve, even if this is not always explicit in the debates. Bureaucratic committees can be gender neutral, but a father can only be a male. For supporters of Ratzinger's position, however, the fact that we can describe contemporary social life as a "fatherless society" evidences the need to affirm fatherhood wherever possible, not dismiss it as a relic of a feudal or otherwise premodern order. Indeed, providing fathers for the fatherless could be construed as a high priority field hospital service.

Returning to Ratzinger's affirmative reference to "diversity" in the life of the Church, an area of ecclesial life historically characterized by diversity in liturgical practices. Since the earliest times, there have been several legitimate rites in usage. This liturgical plurality was accepted by Ratzinger as something positive. His governing principle was that any number of rites were potentially legitimate providing that each such rite was of apostolic provenance. In other words, new rites of the Mass could not be cooked up by committees, but ancient rites of apostolic provenance were not a problem. He saw no "virtue" in a bureaucratic uniformity in matters liturgical.[55] He would, however, have had a problem with different bishops' conferences or national synods promoting different moral theologies: "Whoever denies the Church's final doctrinal competence in this domain [moral theology] forces her to remain silent precisely at the point where the boundary between truth and falsehood is at stake."[56] It is hard to imagine Ratzinger ever being able to accept that if something was morally wrong in Warsaw, it could be a moral good or even a virtue in Berlin. For Ratzinger, the Church's moral teaching is part of the *bloc des idées incontestibles*. A strange factor in contemporary

---

[53] Rahner, *Freiheit und Manipulation*, 50.

[54] Rahner, *Freiheit und Manipulation*, 50.

[55] For a longer account of Ratzinger's thoughts on liturgical plurality, see Tracey Rowland, "Joseph Ratzinger and the Hermeneutic of Continuity," in *The Hermeneutics of Tradition: Explorations and Examinations*, ed. Craig Hovey and Cyrus P. Olsen (Eugene, OR: Cascade, 2014), 193–226.

[56] Benedict XVI, *What Is Christianity? The Last Writings* (San Francisco: Ignatius Press, 2023), 182.

ecclesial life is that those who favor democratization of ecclesial governance tend to favor liturgical uniformity and pluralism in matters pertaining to moral teaching, while those who view the Church as the Body of Christ and have a strong, sacramental ecclesiology are often quite accepting of liturgical pluralism but insist on unity in matters of moral theology.

Much more could be said about how to defend the ecclesial "*bloc des idées incontestibles*" while encouraging diversity of ecclesial communities and cultural (including liturgical) practices within the one Body of Christ. Ratzinger's fellow *Communio* founder, Hans Urs von Balthasar, suggested the Church rests on pillars exemplified by biblical figures as Peter, James, John, and Paul. Only Peter is associated with ecclesial governance. James is a guardian of tradition, John is the exemplar of the contemplative vocation, and Paul is associated with charismatic renewal. Any real ecclesial reforms in our time will need to encompass and engage all four pillars and address how they can simultaneously guard the deposit of faith from corruption while encouraging a "faithful to the tradition" plurality of communities and plurality of genuinely Catholic cultures. For Balthasar, all the pillars have a Marian dimension, above all, a receptivity to the truth. This receptivity means, in turn, that a mark of the Church is unity of belief.

To conclude, in "Die Kirche und das Skandal des sexuellen Missbrauchs" (2019), a letter composed almost fifty years after the publication of *Demokratie und der Kirche*, Pope Benedict wrote,

> Today, the accusation against God focuses above all on discrediting his Church as a whole and thereby turning us away from her. The idea of a better Church of our own creation is really a proposal of the devil, with which he tries to turn us away from the living God by using a deceitful logic that we fall for much too easily.[57]

---

[57] Benedict XVI, *What Is Christianity?*, 195.

CHAPTER 4

Joseph Ratzinger on the Timelessness of Truth[1]

In 1982 Joseph Ratzinger published *Theologische Prinzipienlehre* that was later translated into English and published as *Principles of Catholic Theology: Building Stones for a Fundamental Theology.* On the occasion of Ratzinger's ninetieth birthday, it is useful to re-examine his thoughts on the necessary foundations for the discipline of theology and to juxtapose this with some alternative constructions, including those he associated with the "Hinduisation" of the faith.

In his preface to *Principles of Catholic Theology*, Ratzinger noted that "a frequently recurring problem in the intellectual climate of our age is that of reconciling history with the present—of transforming the events and words of a time now past into the realities and needs of the present."[2] Later, he described the place of history's role in the realm of being as "the fundamental crisis of our age."[3] This crisis questions the notion of a timeless, universal human nature, is there any continuity in "humanness," and can there be perennial truth.

Ratzinger locates the decisive turn to history in the philosophy of Hegel, for whom being itself is now regarded as time and the *logos* becomes itself in history:[4] "Truth becomes a function of time; the true is not that which

---

[1] This essay was first published in *Communio: International Catholic Review* 44, no. 2 (Summer 2017): 242–65. Used with permission.

[2] Joseph Ratzinger, *Principles of Catholic Theology: Building Stones for a Fundamental Theology* (San Francisco: Ignatius, 1987), 9.

[3] Ratzinger, *Principles of Catholic Theology*, 160.

[4] Ratzinger, *Principles of Catholic Theology*, 16.

simply *is* true, for truth is not simply that which *is*, it is true for a time because it is part of the becoming of truth, which *is* by becoming."[5]

> This means that, of their very nature, the contours between true and untrue are less sharply defined: it means above all that man's basic attitude to yesterday's truth consists precisely in abandoning it, in assimilating it into today's truth; assimilation becomes the form of preservation. What was constitutive yesterday is constitutive today only as that which has been assimilated. In the realm of Marxist thought, on the other hand, this ideology of reconciliation (as it might be called) is converted into an ideology of revolution; assimilation becomes transformation. The concept of the continuity of being in the changeableness of time is now understood as an ideological superstructure conditioned by the interests of those who are favoured by things as they are. It is thus a response that runs counter to the logic of history, which demands progress and forbids lingering in the status quo. The notion of truth comes to be regarded as an expression of the vested interests of a particular historical moment; it gives place to the notion of progress: the "true" is whatever serves progress, that is, whatever serves the logic of history.[6]

Ratzinger observes that discussions about theological content remain mere "isolated and losing skirmishes" if no consideration is given to these questions: Is there, in the course of historical time, a recognizable identity of man with himself? Is there a human "nature"? Is there a truth that remains true in every historical time because it *is* true?[7]

While these lines were first published by Ratzinger in 1982, a decade earlier Charles Davis, an English theologian who left the priesthood because of his "intellectual rejection of the papacy," had also identified this choice for or against Hegelian-style notions of truth as the neuralgic point of contemporary Catholic theology. Davis addressed the topic in an article about how in the middle to late twentieth century, Dutch and Belgian Catholic theologians became enthralled with the Critical Theory of the Frankfurt School of Social Research.

The fundamental principles of Critical Theory were formulated by Max

---

5 Ratzinger, *Principles of Catholic Theology*, 16.
6 Ratzinger, *Principles of Catholic Theology*, 16–17.
7 Ratzinger, *Principles of Catholic Theology*, 17.

Horkheimer (1895–1973) in the *Zeitschrift für Sozialforschung* and republished in 1968 as *Kritische Theorie* (Critical Theory). Leszek Kołakowski described Horkheimer's thought as permeated by the Marxist principle that philosophical, religious, and sociological ideas can only be understood in relation to the social interests of those who promote them.[8] Against this background, Charles Davis concluded that the fundamental question that any theologian needs to address is this: "Is theology, as [Edward] Schillebeeckx says, the critical self-consciousness of Christian *praxis*, or is Kołakowski right when he says: 'For theology begins with the belief that truth has already been given to us, and its intellectual effort consists not of attrition against reality but of assimilation of something which is ready in its entirety.'"[9]

The first option—that theology is the critical self-consciousness of Christian *praxis*—leads one down the road of all the varieties of liberation theology, be they Chilean, Honduran, Peruvian, El Salvadorian, Brazilian, Argentinian, Marxist, Peronist, or Feminist. It also leads one down the path of contemporary, second generation Schillebeeckxian theology, with its project of recontextualizing the faith to the culture of postmodernity. Liberation theology that is focused on class and economics is the form that the first option takes in countries that were formerly Spanish or Portuguese colonies. Schillebeeckxian style theology is the form taken in Europe (especially in Belgium and Holland) and in some parts of the Anglosphere. Feminist theology takes a variety of forms depending on the cultural context. In Latin America it is often presented as a particular sub-branch of liberation theology, while in Europe and the Anglosphere it is more a critique of two millennia of Christian tradition from the perspective of contemporary, psychoanalytical theory. Instead of St. Paul meets Juan Perón, we have St. Paul meets Sigmund Freud or Jacques Lacan. Both cases (that is, the various forms of liberation theology and the predominately first-world Schillebeeckxian theology) reject the principle that truth is received within a community which maintains its own hermeneutical framework in favor of truth being constructed within the context of the critical consciousness of an era.

Returning to Davis's observation that the choice is between the position of Schillebeeckx or the position of Kołakowski, Joseph Ratzinger has been the standard bearer for theologians who side with Kołakowski since the 1960s: "The seat of all faith is . . . the *memoria Ecclesiae*, the memory

---

8   Leszek Kołakowski, *Main Currents of Marxism*, vol. 3, *The Breakdown* (Oxford: Clarendon Press, 1978), 347.

9   Charles Davis, "Theology and Praxis," *Cross Currents* 23, no. 2 (Summer 1973): 154–68, at 167.

of the Church. . . . It exists through all ages, waxing and waning but never ceasing to be the common *situs* of faith . . . there can be a waxing or waning, a forgetting or remembering, but no recasting of truth in time."[10]

The "no recasting of truth in time" principle does not, however, mean that the faithful's understanding of truth cannot deepen. How this deepening occurs was a subject of study for St. John Henry Newman, leading to the publication of his essay on the development of doctrine. Newman identified some seven principles for discerning when a new idea represents a legitimate development in understanding some foundational truth and when it represents a corruption. Arguably, the most important of the seven principles is that any legitimate development must take the form of an *organic* development. In other words, an oak tree is an organic development of an acorn, but a fig tree is not. Developments do not contradict previous teaching; they do not repudiate it. Typically, such situations arise in a moment of crisis when some pastoral problem raises questions never previously considered. One can trawl through Catholic history for examples of this phenomenon, and usually some great Doctor of the Church provides a solution that helps develop tradition. Scholar-saints play important roles in this aspect of ecclesial life. Ratzinger not only described John Henry Newman as a hero of his youth but that Newman showed him a way "to build historical thought into theology, or much more, [Newman] taught us to think historically in theology and so to recognise the identity of faith in all developments."[11]

In his *Theology of Karl Barth*, Hans Urs von Balthasar offered a helpful summary of the names and publications of those who from the nineteenth to mid-twentieth centuries engaged with the problem of history's significance for theology:

> The preparations were started by the Tübingen School, in France by Blondel and Laberthonnière, in England by the Oxford movement and by Newman. Then all the leading Catholic thinkers carried on and developed this trend, of whom we can mention only a few: Joseph Bernhart, *Sinn der Geschichte* (1931); Peter Wust, *Dialektik des Geistes* (1928); Theodor Haecker, *Der Christ und die Geschichte* (1935); Karl Buchheim, *Wahrheit und Geschichte* (1935); A. Schütz, *Gott in der Geschichte* (1935); Philipp Dessauer, *Der Anfang und das*

---

[10] Ratzinger, *Principles of Catholic Theology*, 24.

[11] Joseph Ratzinger, "Presentation on the Occasion of the First Centenary of the Death of Cardinal John Henry Newman," April 28, 1990, Rome.

Ende (1939); Oskar Bauhofer, *Das Geheimnis der Zeiten* (1936); Karl Rahner, *Hörer des Wortes* (1941); Alfred Delp, *Der Mensch und die Geschichte* (1948); Karl Thieme, *Gott und die Geschichte* (1948); Michael Schmaus, *Von den letzten Dingen* (1948) with introductory chapters on the temporal-historical constitution of man and on the historicity of revelation; Josef Pieper, *Über das Ende der Zeit* (1950); and nearly the entire work of Guardini and Reinhold Schneider. In France, Henri de Lubac's *Catholicisme* (1937) with its rich citation of material from the great tradition, effected the breakthrough and was followed by the historical and theological work of Gaston Fessard, Yves de Montcheuil, Jean Daniélou. In England, we can cite Christopher Dawson. The reality of history forms the main theme not only of such Catholic thinkers as Th. Haecker, A. Dempf, H. Meyer, A. Wenzl, H. E. Hengstenberg, M. Muller, E. Spiess, B. Welte and so on, but even more so of those theologians who to some extent rediscovered the earlier tradition and were engaged in a creative attempt to work out methodologically and consciously for the first time the historical and theological categories for this issue.[12]

There is, however, a significant difference between the treatment of the history-theology relationship in the scholarship of those listed on Balthasar's honor board above, and the understanding of the same relationship in the publications of those influenced by Hegel or Marx or Critical Theory. Newman and others listed by Balthasar believed that the apostolic generation received the faith in its purity directly from Christ and under the guidance of the Holy Spirit, and that this original deposit of faith does not change as we move through history. In contrast, Erik Borgman, a former student of Schillebeeckx, argues that "what is normative, from the perspective of faith, are not Jesus' words and actions (the apostolic understanding of what was important) but the relationship between the words and the deeds of Jesus on the one hand and their context on the other. Believers here and now are not asked to imitate what Jesus said or did, rather they are to relate to their context as Jesus related to his."[13]

---

[12] Hans Urs von Balthasar, *Theology of Karl Barth* (San Francisco: Ignatius Press, 1992), 335n37.

[13] Erik Borgman, "*Gaudium et spes*: The Forgotten Future of a Revolutionary Document," *Concilium* 4 (2005): 54.

Theologians need to abandon the fiction that the truth of the tradition and the authority of the church form a firm foundation on which they can build further, up to and including the last remnants and traces. Theology has no other foundation than the God of salvation, whose mystery it may and must constantly decipher and clarify. If it takes that completely seriously, it will inevitably change fundamentally, time and again.[14]

Regarding orthopraxis (or correct practice), Borgman claims that it "is not a consequence of a previously given, communal unity of faith, but the manner in which such a communal unity and conviction is realised."[15]

Similarly, Lieven Boeve, a second-generation Schillebeeckxian, argues that the "Christian faith and tradition are not only contained in a specific historico-cultural, socioeconomic and socio-political context, but are also co-constituted by this context."[16] Boeve believes that those who inherit a tradition are not only its heirs but also its testators.[17] He accuses those who hold that Christian faith and tradition do not or should not change do not understand that they are testators as well as heirs.[18]

The use of the testator-beneficiary metaphor for unpacking the concept of tradition was anticipated in the works of Josef Pieper (1904–1997). Contrary to the position now taken by scholars in the line of Schillebeeckx, Pieper argued that what a student learns through his own efforts is his own property, but what he receives from tradition is something more like the loan of a gift. Pieper also endorsed St. Augustine's maxim *quod a patribus acceperunt, hoc filiis tradiderunt*. This means that the last child in line receives from his father exactly the same thing that the first in line handed over to

---

[14] Erik Borgman, *Edward Schillebeeckx: A Theologian in his History*, vol. 1, *A Catholic Theology of Culture (1914–1965)* (London: Continuum, 2004), 381. Also cited by Lieven Boeve in "The Enduring Significance and Relevance of Edward Schillebeeckx: Introducing the State of the Question in Medias Res," in *Edward Schillebeeckx and Contemporary Theology*, ed. Lieven Boeve, Frederiek Depoortere, and Stephan van Erp (London: T & T Clark, 2010), 6.

[15] Edward Schillebeeckx, *The Understanding of Faith: Interpretation and Criticism* (London: Sheed & Ward, 1974), 68.

[16] Gregory Hoskins, "Interview with Lieven Boeve," *Journal of Philosophy and Scripture* 3, no. 2 (Spring 2006): 31–37, at 32.

[17] Lieven Boeve, *Interrupting Tradition: An Essay on Christian Faith in a Postmodern Context*, Louvain Theological and Pastoral Monographs, vol. 30 (Leuven, Belgium: Peeters Press, 2003), 24.

[18] Boeve, *Interrupting Tradition*, 49.

his "son." The *traditum* is does *not* grow in the process of tradition.[19] This is consistent with Henri de Lubac's argument that "whether we are talking about profane or ecclesiastical history, by themselves, historical events bring us no increase in supernatural revelation."[20] Contexts may change and raise new issues, someone might discover a "lost" patristic-era homily which opens up new areas of research similar to the recovery of Aristotelian texts influenced theological scholarship in the medieval period. Technological developments frequently throw up hitherto unimagined moral problems requiring new studies. All these events can foster developments in theological scholarship, but what cannot change is, to use Pieper's word, the *traditum*. The *traditum* is not changed by history—history brings no increase in supernatural revelation.

Nonetheless, Lieven Boeve and Ben Vedder asserted that Schillebeeckx's theology implies that theologians "have to constantly re-evaluate God's presence in the here and now. Tradition is not unchanging; it constantly relates to the spirit of the times."[21]

Following directions set by Schillebeeckx, Boeve is interested in a theological project he calls "re-contextualisation." Whereas Schillebeeckx was interested in correlating the faith to the culture of modernity, Boeve wishes to recontextualize the faith with reference to postmodernity. He defines recontextualization as "a continuous, never-finished theological programme [that] necessitates a continuously undertaken dialogue with the contextual critical consciousness."[22] This consciousness is "an expression of the reflexive potential present in the context, of its sensitivities, attitudes, thinking patterns and ambiguities."[23] It "compels theology towards a contemporary theological critical consciousness."[24] Further, one acquires a sense of Catholic identity through dialogue with the critical consciousness of contemporary culture. As such, one's Catholic identity is socially constructed. It is not received like one's familial identity as a child of father X and mother Y, grandson or granddaughter of grandparents A and B, C and D.

Potentially, there are as many different Catholic identities as there are baptized Catholics. The "recontextualization" project makes Catholic

---

19 Josef Pieper, *Tradition: Concept and Claim* (Wilmington, DE: ISI Books, 2008), 21.

20 Henri de Lubac, *La révélation divine* (Paris: Cerf, 1968), 101.

21 Lieven Boeve, Frederiek Depoortere, and Stephan van Erp, eds., *Edward Schillebeeckx and Contemporary Theology* (London: Bloomsbury, 2012), x.

22 Lieven Boeve, *Theology at the Crossroads of University, Church and Society: Dialogue, Difference and Catholic Identity* (London: Bloomsbury, 2017), 2.

23 Boeve, *Theology at Crossroads*, 2.

24 Boeve, *Theology at Crossroads*, 2.

identity something completely fluid. While national histories have always influenced one's Catholic identity, these various national sensitivities have always been regarded as particular wounds suffered by particular members of the Body of Christ and not central to Catholic identity which is a universal concept: for example, the experience of the Cromwellian era left a deep mark upon the Irish understanding of what it means to be a Catholic, and the experience of the French revolution deeply penetrated the French understanding of what it means to be a Catholic. Since Christ is the same yesterday, today, and forever, since he is the alpha and the omega of human history, since the Incarnation is the very center or high point of human history, what it means to be a Catholic does not fundamentally change from one generation or even one century to another. One takes one's identity from one's sacramental incorporation into this sacred body of Christ; one is claimed by him and drawn into the circle of Trinitarian love and henceforth one is given a particular mission and charism for the service of this body. This mission will differ from person to person and hence there is a place for individuality within the Body of Christ. Nonetheless, the deepest core of one's identity as a son or daughter of Christ is something given at baptism, it is not something constructed in dialogue with whatever happens to be the "critical consciousness of the era" or the Zeitgeist, in other words. Even one's personal spiritual mission is given and discerned through prayer, not self-created. At least this was the classical understanding of Catholic identity, which differs markedly from the notion that one is a testator of whatever one receives in one's basket of Catholic ideas, values, and cultural practices to be "recontextualized," which includes "co-constituted," with reference to contemporary intellectual fashions.

Recontextualizing the Catholic faith to postmodern culture also means, in effect, that theology must be altered to make it capable of a defense before a tribunal of postmodern philosophers. The meme is that just as St. Thomas Aquinas developed a theological framework in response to a new academic context brought about by the retrieval of Aristotelian philosophy in the thirteenth century, today it is not only acceptable but also necessary for theologians to bring Catholic theology into line with fashionable philosophies such as Critical Theory, Postmodern philosophy, and Psychoanalytical Theory. Thus, after rejecting the sacramental theology of St. Thomas Aquinas, Karl Rahner, Hans Urs von Balthasar, and Joseph Ratzinger for its interest in ontology ("ontology" is the nemesis of post-moderns), Boeve suggests that if theology is "to regain contextual plausibility," the sacramentality of life celebrated in the sacraments must no longer be thought of as "participation in a divine being, nor as an anticipation of a self-fulfilling development, but as being involved in the tension arising from the interruption of the divine Other into our human narratives."[25] Boeve concludes that "it goes without saying that such a re-contextualisation will have serious consequences for Christian self-awareness, and that such a sacramental structuring of human existence has implications which go beyond a theology of the sacraments."[26]

Such recourse to the precedent of Aquinas's academic projects fails to engage the issue that the synthesis of Aquinas did not challenge fundamental Church teachings. It did not lead to a revolution in moral theology or ecclesiology that embraced the fundamental principles of Critical Theory or contemporary as postmodern philosophies do. The implications of a Schillebeeckxian approach to tradition and its recontextualization to postmodern culture are well summarized by Thomas Guarino:

> Catholic "foundationalist" thinkers like Rahner and Lonergan . . . thought that some foundationalist ontology is necessary if one is adequately to defend fundamental Catholic positions on doctrine. If one accepts postmodernity more fully, thereby abandoning some form of foundationalist ontology, one's entire understanding of revelation, especially the role of Christian doctrine, is deeply affected. Either the truth of the gospel must simply be asserted, breaking its link with a rationally elaborated infrastructure. Or, by opening a fissure between ontology and theology, one develops a quite different understanding of what the deposit of faith is, how it develops, and the type of continuity and identity proper to it. Particularly affected is the type of truth mediated by it.[27]

---

[25] Lieven Boeve, *Lyotard and Theology* (London: Bloomsbury, 2014), 123.

[26] Boeve, *Lyotard and Theology*, 123. Concrete examples of this theology are offered in *Edward Schillebeeckx*, ed. Boeve, Depoortere, and van Erp. In her eco-feminist contribution, Kathleen McManus, O.P., employs Theodor Adorno's concept of "negative contrast experience" in an "effort to seek out the feminine body of Christ hidden in the tradition," while Mary Catherine Hilkert, O.P., argues that the contemporary context requires that theologians "begin not with an abstract ideal of human nature or assumptions about a pre-existing order in human life, but rather, with the reality of those persons and communities whose well-being is at risk or has been violated." Kathleen McManus, "Suffering, Resistance and Hope: Women's Experience of Negative Contrast and Christology," in Boeve, Depoortere, and van Erp, *Edward Schillebeeckx*, 111–26; and Mary Catherine Hilkert, "The Threatened *Humanus* as *Imago Dei*: Anthropology and Christian Ethics," in Boeve, Depoortere, and van Erp, *Edward Schillebeeckx*, 127–142, at 129.

[27] Thomas Guarino, "Postmodernity and Five Fundamental Theological Issues," *Theological Studies* 57, no. 4, (December 1996): 654–90, at 660–61.

Boeve acknowledges that the general orientation, or one might say "building stones," of Schillebeeckx's theology is contrary to that of Benedict XVI, the *Communio* circle of theologians, members of the largely Protestant Yale School of Divinity, as well as the ecumenical Radical Orthodoxy group led by the Anglican John Milbank. In one way or another these types all line up with Kołakowski and retain the classical understandings of tradition and Catholic identity. Boeve identifies Joseph Ratzinger as his "sparring partner" and a very strong opponent of Schillebeeckxian theology:

> With Ratzinger's theological paradigm we have a subordination of the historical to the eternal, the human to the divine, nature to grace. This also results in a "high" Christology, sacramentality and ecclesiology, in which dialectics is emphasised stronger than dialogue and opposition gets more attention than mediation. It is never from history, nature, reason, or the human that revelation, grace, faith, and the divine can be understood, but decisively the other way around.[28]

While Ratzinger may plead guilty to holding to a high Christology, sacramentality, and ecclesiology, his defense lawyers would no doubt argue that the verb to "subordinate" completely misses the point of Ratzinger's many statements about these critical couplets (history and eternity, humanity and divinity, nature and grace). Ratzinger is neither a Monophysite nor a Nestorian. He is not attracted to sharp either/or options typical of Calvinism, or sharp separations typical of Nestorians, or subordination theories typical of Monophysites. In all these areas he is heavily influenced by de Lubac and Balthasar who were highly critical of Monophysite and Nestorian temptations. A better analysis for his fundamental building stones would be to say that he is hostile to "bastard dualisms" such as "pure nature" without grace, "pure reason" without revelation, or mere history, such as a sociological reading of the "signs of the times," without reference to eschatology. When it comes to these critical couplets, Ratzinger typically holds that we can only understand one pole of the couplet with reference to the other. For example, history is only understood against the backdrop of revelation, but revelation itself is historical. We only have access to one through the other. Similarly, it is hard to find a greater contemporary advocate for reason than Ratzinger. He argues that faith has the right to be missionary only if it transcends all traditions and constitutes an appeal to reason and an orientation toward

---

[28] Boeve, *Theology at Crossroads*, 229.

the truth itself. Nonetheless, his notion of reason is not the same as the truncated conception typical of eighteenth-century philosophy—his notion of reason encompasses the idea of wisdom and hence must always be open to revelation: "I am convinced, in fact, that the crisis we are experiencing in the Church and in humanity is closely allied to the exclusion of God as a topic with which reason can properly be concerned—an exclusion that has led to the degeneration of theology first into historicism, then into sociologism and, at the same time, to the impoverishment of philosophy."[29]

There is, moreover, a strong Christocentrism in his theological structure. As he wrote in his best-selling work *Introduction to Christianity*, ontology (represented Christologically by the theology of the Incarnation) and history (represented Christologically by the theology of the Cross) "reveal polarities that cannot be surmounted and combined in a neat synthesis without the loss of the crucial points in each; they must remain present as polarities that mutually correct each other and only by complementing each other point toward the whole."[30] In contrast to the anti-metaphysical animus of contemporary postmodern philosophy, Ratzinger affirms both history and metaphysics, not metaphysics without history (the pre-conciliar problem) or history without metaphysics (the postmodern temptation). He eschews any dualistic choice between the being-Christology of Chalcedon and the event-Christology of the New Testament.[31] Chalcedon continues to represent the "definitive ecclesial formulation of Jesus' Divine Sonship," which is nothing less than "the pivotal truth that decides everything."[32] "The ontological character of the Trinity is central for the reality-content of Christianity, but it is not in opposition to the event; rather, it is revealed precisely in the event of God's action toward us."[33]

> Man finds his centre of gravity, not inside, but outside himself. The place to which he is anchored is not, as it were, within himself, but without. This explains that remnant that remains always to

---

[29] Ratzinger, *Principles of Catholic Theology*, 316.

[30] Joseph Ratzinger, *Introduction to Christianity* (San Francisco: Ignatius Press, 1990), 230. We are indebted to Dr. Adam Cooper for drawing our attention to this reference. See Adam Cooper, "History as an Ontological Experience," paper presented at the Transcending Dualisms Conference, John Paul II Institute for Marriage and Family, Melbourne, May 10, 2014.

[31] Joseph Ratzinger, *Dogma and Preaching: Applying Christian Doctrine to Daily Life* (San Francisco: Ignatius Press, 2011), 42.

[32] Ratzinger, *Dogma and Preaching*, 42.

[33] Ratzinger, *Dogma and Preaching*, 46.

be explained, the fragmentary character of all his efforts to comprehend the unity of history and being. Ultimately, the tension between ontology and history has its foundation in the tension within human nature itself, which must go out of itself in order to find itself; it has its foundation in the mystery of God, which is freedom and which, therefore, calls each individual by a name that is known to no other. Thus, the whole is communicated to him in the particular.[34]

To borrow a Kantian idiom, Christ was the particular, "concrete universal." For Ratzinger, "truth" is found in the teachings of Christ as presented in the Scriptures as his disciples remembered them under the guidance of the Holy Spirit.[35] Though this truth is timeless, indeed unchanging, it is "not merely a timeless truth—an eternal idea hovering independently over a realm of changing facts."[36] The act of faith in the teachings of Christ introduces the human person into the dynamic circle of Trinitarian love. Since this love "is neither blind will or pure feeling but love as meaning and meaning as love, because it is the creative reason of all reality, it cannot be reciprocated without logic, without thought and word."[37] Love and reason are the "twin pillars" of all reality and "true reason makes itself known, not in the abstraction of thought, but in the purification of the heart."[38] *Lumen Fidei*, which was drafted by Ratzinger, reads, "Theology is more than simply an effort of human reason to analyse and understand, along the lines of the experimental sciences. God cannot be reduced to an object. He is a subject who makes himself known and perceived in an interpersonal relationship."[39] This "spiritual Christology," as Peter McGregor calls it, creates a decidedly different "building block" for Catholic theology from what Ratzinger disparagingly calls "drawing-board theology," presumably theology done with pen and paper but no engagement of the human heart in the circle of Trinitarian love.[40]

The logic of Ratzinger's position is that the reception and understanding and transmission of this "not merely timeless truth" requires several

---

[34] Ratzinger, *Principles of Catholic Theology*, 171.

[35] In this context, Ratzinger makes explicit reference to John 2:22 and 2 John 9.

[36] Ratzinger, *Principles of Catholic Theology*, 26.

[37] Ratzinger, *Principles of Catholic Theology*, 26.

[38] Ratzinger, *Principles of Catholic Theology*, 27.

[39] Francis, *Lumen Fidei* (2013), §36.

[40] For an extensive analysis of this theme in the work of Ratzinger, see Peter McGregor, *Heart to Heart: The Spiritual Christology of Joseph Ratzinger* (Eugene, OR: Pickwick Publications, 2016).

operational factors: revelation of such truth by God the Son, reception of such truth by the members of the apostolic generation, stewardship of this truth by the members of the magisterium across the centuries, openness of members of the Body of Christ to receive this truth, and the Holy Spirit assisting this reception and cognition. As Ratzinger says, "Man's perceptive powers play in concert."[41]

One can observe these factors in operation in Ratzinger's approach to scriptural hermeneutics. Since faith is a gift, indeed a grace, not an intellectual achievement, the study of Scripture requires certain spiritual predispositions in addition to knowledge of the biblical languages and biblical history:

> The notion that God's revelation is identical with literature and that the dissecting knife of the literary critic is the only correct way of disclosing God's secrets misconstrues both the nature of God and the nature of literary criticism. Enlightenment is here transformed into naivete. The Bible itself does not think in this way. It certainly does not teach that the act of faith by which an individual received revelation is located in the encounter between the book and the person's analytical reason. The act of faith is rather a process that frees both the reason and the existence of the individual from the bonds that restrict them; it is the introduction of the isolated and fragmented reason of the individual into the realm of him who is the logos, the reason and the rational ground of all things and all persons. Anyone who construes the essence of the act of faith as the encounter between a book and the thinking of an individual has failed to understand the act of faith. For it is essentially an act of union; it leads into that spiritual realm where unity with the ground of all things and, hence, the understanding of that ground is present in a living community. Intrinsic to the basic structure of the act of faith, in other words, is incorporation into the Church, the common situs of that which binds together and that which is bound. In Romans 6:17, for instance, this act of faith is defined as the process by which an individual submits himself to one particular creed and, in doing so, performs an act of obedience that comes from his heart, that is, from the center of his whole being.[42]

---

[41] Benedict XVI, *Jesus of Nazareth: From the Baptism in the Jordan to the Transfiguration* (New York: Doubleday, 2007), 92–93.

[42] Ratzinger, *Principles of Catholic Theology*, 328–29.

The same ideas can be found in Ratzinger's commentary on Cardinal Robert Sarah's *The Power of Silence*:

> Certainly, in order to interpret Jesus's words, historical knowledge is necessary, which teaches us to understand the time and the language at that time. But that alone is not enough if we are really to comprehend the Lord's message in depth. Anyone today who reads the ever-thicker commentaries on the Gospels remains disappointed in the end. He learns a lot that is useful about those days and a lot of hypotheses that ultimately contribute nothing at all to an understanding of the text. In the end you feel that in all the excess of words, something essential is lacking: entrance into Jesus's silence, from which his word is born. If we cannot enter into this silence, we will always hear the word only on its surface and thus not really understand it.[43]

Much of the above can be summarized in the principle set forth in *Donum Veritatis*, §10, on the ecclesial vocation of the theologian: "When theology employs the elements and conceptual tools of philosophy or other disciplines, discernment is needed. The ultimate normative principle for such discernment is revealed doctrine which itself must furnish the criteria for the evaluation of these elements and conceptual tools and not *vice versa*." It is the responsibility of the magisterium to see that revealed doctrine is passed on from one generation to another uncorrupted. This is consistent with the conclusions of contemporary hermeneutical scholarship, according to which thinking always involves thinking in the context of some particular and specific public, which will normally have its own institutional structure. As Alasdair MacIntyre explained, in each of these structures there will be four conceptions:

1. A conception of truth beyond and ordering particular truths.
2. A conception of a range of senses in the light of which utterances to be judged true or false and so placed within that ordering are to be construed.
3. A conception of a range of genres of utterance, dramatic, lyrical,

---

[43] Benedict XVI, "With Cardinal Sarah, the Liturgy is in Good Hands," *First Things*, May 17, 2017, https://www.firstthings.com/web-exclusives/2017/05/with-cardinal-sarah-the-liturgy-is-in-good-hands. Cf. Robert Sarah, *The Power of Silence: Against the Dictatorship of Noise* (San Francisco: Ignatius Press, 2017).

historical and the like, by reference to which utterances may be classified so that we may then proceed to identify their senses; and

4.   a contrast between those uses of genres in which in one way or another truth is at stake and those governed only by standards of rhetorical effectiveness.[44]

The CDF is the institutional structure which undertakes such judgment on behalf of the Church "public." Such a body is required because the Church "is not a bureaucratic institution, an association of believers, as it were; rather, she is a gift from him who holds the key to death."[45] The Church needs a body of scholars dedicated to the intellectual apostolate who understand how particular truths or dogmas are ordered in relation to one another, how there is a range of theological genres and senses in which the Scriptures can be interpreted, how to make the necessary fine distinctions between similar but different concepts, and how to make judgments about the suitability of different philosophies as "handmaidens" to theology. It is therefore, as Ratzinger argued,

absurd to seek to destroy the bearer of tradition as such, to undertake an ecclesiastical space flight with no ground station, to attempt to produce a new and purer Christianity in the test tube of the mere intellect: a Church that is nothing but a manager is nothing at all: she is no longer tradition, and, in an intellect that knows no tradition, she becomes pure nothingness, a monster of meaninglessness.[46]

Regarding the claim that disrupting tradition is actually a Christian act—an idea found in several contemporary Christologies with affinities to liberation theology, Ratzinger observed,

Despite the diversity of tradition, one fact is uniformly recognizable: although Jesus fought determinedly against the dogmatization of a casuistical tradition, he stood firmly rooted in the foundation of Old Testament faith, that is, in the foundation of the law and the

---

[44] Alasdair MacIntyre, *Three Rival Versions of Moral Enquiry* (London: Duckworth, 1990), 200–201.

[45] Ratzinger, *Principles of Catholic Theology*, 40.

[46] Ratzinger, *Principles of Catholic Theology*, 100–101.

prophets. . . . He did not abandon the Old Testament as something antiquated and now superseded.[47] . . .

[Christ's] No to the traditions of the Pharisees is by no means the prelude to a generally liberal position with regard to the law but, upon occasion, even heralds an unprecedented intensification of its demands, as, for, example, in his position with regard to the indissolubility of marriage, the demands of love of neighbour or the requirements of discipleship.[48]

Contrary to the whole orientation of Schillebeeckxian theology, Ratzinger rejects the principle of the priority of *praxis*:[49]

Christian *praxis* is nourished by the core of Christian faith, that is, the grace that appeared in Christ and that is appropriated in the sacrament of the Church. Faith's *praxis* depends on faith's truth, in which man's truth is made visible and lifted up to a new level by God's truth. Hence, it is fundamentally opposed to a *praxis* that first wants to produce facts and so establish truth.[50] . . .

If the word "orthopraxis" is pushed to its most radical meaning, it presumes that no truth exists that is antecedent to *praxis* but rather than truth can be established only on the basis of correct *praxis*, which has the task of creating meaning out of and in the face of meaninglessness. Theology becomes then no more than a guide to action, which, by reflecting on *praxis*, continually develops new modes of praxis. If not only redemption but truth as well is regarded as "*post hoc*," then truth becomes the product of man. At the same time, man, who is no longer measured against truth but produces it, becomes himself a product.[51]

---

[47] Ratzinger, *Principles of Catholic Theology*, 95.

[48] Ratzinger, *Principles of Catholic Theology*, 98.

[49] *Theoria, Praxis*, and *Poiesis* are Greek philosophical terms generally translated as seeing, doing, and making. See Nikolas Lobkowicz, *Theory and Practice: History of a Concept from Aristotle to Marx* (Notre Dame, IN: University of Notre Dame Press, 1967); Robert Kress, "Praxis and Liberation," *Communio* 6, no. 1 (Spring 1979): 113–34; and Hans Urs von Balthasar, "Current Trends in Catholic Theology and the Responsibility of the Christian," *Communio* 5, no. 1 (Spring 1978): 77–85. In the latter, Balthasar argues that the three basic trends of European Catholic theology are all at pains to stress the unity of theory and practice.

[50] Ratzinger, *Principles of Catholic Theology*, 70.

[51] Ratzinger, *Principles of Catholic Theology*, 318.

Ratzinger traced the contemporary priority of *praxis* issue to what he called a thirteenth-century controversy. According to the Thomistic view, theology is to be regarded as a *scientia speculativa*; according to the Franciscan view, it is to be regarded as a *scientia practica*. Unfortunately, Ratzinger does not identify which particular Franciscan or Franciscans took a strong *scientia practica* position, but he positively endorses St. Bonaventure's mature post-1259 position, which he reads as an endorsement of the Thomistic ontological character of theology and an insistence that theology is also a spiritual science:[52] "Just as we cannot learn to swim without water, so we cannot learn theology without the spiritual praxis in which it lives."[53] Theology, he asserts, cannot become "academically neutralised," that is, cut off from the operation of the human heart and its spirituality. Theology is thus both a science and a practice; indeed, it is a science that requires a very particular kind of practice. This means, in turn, that while "faith is not to be placed in opposition to reason . . . neither must it fall under the absolute power of enlightened reason and its methods."[54]

The most extreme form of the priority of *praxis* principle has come from Latin American liberation theology and, in particular, its attacks on the CDF. The priority of *praxis* principle is a weapon designed by one group of elites (professional liberation theologians) to wield against another group of elites, specifically those so-called euro-centric theologians who insist on the priority of *logos* over *ethos*, of *theoria* over *praxis*. In other words, if the guiding principle of all forms of liberation theology is the priority of *praxis* over theory, and if this is strongly opposed by theologians who are critical of Marxism, then one way to legitimize this diversion from the priority of *logos* or reason principle is to ground the priority of *praxis* in the supposed epistemic virtue of those who are uneducated. Instead of entering into intellectual disputes with scholars based at the CDF, the Vatican department which deals with deviations from sound Church teaching and which has been at the center of criticisms of the liberation theology movement, one attempts to delegitimize the CDF by arguing that its members have no epistemic standing. Or, that they at least are of questionable epistemic standing because they are all from middle-class or, even worse, aristocratic families and hold several university degrees and speak multiple languages. The Frankfurt school argument that all systems of thought are mere epiphenomena of the class interests of the promoters of the system is turned

---

[52] Ratzinger, *Principles of Catholic Theology*, 320–21.
[53] Ratzinger, *Principles of Catholic Theology*, 322.
[54] Ratzinger, *Principles of Catholic Theology*, 325.

against the hierarchy of the Catholic Church, especially the CDF, in the name of the epistemic purity of the judgments of the poor and the socially marginalized. Only those without a stake in the present economic and political order, including the hierarchical order of the Catholic Church, can be relied upon to discern the signs of the times in a Christian way, or so the argument goes.

The CDF addressed this mentality in *Instruction on Certain Aspects of the "Theology of Liberation"* (1984), §10:

> The partisan conception of truth, which can be seen in the rev-olutionary 'praxis' of the class, corroborates this position [the challenge to the sacramental and hierarchical structure of the Church]. Theologians who do not share the theses of the "theology of liberation," the hierarchy, and especially the Roman Magisterium are thus discredited in advance as belonging to the class of the oppressors. Their theology is a theology of class. Arguments and teachings thus do not have to be examined in themselves since they are only reflections of class interests. Thus, the instruction of others is decreed to be, in principle, false.[55]

Using an expression from the psychoanalyst Albert Görres, Ratzinger argued that the mentality that wants to prioritize *ethos* over *logos* represents the "Hinduisation" of the faith. By "Hinduisation" is meant a "situation where faith propositions no longer matter because the important thing is contact with a spiritual atmosphere which leads beyond everything that can be said."[56] Without timeless, binding, faith propositions, there is nothing to judge the elements within the spiritual atmosphere, nothing to distinguish the Christian-friendly elements from the Christian-toxic elements.

Undergirding the priority of *praxis* and recontextualization projects is a strong social constructivism. Humans ultimately construct their own truth and their own identity with reference to the fashions of the prevailing culture. Whatever appears to be reasonable according to the contemporary critical consciousness may be hooked up with fragments of the Christian tradition to make a new "open narrative." Belgium, home of this theology, leads the

---

55 Congregation for the Doctrine of the Faith, *Instruction on Certain Aspects of the "Theology of Liberation"* (1984), §10, para. 1.

56 Albert Görres, "Glaubensgewissheit in einer pluralistischen Welt," *IKaZ* 12 (1983): 117–32, at 129; and Joseph Ratzinger, *Gesammelte Schriften*, vol. 9 (Freiburg: Herder & Herder, 2016), 227.

world in the provision of liberal euthanasia laws. In Belgium, even children can be killed by lethal injections intended for no other purpose than to end their lives. Is it now acceptable for Catholics to be pro-euthanasia because the contemporary "critical consciousness" of social elites based in Brussels and Leuven affirms this practice as enlightened and reasonable? And what about the critical consciousness of people in non-European cultures? If there are no timeless, binding, faith propositions which inform our understanding of what practices are consistent with Christian beliefs and which are not, is there any reason why Christians living in India or Thailand, where there are influential elements of Hinduism in the prevailing culture, cannot effect a synthesis of Christian habits with a belief in cows, karma, and the caste system? How can the faith be anything but meaningless without an operation ground control?

Ratzinger's theological contribution to the resolution to this crisis of mediation of history in the realm of ontology is significant because it addressed the historical end of the pole and thus counter-balanced the tendency of baroque-era Scholasticism to ignore the historical end as a dangerous Protestant fixation. But he did so presupposing the continuing value of ontology. Throughout his life, Ratzinger found himself between a double-fronted criticism: criticism from the "right" strict-observance Thomist camp, which is hostile to the consideration of the historical end of the pole, and criticism from the "left" liberal and postmodern camps critical of metaphysical thinking. Ratzinger's attempt to hold the historical and ontological poles in tension caused him no end of grief. As future generations look back at this moment in ecclesial history, they may decide to grant Joseph Ratzinger the title "Doctor of the Church" for his heroism in refusing to genuflect before the Zeitgeist of the 1960s and, moreover, for his intellectual analysis of the pitfalls in the priority of *praxis* principle and the Frankfurt school's stance toward truth and tradition. Of all the thousands of paragraphs written by Ratzinger on the building stones of Catholic theology, perhaps the following best summarizes his approach, and could equally be said of him as well as of St. Paul:

> The text on the Resurrection, contained in chapter 15 of the *First Letter to the Corinthians*, emphasises the connection between receiving and transmitting. St. Paul attributes great importance to the literal formulation of the tradition, and at the end of the passage under consideration underlines, "so we preach, and so you believed." . . . St. Paul's Christology is never original at the expense of faithfulness to the tradition. The kerygma of the apostles always

presides over the personal re-elaboration of Paul; each of his arguments moves from common tradition, and in them he expresses the faith shared by all the Churches, which are one single Church. In this way St. Paul offers a model for all time of how to approach theology and how to preach. The theologian, the preacher, does not create new visions of the world and of life, but he is at the service of truth handed down, at the service of the real fact of Christ, of the Cross and of the Resurrection.[57]

---

[57] Benedict XVI, "General Audience," St. Peter's Square, November 5, 2008.

CHAPTER 5

Between the Theory and the Praxis of the Synodal Process[1]

In recent years the term "synodality" has flourished under the papacy of Francis but has also become something of a "weasel word" in the sense that the concept means different things to different people. Just as weasels are good at using their slender elongated bodies to duck, weave, and slither under fences into chicken coops and other places where they are not wanted, the word "synodality" can change its theological shape depending upon the precise theological content given it by the person using the concept, and thereby justifying more than one form of ecclesial governance.

Clearly there is an understanding of synodality that is consistent with centuries of ecclesial tradition. The word *synod* comes from the Greek σύνοδος meaning "assembly" or "meeting" and is analogous with the Latin word *concilium* from which we get our English word "council." Synods have occurred throughout Christian history at least as far back as the second century. What is distinctive about the current enthusiasm for this term of ecclesial governance is its association with new criteria for choosing the delegates and the protocols for governing the discussions within synodal gatherings. In the past, bishops were typically invited to participate in the discussions, whereas synods in the pontificate of Francis have included large numbers of lay Catholics and are open to "discussing" and "exploring" matters of long settled magisterial teaching.

Extending the catchment field for synod delegates is defended by reference to the concept of the *sensus fidelium*. This concept is relatively new

---

[1] This essay was first published in *The Thomist* 87, no. 2 (April 2023): 233–254. Used with permission.

in Catholic scholarship, and many authorities trace its classic expression to Newman's essay *On Consulting the Faithful in Matters of Doctrine* (1859). At the time of its publication, Newman was the editor of *The Rambler* and there were tensions between prominent lay people and members of the episcopacy about aspects of Catholic education. The bishops of the era did not think that lay people should interfere in decisions they were making about the education of Catholic children. Newman differed from the bishops in his judgment:

> I think I am right in saying that the tradition of the Apostles, committed to the whole Church in its various constituents and functions *per modum unius*, manifests itself variously at various times: sometimes by the mouth of the episcopacy, sometimes by the [church] doctors, sometimes by the people, sometimes by liturgies, rites, ceremonies, and customs, by events, disputes, movements, and all those other phenomena which are comprised under the name of history. It follows that none of these channels of tradition may be treated with disrespect; granting at the same time fully, that the gift of discerning, discriminating, defining, promulgating, and enforcing any portion of that tradition resides solely in the *Ecclesia docens*.[2]

This statement of principle has two limbs. First, the tradition of the apostles, the deposit of faith, manifests itself in many ways, through many agencies, including the beliefs of the lay faithful. Second, "the gift of discerning, discriminating, defining, promulgating, and enforcing any portion of that tradition resides solely in the *Ecclesia docens*."[3] These two concepts, the "apostolic tradition" and the "*ecclesia docens*," the latter more commonly called the magisterium, are extremely important. If these two "planks" in the barque of Peter are splintered, then it is hard to see how it can possibly keep afloat.

Newman thought that the barque had almost sunk in the fourth century during the Arian crisis because the *ecclesia docens* failed to remain true to the deposit of faith:

---

2 John Henry Newman, "On Consulting the Faithful in Matters of Doctrine," *The Rambler* (July 1859): §2.

3 For a more extensive analysis of the author's treatment of Newman's concept of the *sensus fidelium* see Tracey Rowland, 'On the Development of Doctrine: A Via Media between Intellectualism and Historicism,' in *A Guide to John Henry Newman: His Life and Thought*, edited by Juan R. Vélez, (Washington, DC: Catholic University of America Press, 2022), 352–73.

There was a temporary suspense of the functions of the "Ecclesia docens." The body of Bishops failed in the confession of the faith. They spoke variously, one against another; there was nothing, after Nicæa, of firm, unvarying, consistent testimony, for nearly sixty years. There were untrustworthy Councils, unfaithful Bishops; there was weakness, fear of consequences, misguidance, delusion, hallucination . . . extending itself into nearly every corner of the Catholic Church. The comparatively few who remained faithful were discredited and driven into exile; the rest were either deceivers or were deceived.[4]

Clearly there are similarities between the Church of the fourth century and the Church of the twenty-first. Certainly, one can confirm that there has been, at least in relation to some aspects of magisterial teaching, nothing of firm, unvarying, consistent testimony for nearly sixty years. Bishops today are scarcely in agreement on the fundamental building blocks of theology, and if there is no common agreement on the building blocks there are disagreements in all of its subfields. Professional theologians, lay and clerical, also disagree about the building blocks, and in many cases the divisions begin within the Catholic academies educating future priests and bishops. The lack of "unvarying, consistent testimony" among those in Holy Orders is but one consequence or epiphenomenon flowing from disagreements among academics. To put it plainly, the primary teaching bodies of the Church are fractured across a range of fault lines.

One major fault line, at least since the 1960s, is the issue of what is to be made of contemporary social theory. The Catholic intellectual tradition has always operated in partnership with philosophy and today the regnant philosophies are suspicious of reason, while contemporary social theories, many spun out of the Marxist tradition, are completely hostile to Christian moral teachings and the theological anthropology that underpins them. A major split in the 1960s divided Catholic theologians who thought that ecclesiology and moral theology needed to undergo a revolutionary transformation in light of such contemporary social theories from those who believed the theories were but the latest ideological experiments conducted in the social engineering laboratories of the disciples of Marx, Freud, and Nietzsche, the great triumvirate of anti-Christian thinkers of the nineteenth and twentieth centuries.

In 1973 Charles Davis published "Theology and Praxis," explaining the

---

4   Newman, "Consulting the Faithful," §3.

fault line. He described the magnetic attraction of the Frankfurt school's Critical Theory to Belgian and Dutch theologians in the immediate post-conciliar era in the following terms:

> Fundamental for them as a consequence of their acceptance of the Marxist unity of theory and *praxis* is a conviction that the permanent self-identity of the Christian faith cannot be presupposed. . . . They reject a theoretical system of identity. There is no purely theoretical centre of reference, which can serve in an abstract, speculative way as a norm of identity. Truth does not yet exist; it cannot be reached by interpretation, but it has to be produced by change. For these theologians therefore, faith is in a strong sense mediated in history through *praxis*. *Praxis* is not the application of already known truth or the carrying out of a trans-historical ideal; it is that process in and through which one comes to know present reality and future possibilities. If faith is mediated in *praxis*, it must renounce an a priori claim to self-identity and universality.
>
> However, if the mediation of faith through *praxis* is consistently accepted, that means the destruction of theology in the current sense of the articulation of the immanent self-understanding of faith. Theology loses its boundaries as an independent discipline, because the only appropriate context for the conscious articulation of *praxis* is a theory of the development of society in its total reality. Included within such a comprehensive theory would be a critique of theological consciousness, replacing theology as a separate science.[5]

In his final paragraph, Davis points to the significance of this appropriation of the Critical Theory of the Frankfurt School for theology with this rhetorical question: "Is theology, as [Edward] Schillebeeckx says, the critical self-consciousness of Christian *praxis*, or is [Leszek] Kołakowski right when he says: 'For theology begins with the belief that truth has already been given to us, and its intellectual effort consists not of an attrition against reality but of an assimilation of something which exists already in its entirety.'"[6]

If Critical Theory or some other version of a priority of *praxis* theory

---

[5] Charles Davis, "Theology and Praxis," *Cross Currents* 23, no. 2 (Summer 1973): 154–68, at 167.

[6] Davis, "Theology and Praxis," 167. These two paragraphs were also cited in chapter 4 of Tracey Rowland's *Catholic Theology* (London: Bloomsbury, 2017) on the *Concilium* scholars.

becomes the intellectual partner for theology, then almost every branch of theology is open for a radical revision. This was recognized by Joseph Ratzinger in his *Principles of Catholic Theology*:

> If the word "orthopraxis" is pushed to its most radical meaning, it presumes that no truth exists that is antecedent to praxis but rather that truth can be established only on the basis of correct praxis, which has the task of creating meaning out of and in the face of meaninglessness. Theology becomes then no more than a guide to action, which, by reflecting on praxis, continually develops new modes of praxis. If not only redemption but truth as well is regarded as "post hoc," then truth becomes the product of man. At the same time, man, who is no longer measured against truth but produces it, becomes himself a product.[7]

Ratzinger further endorsed Albert Görres's judgment that "there is no doctrine of Jesus without a skeleton, without dogmatic principle," and his description that the belief that "faith propositions do not matter because the important thing is contact with a spiritual atmosphere" is the "Hinduisation of the faith."[8]

We will return to this theological division later in this paper, but suffice to say, one's understanding of synodality depends upon the position one takes regarding theological method. If one endorses some form of the priority of *praxis* principle, one will not follow anything like John Henry Newman's idea of the relationship between the *ecclesia docens* and the *sensus fidelium* or his understanding of the development of doctrine.

To gain a more comprehensive understanding of what a Newmanian understanding of the operation of the *sensus fidelium* within a synod might look like, it is important to refer to other contributions to the notion of the *sensus fidelium*. Newman's ideas were in some ways anticipated by Johann Adam Möhler who was based at the University of Tübingen. In his *Unity in the Church* (1825),[9] Möhler describes the Church as the organic development of the Holy Spirit through history. Its focus was to explain how the

---

7. Joseph Ratzinger, *Principles of Catholic Theology: Building Stones for a Fundamental Theology* (San Francisco: Ignatius Press, 1987), 318.

8. Joseph Ratzinger, *The Nature and Mission of Theology: Approaches to Understanding Its Role in the Light of Present Controversy* (San Francisco: Ignatius Press, 1995), 91.

9. Johann Adam Möhler, *Unity in the Church, or, The Principles of Catholicism: Presented in the Spirit of the Church Fathers of the First Three Centuries*, trans. Peter C. Erb (Washington, DC: Catholic University of America Press, 2016); first published in 1825.

Holy Spirit works in history to see that the original deposit of faith, revealed by Jesus Christ, is handed down uncorrupted from one generation to the next. Here the theological issue is the relationship between Christology and pneumatology, the work of Christ and the work of the Holy Spirit in the economy of salvation. Also necessary is an understanding of theological anthropology, specifically how the Holy Spirit works within the soul to bring about the *sensus fidei*.[10]

In *Sensus Fidei*, the ITC said that in Möhler's view, "it is the Holy Spirit who animates, guides, and unites the faithful as a community in Christ, bringing about in them an ecclesial 'consciousness' of the faith (*Gemeingeist* or *Gesamtsinn*), something akin to a *Volksgeist* or national spirit."[11] This *sensus fidei*, "which is the subjective dimension of Tradition, necessarily includes an objective element, which is the Church's teaching, for the Christian 'sense' of the faithful, which lives in their hearts and is virtually equivalent to Tradition, is never divorced from its content."[12] The Holy Spirit never teaches one thing and Christ another.

> The *sensus fidei fidelis* is a sort of spiritual instinct that enables the believer to judge spontaneously whether a particular teaching or practice is or is not in conformity with the Gospel and with apostolic faith. It is intrinsically linked to the virtue of faith itself; it flows from, and is a property of, faith. It is compared to an instinct because it is not primarily the result of rational deliberation, but is rather a form of spontaneous and natural knowledge, a sort of perception (*aisthesis*).[13]

The point is significant because the instinctual element is sometimes used to defend the idea that actual knowledge of the Church's intellectual tradition is not necessary for the possession of the *sensus fidelium*. Au contraire, since the virtue of faith itself is not without content, it presupposes a degree of knowledge of the apostolic faith as presented in the gospels.

Notwithstanding all the above, "the correct intuitions of the *sensus fidei* can be mixed up with various purely human opinions, or even with errors

---

[10] Andrew Meszaros included a whole section on the significance of sanctifying grace and the gifts of the Holy Spirit for the effective operation of the *sensus fidelium* in *The Prophetic Church: History and Doctrinal Development in John Henry Newman and Yves Congar* (Oxford: Oxford University Press, 2016).

[11] International Theological Commission, *Sensus Fidei* (2014), §35.

[12] *Sensus Fidei*, §35.

[13] *Sensus Fidei*, §49.

linked to the narrow confines of a particular cultural context."[14] Some people are simply not well catechized. They understand bits of the tradition, pieces of the apostolic faith, but there may be gaps in their understanding, which leave them open to appropriating ideas from hostile traditions without knowing the incongruities. "Not all the ideas which circulate among the People of God are compatible with the faith,"[15] a problem acknowledged by St. John Paul II, Pope Benedict XVI, and Pope Francis. In *Familiaris Consortio* §5, St. John Paul II declared,

> The [*sensus fidei*] does not consist solely or necessarily in the con-
> sensus of the faithful. Following Christ, the Church seeks the truth,
> which is not always the same as the majority opinion. . . . The Church
> values sociological and statistical research, when it proves helpful
> in understanding the historical context in which pastoral action
> has to be developed and when it leads to a better understanding
> of the truth. Such research alone, however, is not to be considered
> in itself an expression of the sense of faith.[16]

Moreover, during a retreat conducted by Peter-Hans Kolvenbach, S.J., in 1987, St. John Paul II wrote in his retreat notebook that "reading the signs of the times," a phrase often used in the context of all forms of ecclesial deliberations, "must not be done according to an ideological key." One must not forget that the interpretation of the signs of the times is always liable to fall into the traps of "the father of lies," and the "only key with which the Church and humankind should open 'the signs of the times' is the crucified and risen Christ."[17] In other words, contemporary social phenomena needed to be analyzed from the perspective of the Christian kerygma rather than the kerygma finding itself under review by the proponents of contemporary social theories.

Similarly, Yves Congar wrote,

> The history of modern culture is dominated by various forms of
> immanentism, rationalism, the spirit of Faust; and eventually there
> is Marxism, the most consistent endeavour that has ever been

---

[14] *Sensus Fidei*, §55.

[15] *Sensus Fidei*, §55.

[16] John Paul II, *Familiaris Consortio* (1981), §5.

[17] Karol Wojtyła, *In God's Hands: The Spiritual Diaries of Pope St. John Paul II* (New York: Harper Collins, 2017), 272–73.

made to give the world a purely immanent meaning, excluding all transcendence, an endeavour to overcome all contradictions and to attain integrity without any reference whatever to God. Even things that are in themselves good and true, authentic earthly values, are susceptible of becoming idols and a 'home-ground' for the Prince of this world. Think what can happen to country, production, progress, class, race, the body and sport, domestic comfort; and how many names can be given today to Egypt, Canaan or Babylon.[18]

Hence, in an address to the ITC, Pope Benedict XVI remarked that it is important to clarify the criteria used to distinguish the authentic *sensus fidelium* from its counterfeits. The *sensus fidelium* is not "some kind of public opinion of the Church, and it is unthinkable to mention it in order to challenge the teachings of the Magisterium, this because the *sensus fidei* cannot grow authentically in the believer except to the extent in which he or she fully participates in the life of the Church, and this requires a responsible adherence to her Magisterium."[19]

These limitations echo previous comments made by young Professor Joseph Ratzinger in the late 1960s, referencing *Dei Verbum*, §10:

It is to be regarded as a fortunate decision of the Council that, in emphasizing the share of the laity in the work of keeping the word pure, it did not become involved with the theory of the consensus of faith, which, in connection with the dogmas of 1854 and 1950, resulted in the acceptance of the view that the whole Church has a share in the making manifest of the word. For there is still too much that needs clarification in this theory before it can be regarded as a safe expression of this particular point.[20]

With this caveat in mind, at least one issue requiring clarification is the criteria for choosing lay participants in synods.

Continuing this line of papal caveats, Pope Francis exhorted the members to develop criteria that allow the authentic expressions of the *sensus fidelium* to be discerned since "the *sensus fidelium* cannot be confused with the

---

[18] Yves Congar, *Lay People in the Church* (London: Geoffrey Chapman, 1965), 100.

[19] Benedict XVI, Address to the International Theological Commission, Hall of the Popes, December 7, 2012.

[20] Joseph Ratzinger, "The Transmission of Divine Revelation," in *Commentary on the Documents of Vatican II*, ed. Herbert Vorgrimler (New York: Herder & Herder, 1969), 196.

sociological reality of a majority opinion."[21] In response, the ITC's theologians argued that individual Catholics needed to possess at least the following six dispositions: (1) participation in the life of the Church, (2) listening to the word of God, (3) openness to reason, (4) adherence to the magisterium, (5) holiness, and (6) seeking the edification of the Church.[22] *Synodality in the Life and Mission of the Church* elaborates further:

> The same dispositions that are required to live and bring to maturity the *sensus fidei*, with which all believers are endowed, are also required to put it to use on the synodal path. This is an essential point in forming people in a synodal spirit, since we live in a culture where the demands of the Gospel and even human virtues are not often the object of appreciation or sufficient preparation. . . .
>
> The Eucharistic synaxis is the source and paradigm of the spirituality of communion. In it are expressed the specific elements of Christian life that are called to mould the *affectus synodalis*.[23]

Five specific elements are then mentioned: (1) the importance of the Trinity and especially the gifts of the Holy Spirit; (2) the importance of reconciliation; (3) the importance of listening to the Scriptures and participating in the sacraments, especially the Eucharist; (4) "Communion," by which is meant something like a harmonious symphony of different gifts and charisms; and (5) the importance of possessing a missionary disposition.

In theory, all participants in synods should show evidence of the full set of dispositions listed in the ITC documents qualifying them for the trust that the synod leaders place in their judgment. In practice, however, a survey of lay persons chosen to be synod delegates in recent times is likely to reveal that the overwhelming majority fall short of this standard, especially in the disposition of fidelity to magisterial teaching. In fact, a common currently held criteria for selection as a synod delegate has been employment by the Catholic Church. Synods are very time-consuming events and those chosen to attend are not paid to do so. Most working Catholics or Catholic mothers rearing children do not have the ability, either in terms of time or financial capacity, to simply drop everything and spend a couple of weeks attending

---

[21] Francis, Address to the International Theological Commission, Hall of Popes, December 6, 2013.

[22] *Sensus Fidei*, §§89–105.

[23] International Theological Commission, *Synodality in the Life and Mission of the Church* (2018), §§108–9.

a meeting, which may well involve considerable time and expense. Most employers would not tolerate such absences. Those already on the Church's payroll have no such problems. Yet being on the Church's payroll is scarcely synonymous with an education in the Church's theological tradition, or even with regular Mass attendance, or familiarity with Sacred Scripture, or with the life of prayer conducive to holiness of life.

Corporate executives occupying senior management positions in Catholic curial offices or social welfare agencies, as well as educational and medical institutions, are more likely to hold degrees in management theory, or health sciences, or pedagogy along with qualifications in business management than in any deeply grounded theological discipline. This is especially so in countries where the Church is comparatively wealthy and manages numerous institutions, such as Germany and Australia. It is perhaps, therefore, no surprise that these two countries have held a national synod or plenary, two countries where the Catholic Church is the largest private employer in the entire employment sector. One journalist described the Australian Plenary Council of 2022 as a gathering of the Church's "HR [Human Resources] Department," an event marketed as an exercise in synodality.

German Catholics have led the way in calls for ecclesial governance by national synods. This is not a recent development of the pontificate of Francis but can be traced back to the immediate post-conciliar years when Karl Rahner was the biggest name in post-conciliar theology, busily writing works such as *The Shape of the Church to Come*, while Hans Küng was publishing books such as *Structures of the Church* (1965), dedicated to Karl Rahner, and *Reforming the Church Today* (1990).[24] In the traumatic wake of the Nazi era, the German generation of 1968 passionately promoted democracy and was correspondingly critical of all forms of hierarchical governance. Yet what was often missing in these calls for democratic talk fests is the notion that the persons taking part in the discussions needed a high level of sanctity and understanding of the ecclesial tradition.

Many calls for synods or national plenaries appear to be motivated not by a desire to seek the wisdom of the holy but to promote the democratization of ecclesial governance because of a preference for democratic forms of governance as a general social principle. Such a preference is easily defended by reference to the history of episcopal negligence in the child abuse tragedy. The resultant attitude is not that the episcopacy needs to be

---

[24] Hans Küng, *Structures of the Church* (London: Burns & Oates, 1965); *Reforming the Church Today: Keeping Hope Alive* (New York: Crossroad, 1990); and Karl Rahner, *The Shape of the Church to Come* (London: SPCK, 1974).

reformed in such a way that bishops actually shoulder the responsibilities they have been given, symbolized by the pallium given to an archbishop, but that bishops need to be reduced to corporate CEO's, answerable to boards of directors and circumscribed in the exercise of their prudential judgment by an encroaching labyrinth of bureaucratic protocols. More bureaucracy—not more sanctity—is the proposal of many advocates of synodality, with the advantage that one does not require any of the dispositions mentioned by the ITC to formulate and proliferate bureaucratic protocols.

Two of the leading theological names who opposed calls to democratize decision-making within the Church were Joseph Ratzinger and Hans Maier.[25]

In *Demokratie in der Kirche* and in his replies to reviews of his best-selling *Introduction to Christianity* (1968), Ratzinger argued that the enthusiasm for synods and the democratization of ecclesial governance was a way of avoiding the really important tasks the Church is called to perform:

> For me, the properly practical task of theology lies in teaching men to believe, to hope and to love and thereby opens up meaning which helps him to live. It does not lie in inventing new costumes for clerics, new forms of ecclesial organization and new forms of liturgical celebration. . . . Its proper praxis consists in giving man something which other "organisations" are not in a position to give. It seems to me a dangerous instance of diminution if one thereby loses sight of that which is truly "practical" with regard to faith and in exchange one escapes into introspective activity that soon devolves into idleness.[26]

The Church, in other words, operates differently from other institutions because its mission is completely different. According to the Catechism,

> Episcopal consecration confers, together with the office of sanctifying, also the offices of teaching and ruling. . . . In fact . . . by the imposition of hands and through the words of the consecration, the grace of the Holy Spirit is given, and a sacred character is impressed in such wise that bishops, in an eminent and visible manner, take

---

[25] A collection of their critical essays was published in *Demokratie in der Kirche: Möglichkeiten und Grenzen*, (Limburg: Lahn-Verlag, 2000).

[26] Joseph Ratzinger, "Glaube, Geschichte und Philosophie Zum Echo auf meine 'Einführung in das Christentum,'" in *Gesammelte Schriften*, vol. 4 (Freiburg: Herder & Herder, 2014), 323–39, at 330.

the place of Christ himself, teacher, shepherd, and priest, and act as his representative (*in Eius persona agant*). By virtue, therefore, of the Holy Spirit who has been given to them, bishops have been constituted true and authentic teachers of the faith and have been made pontiffs and pastors. (CCC, §1558)

Many other paragraphs could be quoted from the Catechism which, like this one, make it clear that the Church as an institution is completely *sui generis*. She is not just another provider of philanthropy, health care, and education. Thus, Ratzinger wrote,

> The Church is not about distributing shares in common products fairly and protecting or exercising the corresponding rights of individuals and the whole, but about keeping the irreducible Word of God present as a claim on people and as a hope for them. This in turn means that the ecclesiastical government does not have the same structural position in the structure of the church as state institutions have in the political community.[27]

He also noticed that not all lay Catholics were enthusiastic about synods. Some lay Catholics argue that the two classes in the Church today are not the clerics and the laity but the bureaucrats (lay and clerical) and the non-bureaucrats. The latter group includes faithful leaders of families, parish priests, and priests in religious orders focused on pastoral and intellectual work. Priests who are not in bureaucratic roles often feel as marginalized as the laity who are not in bureaucratic roles. Speaking of the 1999 European Synod of Bishops, Ratzinger wrote,

> There are complaints that the majority of believers generally show little interest in dealing with the Synod. I have to admit that this reluctance seems to me to be more of a sign of health. From a Christian point of view, i.e. for what is actually meant by the New Testament, little is gained by people passionately grappling with the problems of the Synod—just as little does anyone become a sportsman as a result of being deeply involved in the structure of the Olympic Committee.[28]

---

[27] Ratzinger, *Demokratie in der Kirche*, 19.
[28] Ratzinger, *Demokratie in der Kirche*, 20.

Ratzinger was also critical of the idea that lay participants in synods should have the same voting rights as bishops. Referring to Karl Rahner's idea of an all-German (or a national) synod of bishops, priests, and lay people, which would be the supreme governing body of individual, national churches to which the bishops should also be subject, Ratzinger remarked,

> Such an idea is as alien to the New Testament as it is to Church-wide tradition, and this is not as valid for the Church, which is based on tradition, as it may be for draft constitutions. The assertion that the early church councils were made up of lay people and bishops and that only Trent or even Vatican I completed the transition to a pure bishop's council is, from a historical perspective, quite simply wrong: It also does not apply to the concept according to which in Acts 15 the assembly in Jerusalem is drawn, which decided on the question of the relationship between Jewish and Gentile Christians. Rather, Luke represents this meeting according to the model of the ancient people's assembly. The property of the ancient assemblies consisted (sounding quite modern) in their fundamental public nature, which of course presupposes the distinction between the decision-making body and the public present. The public is by no means condemned to passivity: through its (positive and negative) "acclamations" it has often decisively influenced events without directly taking part in the suffragium (vote).[29]

In this passage Ratzinger is drawing a distinction between what Newman would call "consulting the faithful in matters of doctrine" and the special charisms of the episcopacy, the *ecclesia docens* in Newman's terms, who enjoy the privilege of voting.

In the following passage Ratzinger underscores this point and then makes another argument about the medieval period when monarchs and other nobles were sometimes invited to Church councils, distinguishing between these medieval councils and the notion of consulting the faithful in matters of doctrine:

> According to Acts 15, the Council of the Apostles met according to this model: It took place in front of the public of the whole "ekklesia," but only "apostles and presbyters" are designated as its decision-makers (15.6 and 15.22). The early church adhered to

---

[29] Ratzinger, *Demokratie in der Kirche*, 30.

this form in its councils from beginning to end, and any assertion to the contrary is simply without historical basis. Of course, the medieval councils were not only church councils, but also general assemblies of Latin Christianity, which attempted to use them to regulate their foreign affairs in a uniform manner. To interpret the representation of the members of the Corpus Christianum at these meetings as lay people participating in the Council means misjudging the historical perspectives. The basic concept that the council is an assembly of bishops (which as such can of course also grant voting rights to non-bishops) remained unchanged during the Middle Ages. The naturalness with which Trent, which only had to work as a council and not as a political-economic assembly, met again as a pure bishops' assembly would remain incomprehensible in any other case.[30]

Ratzinger concluded his discussion on the alleged historical precedents for including the laity in the *ecclesia docens* (not merely consulting the laity on matters of doctrine but raising their judgments to magisterial levels) with the following declaration:

The idea of the mixed synod as a permanent supreme governing body of the national churches is a chimerical idea in terms of the tradition of the church as well as its sacramental structure and its specific goal. Such a synod would lack any legitimacy and therefore obedience to it has to be decisively and unequivocally denied.[31]

As if this declaration were not the end of the matter, Ratzinger further argued that "the so-called synodal idea . . . seems strangely obsolete against the background of general social and political developments."[32] Whereas in the world at large the movement is against increasingly high levels of bureaucratization, the call for the democratization of the Church will lead, as bureaucratization inevitably does, to more uniformity and less real freedom, as some of the Catholic student experiments at the German universities demonstrated.

---

[30] Ratzinger, *Demokratie in der Kirche*, 31.
[31] Ratzinger, *Demokratie in der Kirche*, 31.
[32] Ratzinger, *Demokratie in der Kirche*, 31.

In the church today, the exact opposite is being proposed to us: Total integration of all initiatives into an all-encompassing synodal regime, which regulates everything in the fully integrated congregation, from worship to political mandate, which in turn seems to overshadow all other tasks. This program, which is being heralded to us as the prospect of future reforms at the national level, has meanwhile been zealously exercised in the nuclei of such ideas, in the student communities: active minorities who, to the silence of their fellow students who are disinterested in such experiments, present themselves as a "General Assembly" and thus as "democratically legitimized" representatives of the whole, who have worked out "synodal" constitutions for the congregations, in which the totalitarian consequences of this conception became frighteningly clear: the church at the university no longer meant the free offer of word and sacrament, but the unrequested confiscation of all Christians in the university by a group of "committed people" defined completely independently of belief. Because of the synodal constitution, it is always the congregation as a whole that expresses itself, and this congregation also expresses itself about the whole, i.e. about everything.[33]

Ratzinger noted that in Cologne, Catholic students "resolutely rejected" the "synodal conspiracy" (*synodale Komplott*) since they wanted their community to be bound together by the one commonality: "The gospel of Jesus Christ, as the faith of the church professes."[34]

In summary, one might argue that under the banner of synodality, three completely different reasons are found for consulting the laity. The first reason, Newman's, is that sometimes the *ecclesia docens* fails in its duty. This plank in the barque of Peter becomes weak or rotten or broken and the *sensus fidelium* needs to be found among the lay saints. The second reason—that of the generation of 1968 Germans—is war guilt and a corresponding faith in democracy as the highest or only legitimate form of governance in any context. This is notwithstanding that the ascendency of National Socialism was enabled by a democratic vote of the German people. The worst thing about Nazism was not that it was lacking in democratic elements but that it posted itself beyond the Ten Commandments, that is, above divine law and above truth.

---

[33] Ratzinger, *Demokratie in der Kirche*, 32.
[34] Ratzinger, *Demokratie in der Kirche*, 33.

Throughout his many publications, Ratzinger was consistently hostile to the idea that the truth could be subjected to the majority principle:

> Indeed, by its very nature, faith is suspended where it is subjected to the majority principle: Why should Mr. Muller or Mrs. Huber be able to oblige me to believe this or that which they more or less happen to think is right? Why should I be obliged to believe what a majority passes today that might tomorrow be replaced by an opposing majority? Either there is a different authorization in the faith of the church than that of human opinion, or there is not. If not, then there is no belief, but everyone thinks up whatever he thinks is right.[35]

On the contrary, "if God has really told us something and also created the organs that stand for fidelity to his word, then this or that random majority does not count."[36] Ratzinger further noted that "the crisis in the Anglican Church was not triggered by the ordination of women as such, but by the fact that, contrary to the previous tradition, questions of faith were also subjected to a majority vote. . . . Where this prevails, faith is actually at an end."[37]

A third reason is the idea that the episcopacy not only failed to exercise its teaching responsibilities but also failed to shoulder its pastoral responsibilities, most notoriously in context of the care of children in its educational and welfare institutions. Here, the argument is that lay leadership is needed—not so much at the level of doctrinal development but at the level of the provision of boards of overview and general protocol compliance. As mentioned above, the general attitude is that more bureaucracy not more sanctity solves this problem. In Ratzinger's words, "The apostolic element disappears behind the structural."[38]

While Ratzinger's arguments addressed the problems latent in the various calls for the democratization of ecclesial decision-making, Hans Maier's publications focused more on the genealogy of these arguments, on their theological sources and modes of unfolding within the culture of the Church. Like Charles Davis and Ratzinger, he too noticed that a central issue is what he calls "a new relationship between theory and practice":

---

[35] Ratzinger, *Demokratie in der Kirche*, 88.
[36] Ratzinger, *Demokratie in der Kirche*, 89.
[37] Ratzinger, *Demokratie in der Kirche*, 89.
[38] Ratzinger, *Demokratie in der Kirche*, 86.

Theologians such as Jürgen Moltmann or Johann Baptist Metz discuss the problem of democracy today primarily in the context of a modern history of freedom and emancipation. For Metz it begins with the Enlightenment, in which the old unity of religion and society is destroyed, and it continues in the political attempt to create the social prerequisites for the public use of reason and the mobilisation of all institutions—including the church—towards a "second reflection" on human freedom. A new relationship between theory and practice, knowledge and morality, reflection and revolution is effective, which must also determine theological consciousness if it is not to fall back to an earlier, pre-critical level of consciousness. In the future, practical and—in the broadest sense of the word—political reason, must be involved in all critical reflections on theology.[39]

Given all that has been outlined above, we may conclude that the meaning of "synodality" is not something that is settled Church teaching. It is a concept that is given different content by different theologians. For Möhler, Newman, St. John Paul II, and Ratzinger, there is a clear distinction between the *ecclesia docens*, the magisterium, and the *sensus fidelium* of the lay faithful. While in times of crisis it may be valuable to consult the laity on matters of doctrine, as Newman argued, it is not suggested by these authorities that the lay faithful themselves should be regarded as members of the *ecclesia docens*.

Moreover, not just any baptized person is regarded by these authors as worthy of consultation. In order to manifest the *sensus fidei*, persons need to have at least the dispositions mentioned by the members of the ITC, not omitting the disposition of fidelity to magisterial teaching.

It is worth a moment considering the dispositions of those lay saints in the fourth century who proved faithful when many of the episcopacy did not. They had a radically *un*-worldly faith. In a prevailing atmosphere of conforming oneself to prevailing imperial or political, social, and intellectual norms, they knew where "the sword piercing to the division of soul and spirit" (Heb 4:12) fell, and they were prepared to pay the cost. They and the minority of pastors and bishops who stood firm. "You are the children of martyrs," said St. Basil to such faithful. Their faith had what Ratzinger has called "the eschatological edge," inherited from their forebears.

---

[39] Hans Maier, "Vom Getto der Emanzipation. Kritik der 'demokratisierten' Kirche," *Hochland* 62 (1970): 385–99, at 387.

If, however, one follows the trajectory of theologians who have flipped the relationship between *logos* and *ethos*, giving priority to *ethos* or *praxis*, or those otherwise influenced by social theories with a Marxian pedigree, including contemporary proponents of gender fluidity, then one reaches a different conclusion: the entire theological tradition of the Church requires a revolution, especially in the fields of moral theology and ecclesiology, and the revolution in ecclesiology is eliminating the idea that only bishops are the bearers of magisterial authority. Why anyone would present themselves as candidates for Holy Orders if it means being reduced to chief executive officers of a vast welfare institution—at best—is a practical question yet to be addressed. But its "practicality" may explain why seminaries in some dioceses, which are maintaining the priority of *logos*, are still attracting candidates, if not in large numbers, while seminaries in dioceses where priority of *praxis* theologies dominate are often empty or closed.

In the fifth century, the importance of the *ecclesia docens* was addressed by St. Cyril of Alexandria in his *Commentary on the Gospel of St. John*:

> Our Lord Jesus Christ has appointed certain men to be guides and teachers of the world and stewards of his divine mysteries. Now he bids them to shine out like lamps and to cast out their light not only over the land of the Jews but over every country under the sun and over people scattered in all directions and settled in distant lands. That man has spoken truly who said: No one takes honour upon himself, except the one who is called by God, for it was our Lord Jesus Christ who called his own disciples before all others to a most glorious apostolate. These holy men became the pillar and mainstay of the truth, and Jesus said that he was sending them just as the Father had sent him.[40]

Perhaps one question for aspiring synod delegates, one criterion of suitability for participation in a synod, could be something along the lines of "do you agree with this statement from St. Cyril?" The question would at least be a quick way to discern what version of the "synodality" drum a proposed delegate is marching to.

Newman quoted St. Jerome as saying that by AD 361, "nearly all the churches in the whole world, under the pretence of peace and the emperor, are polluted with the communion of the Arians."[41] One is tempted to suggest

---

[40] Cyril of Alexandria, *Commentary on the Gospel of St. John* (Lib. 12,1: PG, 74:707–10).

[41] John Henry Newman, "The Orthodoxy of the Body of the Faithful during the Supremacy

that today the Arians have been replaced by two dominant groups. The first consists of an assortment of people Görres would describe as wanting to "Hinduize" Christianity in the sense of leaving behind the Church's doctrinal tradition, and who are going about this by adopting Marxian notions of truth and anthropology, above all by insisting upon the priority of *praxis*. These types speak a lot about "listening to the Spirit" but ignore the teachings of Christ or write them down as only relevant for a particular time and culture. This disjunction between the Second Person and Third Person of the Trinity is a contemporary form of Joachimism, the idea that the era of Christ is superseded by the era of the Holy Spirit. This first group is mostly concerned to overturn millennia of teaching in the fields of moral and sacramental theology, and its proponents are often found in academies of theology.

The second group consists of people who wish to base ecclesial governance upon the latest fashionable practices in business management schools. Many in this group would also agree with members of the first group about issues of moral and sacramental theology, but their primary focus is ecclesiology, not moral or sacramental theology. The members of this group want to overturn millennia of teaching in the field of ecclesiology because they believe that the current "business model," conferring a sacred authority upon bishops, has clearly failed. Those in this category are often members of the laity who occupy senior management positions in Catholic educational, health, and social welfare institutions. While some theologians in the tradition of Hans Küng would strongly agree with them, the agenda of this group is largely driven by management theory, not theology. For both groups, synodality becomes a means to effect revolutionary change in Catholic teaching and practice.

There are many lay faithful, however, who wholly concur with the assessments of Ratzinger, and who simply want bishops to see that the apostolic teaching is passed on uncorrupted to the next generation, and that institutions falling under the governance of bishops are run according to Christian principles. Those in this camp are far from happy with the current situation and would agree with those in the other two groups that we are living through a great crisis and that the episcopacy is at the center of that crisis. Their solution, however, is not to trash the tradition, not to buy a new "boat," but to do something about the "splintered planks," to throw their support behind those they perceive to be the saintly bishops of our time, the

of Arianism," historical point 17, *Newman Reader*, https://www.newmanreader.org/works/arians/note5.html.

contemporary confessors of the faith. They have no opposition to synods undertaken according to something like the Newmanian model described above, since synods of this nature presuppose that magisterial teaching can be developed but not trashed. They also presuppose that the Second Person and Third Person of the Trinity work together in the economy of salvation. In the words of Archbishop Charles Chaput, "Our one unique responsibility as bishops is to proclaim and protect the apostolic tradition of the Church."[42]

---

[42] Charles Chaput, "Only Worthy Agenda for Synod Is One Given to Us by Jesus in the Gospels," interview by Kelsey Wicks, *Catholic News Agency*, February 10, 2023, https://www.catholicnewsagency.com/news/253604/synod-on-synodality-archbishop-chaput-asks-bishops-only-to-use-jesus-agenda.

CHAPTER 6

Four Models of What the Church Is Not in the Ecclesiology of Joseph Ratzinger[1]

INTRODUCTION: *COMMUNIO* VS. *CONGREGATIO*

"One of the most crucial tasks in the study of the conciliar legacy today . . . will be to reveal anew the sacramental character of the church," wrote Ratzinger.[2] Ratzinger has constantly probed this sacramental character throughout the long history of his publications, from his doctoral dissertation through to his commentaries on the Council, to the documents he promulgated as prefect for the CDF, down to his many papal homilies. A common thread is the recurring theme of *communio*.

As David L. Schindler explains, "The notion of the Church as '*communio*' contrasts with the notion of the Church as '*congregatio*.' While 'Communio' emphasizes the nature of the Church as a gift from God, established 'from above,' '*congregatio*' indicates a community that comes to be 'from below' by virtue of the decision of the individual wills of the community, in the manner of a democratic body."[3] In contrast to those who propose a sociological vision of the Church as a form of *congregatio*, the "theocentric ['Communio']

---

1   This paper was first presented at a conference on the ecclesiology of Joseph Ratzinger sponsored by the Ratzinger Foundation and hosted by the Franciscan University of Steubenville in 2022. Used with permission.

2   Joseph Ratzinger, *Principles of Catholic Theology: Building Stones for a Fundamental Theology* (San Francisco: Ignatius Press, 1987), 55.

3   David L. Schindler, "David Schindler on Cardinal Ratzinger's Ecclesiology," interview with editor of *Communio*, Zenit, May 1, 2005, para. 15, https://zenit.org/2005/05/01/david-schindler-on-cardinal-ratzinger-s-ecclesiology/.

understanding of the Church as the sacrament of Christ's love has been an abiding feature of Ratzinger's life."[4]

From this sacramental understanding of the Church flows the judgment that a number of ecclesial models are simply wrong or defective. Many of Ratzinger's publications in ecclesiology take either a positive form of sketching the sacramental relationships or a negative form of offering critiques of the wrong or defective models. This paper will focus on the negative critiques. It will address four "contra Communio" ecclesiologies that are prominent in countries of the Anglosphere and parts of Europe, that is, prominent in parts of the world where the Church has been, until quite recently, a wealthy and powerful institution.

THE CHURCH IS NOT A DEMOCRACY

First, the church is not a democracy. As Ratzinger remarked, "The Church of Christ is not a party, not an association, not a club. Her deep and permanent structure is not democratic but sacramental, consequently hierarchical."[5]

> The Church cannot conceptualize for herself how she wants to be ordered. She can only try to understand ever more clearly the inner call of faith, and to live from faith. She does not need the majority principle, which always has something atrocious about it: the subordinated part must bend to the decision of the majority for the sake of peace even when this decision is perhaps misguided or even destructive. In human arrangements, there is perhaps no alternative. But in the Church the binding to the faith protects all of us: each is bound to faith, and in this respect the sacramental order guarantees more freedom than could be given by those who would subject the Church to the majority principle.[6]

In "Freedom and Constraint in the Church," Ratzinger associated calls for a more democratized Church with a misunderstanding of the "People of God" concept and with a general social discontent with large impersonal associations. He agreed that "a communal responsibility for one another and for the Christian cause, the experience of faith-based practical fellowship, the

---

4 Schindler, "Ratzinger's Ecclesiology," para. 16.
5 Joseph Ratzinger, *The Ratzinger Report* (San Francisco: Ignatius Press, 1985), 49.
6 Benedict XVI, *Images of Hope: Meditations on Major Feasts* (San Francisco: Ignatius Press, 2006), 33–34.

oasis of fraternity and intimacy amid the pressures of an impersonal world . . . are values in which Christian freedom can express itself" in parish or other local communities.[7] However, "when the element of local community is isolated and set apart from the mainstream of sacramental communion of the whole Church, the community's freedom is reduced to triviality and becomes empty. The autonomous community is reduced to a group for purely social concerns and leisure activities; its act of worship becomes irrational or a mere rite of fellowship that celebrates itself."[8] This, he argues, is not a Christian conception of freedom.

In Europe many of the democratization movements such as *Wir Sind Kirche* have their intellectual foundations in the theology of Hans Küng. As the great German philosopher Robert Spaemann (1927–2018) explained,

> Hans Küng [is] in the tradition of the modern instrumentalization of religion in the service of morality and morality in the service of state preservation. He can only interpret ecclesiastical structures in state-political categories and therefore cannot accept the strangeness of Christianity in the world of which the New Testament speaks. [According to Küng] the church must be adapted to the respective state structures, i.e., today it must be democratized.[9]

For Ratzinger, in contrast, the hierarchical structure of the Church is something divinely ordained. It is not a matter of human construction. As the Catechism affirms,

> The Lord Jesus endowed his community with a structure that will remain until the Kingdom is fully achieved. Before all else there was the choice of the Twelve with Peter as their head. Representing the twelves tribes of Israel, they are the foundation stones of the new Jerusalem. (CCC, §765)

In one of his Carinthia lectures, Ratzinger explained, somewhat more poetically, "The Church is not a human association formed on a lost planet somewhere, but rather, extends into the reality of creation. In the ultimate and definitive history of the universe, the Twelve are to be, as it were, the

---

7   Joseph Ratzinger, *Church, Ecumenism, and Politics: New Endeavors in Ecclesiology* (San Francisco: Ignatius Press, 2008), 185.

8   Ratzinger, *New Endeavors*, 185.

9   Robert Spaemann, "Weltethos als 'Projekt,'" *Merkur* 50 (1996): 893–904, at 903.

new 'signs of the zodiac.'"[10] In this statement, ecclesiology is linked to cosmology and the theology of history.

Charismatic Authority and Corporate Managerialism

A problem the Church faces in the era of child abuse trauma is that it is often hard for the faithful to think of bishops as anything so exalted as Christian analogues of the twelve signs of the zodiac. Here the problem is not so much the theology underpinning the episcopate as issues of a more socio-political nature that currently constrain a proper execution of episcopal responsibilities. To use sociological shorthand, the charismatic authority of the episcopacy is constantly undermined by the power of bureaucratic authority. Instead of behaving like medieval feudal lords who deemed themselves to be personally responsible for the welfare of their subjects, or, in an even older scriptural image, behaving like shepherds personally responsible for each and every sheep in their pasture, there is a tendency for bishops to behave instead like chief executive officers of modern corporations. They surround themselves with lawyers, accountants, and in some of the wealthier dioceses with professional "spin-doctors," *alias* public relations advisers. The lawyers encourage them to be risk adverse. In effect, that aspect of their stewardship requiring them to take risks for the sake of the sheep is thwarted. The accountants tell them that they must conserve their capital and increase their capital fund, while urgent pastoral works are put on the back burner. The public relations agents tell them that they must "market" the Church to the world as an agent of philanthropy and remain quiet about aspects of the Church's teaching likely to be unpopular with powerful interest groups. Simultaneously, the modern state seeks to impose more and more control over the institutions of civil society, of which the Church is one. This has two nefarious consequences: 1) ecclesial leaders lose the freedom to choose the personnel employed in Church agencies and determine internal policies of Church agencies; and 2) bishops become responsible for any infringements of government regulations. Furthermore, bishops spend considerable time sitting as chairmen of the diocesan corporate boards and sitting at their desks ensuring every bureaucratic box has been ticked by the ecclesial agencies, for which they are responsible under civil law. For many bishops in large, first-world dioceses, a degree in business administration

---

[10] Joseph Ratzinger, *The Divine Project: Reflections on Creation and the Church* (San Francisco: Ignatius Press, 2023), 133.

and constitutional law would be more related to their daily tasks than the licentiate and doctorate in sacred theology.

This difference between charismatic and bureaucratic authority gives rise to the problem described by the Anglican theologian Lyndon Shakespeare: how is it possible to be the Body of Christ in the age of management?[11] In theory, charismatic authority is linked to character, and character is linked to prudential judgment, and prudential judgment is linked to holiness. Merely bureaucratic authority, however, is linked to nothing higher than the administrative skills needed to see that policy guidelines are observed, that the checklist is diligently followed through. Bureaucratic authority stands opposed to charismatic authority insofar as bureaucratic authority is opposed to prudential judgment. Charismatic authority always carries a non-democratic element because not all people are equally prudent. Some people have better prudential judgment than others. As the political philosopher Leo Strauss once explained, the opinions of Socrates and the Athenian town drunk are not of equal merit! Promotion within a hierarchy based on charismatic authority is related to a person's reputation for excellent prudential judgment, among other virtues. With bureaucratic authority, no special reputation for virtue is required. One simply must follow guidelines and say, in the words of a British comedy show that has entered popular parlance, "the computer says No."

Bureaucratic authority is often easier to "market," at least to a society imbued with democratic values, because, on its surface at least, it appears to be open, inclusive, and anti-elitist. Although it appears more democratic, sociological evidence shows the more an institution is governed by bureaucratic authority, the less freedom there is. This is true both of administrators and of those subject to their decisions. Bureaucratic institutions are not more democratic than institutions based on charismatic authority because behind the public facade of openness, inclusivity, and equality are the persons who write the policies, set the agenda of the institution, determine the ethos of the institution, and organize compliance. In large archdioceses of wealthy countries, these are typically the lawyers, accountants, and public relations officers employed by the archdiocese. Their elite power, in operation behind the scenes, is understood (sadly, all too well), by many faithful lay Catholics and holy priests who unhappily refer to them as the "professional Catholics," the "company men," the "men in gray cardigans," or the "business suit nuns."

The archdiocese this sociological caricature embodies is not the Church

---

[11] Lyndon Shakespeare, *Being the Body of Christ in the Age of Management* (Eugene, OR: Cascade, 2016).

as the Bride of Christ, or as a mother, or as a sacred communion of people with charisms and spiritual missions, but the Church as Catholic Inc. The late Fr. Benedict Groeschel, co-founder of the Franciscans of the Capuchin Friars of the Renewal, had a word for Catholic Inc. He called it the "hippopotamus" and he advised his friends to steer clear of the hippopotamus *at both ends!*[12] In other words, it is not prudent to become dependent on the hippopotamus or to expect it to make provision for the spiritual needs of the faithful, and it is not prudent to become personally entangled in its operations, many of which are not only unrecognizable as Christian but are anti-Christian. Catholics supporting a large family become redundant by archdiocesan business managers who treat the Church's social teachings as immaterial to the sound management of the hippopotamus, which attests to Fr. Groeschel's wisdom.

Although Ratzinger is not a sociologist, he personally experienced a totalitarian government, and thus when he says that the divinely ordained ecclesial structures will give the faithful more freedom than a democratized Church, he speaks with background knowledge of how bureaucratic authority, though apparently populist and democratic, is a hallmark of totalitarian governments. The "something atrocious" democracy has is prioritizing the principle of extrinsic equality over inherent excellence, whereas bureaucratic authority has no capacity to treat persons as individuals with unique needs. Bureaucratic authority is about making life easy for the elites who coral the herd. Charismatic authority is about shepherds laying down their lives for their flock.

Concrete case studies between these two approaches to episcopal authority may be found in how different bishops reacted under twentieth-century totalitarian governments. Some accommodated or capitulated to the state while others took the stance of Cardinal Mindszenty—the Prince Primate of Hungary—who said, "I will keep on fighting [Communists] until the coffin closes above me."[13]

A case study of different exercises of episcopal authority under totalitarian governments would also highlight another implication of Ratzinger's

---

[12] We are indebted to Fr. Martin Onuoha, author of *Mary, Daughter Zion: An Introduction to the Mariology of Joseph Ratzinger* (New York: Peter Lang, 2021), and Actio Divina: *The Marian Mystery of the Church in the Theology of Joseph Ratzinger* (New York: Peter Lang, 2021), for this anecdote about the ecclesial wisdom of Fr. Groeschel. We do not know whether, in adopting this metaphor, Fr. Groeschel was inspired by T. S. Eliot's poem "The Hippopotamus" (1919), composed before Eliot's conversion to the faith of the Church of England.

[13] Margit Balogh, *"Victim of History": Cardinal Mindszenty, a Biography* (Washington, DC: Catholic University of America Press, 2021), 10.

ecclesiology: the ambivalent value of national bishops' conferences. In theory, each bishop is personally responsible for the welfare of the faithful within his diocese, but in practice, in many countries, individual bishops feel compelled to follow the policies of the national bishops' conference. From a sociological perspective, bishops often allow the national policies set by the conference to curb their exercise of prudential judgment. The policies become yet another example of the triumph of bureaucratic authority over charismatic authority and especially over prudential judgment. Group policy documents are rarely, if ever, the fruit of heroic sanctity. They represent the lowest common denominator agreement of a large number of people. The expectation that a bishop will follow policy guidelines enacted by a national bishops' conference is yet another fetter around the exercise of his prudential judgment and personal responsibility for the welfare of the faithful within his jurisdiction.[14] Ratzinger remarked that "the search for agreement between the different tendencies and the effort at mediation [that takes place at national bishops' conferences] often yield flattened documents in which decisive positions (where they might be necessary) are weakened."[15] During the period of National Socialism, "the really powerful documents were those that came from individual courageous bishops."[16]

Courage is one of the chief qualities required in bishops, Ratzinger remarked, and bishops "have to be people with qualities of intellect, professionalism and humanity, so that they can lead and draw others into a close-knit community."[17] It was important for him as the prefect for the CDF to generate a sense of community among his staff, such as one finds in a family. The Church Ratzinger loves is not a bureaucratic machine: "Saints reformed the Church in depth, not by working up plans for new structures, but by reforming themselves," and thus "what the Church needs in every age is holiness, not management."[18] Ratzinger observed that the saints were all people of imagination, not functionaries of apparatuses,[19] and that the Apostle Paul was effective "not because of brilliant rhetoric and sophisticated strategies, but rather because he *exerted* himself and left himself vulnerable

---

[14] For analyses of the power of bishops' conferences, see Henri de Lubac, *The Motherhood of the Church* (San Francisco: Ignatius Press, 1982); Ratzinger, *Ratzinger Report*, 59–60; and John Paul II, *Apostolos Suos* (1998).

[15] Ratzinger, *Ratzinger Report*, 61.

[16] Ratzinger, *Ratzinger Report*, 61.

[17] Benedict XVI, *Light of the World: The Pope, the Church and the Signs of the Times* (San Francisco: Ignatius Press, 2010), 85.

[18] Ratzinger, *Ratzinger Report*, 53.

[19] Ratzinger, *Ratzinger Report,* 67.

in the service of the Gospel."[20] "I have said very often that I think we have too much bureaucracy. Therefore, it will be necessary in any case to simplify things. Everything should not take place by way of committees; there must also be the personal encounter."[21] "The more administrative machinery we construct, be it the most modern, the less place there is for the Spirit, the less place there is for the Lord, and the less freedom there is." In Ratzinger's opinion, "We ought to begin an unsparing examination of conscience on this point at all levels in the Church."[22]

According to Fr. Martin Onuoha, "Joseph Ratzinger fights tooth and nail this vision of the Church as a [bureaucratic] structure or programme for action."[23] Quite simply, the Church, when being true to her divine mission, runs according to the logic of sacramental grace in sacramental relationships, not the logic of corporate management theory specifically designed to eliminate personal responsibility and personal treatment.

The Church Is Not a Debating Society

Regarding this second and related implication of understanding the Church as *Communio*, Balthasar wrote,

> Since the Council the Church has to a large extent put off its mystical characteristics; it has become a Church of permanent conversations, organizations, advisory commissions, congresses, synods, commissions, academies, parties, pressure groups, functions, structures and restructurings, sociological experiments, statistics: that is to say, more than ever a male Church, if perhaps one should not say a sexless entity, in which a woman may gain for herself a place to the extent that she is ready herself to become such an entity.[24]

Balthasar concluded that "the masses run away from such a Church." Such a Church is no longer the Church militant, a community of pilgrims journeying to their eternal home and fighting spiritual battles against the

---

[20] Joseph Ratzinger, *Images of Hope: Meditations of Major Feasts* (San Francisco: Ignatius Press, 2006), 26.

[21] Joseph Ratzinger, *Salt of the Earth: The Church at the End of the Millennium. Interview with Peter Seewald* (San Francisco: Ignatius Press, 1996), 266.

[22] Joseph Ratzinger, *Called to Communion: Understanding the Church Today* (San Francisco: Ignatius Press, 1996), 90.

[23] Onuoha, *Actio Divina*, 60.

[24] Hans Urs von Balthasar, *Elucidations* (San Francisco: Ignatius Press, 1998), 70.

enemies of Christ, those St. Paul called *the powers and the principalities*. But, ever so mundanely, she is a "photocopying Church"—an *ecclesia photocopiens*—to cite the Latin transcription of Aidan Nichols.[25]

A debating society presupposes the *raison d'etre* of the institution is endless intellectual discussion, but such is not the Church's understanding of revelation and Tradition. Certainly, there is a place for theological scholarship, and the Church's account of her Tradition develops as she moves through time and history, but the deposit of faith itself is not up for debate. In his homily on the Feast of St. Irenaeus in 2007, Pope Benedict addressed this principle:

> St. Irenaeus did not doubt that the content of the faith transmitted by the Church is that received from the Apostles and from Jesus, the Son of God. There is no other teaching than this. Therefore, for anyone who wishes to know true doctrine, it suffices to know "the Tradition passed down by the Apostles and the faith proclaimed to men": a tradition and faith that "have come down to us through the succession of bishops" (*Adversus Haereses*, 3, 3, 3–4). Hence, the succession of Bishops, the personal principle, and the Apostolic Tradition, the doctrinal principle, coincide.
>
> Apostolic Tradition is "one." Indeed, whereas Gnosticism was divided into multiple sects, Church Tradition is one in its fundamental content, which—as we have seen—Irenaeus calls precisely *regula fidei* or *veritatis*: and thus, because it is one, it creates unity through the peoples, through the different cultures, through the different peoples; it is a common content like the truth, despite the diversity of languages and cultures.[26]

The apostolic tradition is "pneumatic."[27] In the economy of salvation, the Holy Spirit works to enlighten the minds of those responsible for the faith's transmission.

These principles all have implications for the conduct of the Petrine office. Ratzinger observed that the pope is not an absolute monarch who can do whatever he likes, but rather a pope is more like a constitutional

---

[25] Hans Urs von Balthasar, *The Office of Peter and the Structure of the Church* (San Francisco: Ignatius Press, 2007), 40.

[26] Joseph Ratzinger, "General Audience," Saint Irenaeus of Lyons, Vatican, March 28, 2007, §§7–8.

[27] Ratzinger, "General Audience," March 28, 2007, §9.

monarch whose powers are circumscribed by a constitution, though in this case, the place of a constitution is occupied by Scripture and Tradition.[28]

Furthermore, like a monarch, the papal office is a *personal* office, not a bureaucratic position. According to Ratzinger,

> There is no anonymous leadership of the Christian community. Paul writes in his own name as the one ultimately responsible for his congregations ... [and] lists of bishops were compiled already at the beginning of the second century (Hegesippus) so as to emphasize for the historical record the particular and personal responsibility of those witnesses to Jesus Christ. This process is profoundly in keeping with the central structure of the New Testament faith: to the *one witness*, Jesus Christ, correspond the many witnesses who, precisely because they are witnesses, stand up for him by name. Martyrdom as a response to the Cross of Christ is nothing other than the ultimate confirmation of this principle of uncompromising particularity, of the named individual who is personally responsible.[29]

The pope is thus neither an absolute monarch nor the chairman of a debating society, but the one who must personally witness to the undiluted faith of Jesus Christ even to the point of martyrdom. Again, in Ratzinger's words, "Peter becomes the Rock of the Church as the bearer of the *Credo*, of her faith in God, which is a concrete faith in Christ as the Son and by that very fact faith in the Father and, thus, a trinitarian faith, which only the Spirit of God can communicate."[30] "The fact that martyrdom can find no place in Hans Küng's *On Being a Christian* ... is, from this perspective, quite telling."[31]

If the Church is not a debating society, then how does this principle relate to the currently fashionable synodality? To do adequate justice to such a question would require a separate paper on this issue alone, but suffice to say that Ratzinger's essay "The Structure and Duties of the Synod of Bishops" offers valuable sociological reflections in this context.[32] Ratzinger's

---

[28] Joseph Ratzinger, foreword to *The Organic Development of the Liturgy: The Principles of Liturgical Reform and their Relation to the Twentieth-Century Liturgical Movement Prior to the Second Vatican Council*, by Alcuin Reid (San Francisco: Ignatius Press, 2005).

[29] Ratzinger, *New Endeavors*, 40–41.

[30] Ratzinger, *New Endeavors*, 40–41.

[31] Ratzinger, *New Endeavors*, 41n14.

[32] Note, this essay is only about a synod of bishops, not about synodality generally speaking, which includes lay participants.

general assessment is that a perpetual synod of bishops would simply have the effect of creating a second Curia. Bishops are required by canon law to be resident in dioceses, and the amount of time they can attend deliberative events in Rome is limited. Ratzinger summarized his negative assessment of the value of a perpetual synod with this syllogism:

> Within the limited time of a synod—aside from special cases—deliberative power cannot be exercised responsibly.
>
> Lengthening the session so that this becomes possible is incompatible with the intrinsic nature of the episcopal ministry ("iuris divini").
>
> Consequently, the use of deliberative power cannot be the normal canonical form of the synod of bishops. In other words, bishops remain bishops, responsible to their particular Churches. It is not an optional feature of the Church's constitution to erect a second central power within it; that would be much less detrimental to the importance of the papal ministry than to the ministry of the bishops; indeed, it would go so far as to rescind the latter.[33]

In other words, Ratzinger argues that a Church that lurches from one synod to the next takes bishops away from their primary responsibilities in their dioceses. If, however, the time spent at a synod in Rome is short, his concern is that insufficient time will be given to analyzing complex theological and sociological issues. Further, he cannot see how a permanent synod could become anything other than another layer of curial bureaucracy. While these sociological observations all related to the notion of a permanent synod of bishops only, they would also apply to synods including lay and episcopal participants because certain bishops would still be required to focus on meetings and discussions in Rome, not on the day-to-day care of the faithful in their dioceses or archdioceses.

There is, no doubt, a way of understanding the synodality concept consistent with Ratzinger's fundamental theology, but it is rooted in a *Communio* ecclesiology not a congregational ecclesiology. Within *Communio* ecclesiology there is a special place or a special charism for those who are the guardians of the tradition, the guardians of what Ratzinger calls *"the memoria ecclesiae."*[34] One might call this the Jacobite charism that counterbalances the Pauline charism. The work of what was once called the

[33] Ratzinger, *New Endeavors*, 59.
[34] Ratzinger, *Principles of Catholic Theology*, 23.

"Sacred Congregation of the Holy Office," then the "Sacred Congregation for the Doctrine of the Faith," then the "Congregation for the Doctrine of the Faith," and now the much demoted "Dicastery for the Doctrine of the Faith" exemplifies the operation of the Jacobite charism.

THE CHURCH IS NOT A HABERDASHERY SHOP

Third, Ratzinger's *Communio* ecclesiology implies the Church is not what Ratzinger calls a "haberdashery shop," that is, a business that updates its windows with new merchandise at the arrival of each new fashion season. This has important implications for Ratzinger's understanding of evangelization. He never supported the pastoral strategy known as "correlationism": the idea of marketing the faith by finding what Marie-Dominique Chenu, O.P., called "toothing stones" in the culture—popular cultural elements not overtly contrary to Christianity—and then tying the faith to these stones so the Church presents herself as the champion of this or that popular idea.

> When reform is dissociated from the hard work of repentance, and seeks salvation merely by changing others, by creating ever-fresh forms, and by accommodation to the times, then despite many useful innovations it will be a caricature of itself. Such reforms can touch only things of secondary importance in the Church.[35]

Ratzinger's theology of culture, like the rest of his theology, avoids extrinsic constructions. Concerning the relationship between faith and culture, he is highly critical of culture as a "wrapping" for the faith—something peripheral to it or an external marketing device. He uses "shell" in the sense of a carapace and suggests that culture as a shell for the faith is wrong. On the contrary, he understands culture as the *epiphenomena* of religious ideas and their associated practices. Therefore, there may be Buddhist cultures, Islamic cultures, Catholic cultures, Calvinist cultures, liberal cultures, Marxist cultures, and so on. There may be a culture of the Incarnation, and a culture built upon hostility to Christ. For a culture to be truly Catholic, its practices must be linked to the transcendental properties of the true, the beautiful, and the good.

Instead of correlating the faith to modernity or recontextualizing the faith to postmodernity—two approaches to evangelization fostered by

---

[35] Joseph Ratzinger, *Why I Am Still in the Church*, in *Two Say Why*, by Joseph Ratzinger and Hans Urs von Balthasar (Chicago: Franciscan Herald Press, 1973), 70.

Schillebeeckxian theology, and other scholars from the tragically dechristianized "low countries"—Ratzinger's approach is better described as "Trinitarian transformation": a process whereby a culture is built upon Eucharistic and pneumatic graces. This is most evident in Ratzinger's liturgical theology, where he insists upon the importance of beauty and self-transcendence. The idea of bringing God down to the level of the culture of the people is nothing less than a form of apostasy, exemplified by the Hebrews' worship of the golden calf.[36] Just as Ratzinger is critical of the bureaucratic model of the Church, he is critical of evangelization considered as a marketing exercise and conceptions of the faith and culture relationship that treat culture as a mere "shell" for the faith rather than the fluorescence of it. As Bishop Robert Barron observed, does "culture position Christ or does Christ position culture?"[37]

The Church Is Not Another NGO Aid Agency

Fourth, Ratzinger made it clear that the Church is not just another non-government organization offering philanthropy. Some might distinguish between or dichotomize the Church's spiritual and doctrinal priorities, and her social, political, and humanitarian interests, suggesting the first is the province of theologians, the second the province of professional administrators. For Benedict XVI, these two missions are always intertwined. This was a central message of his social encyclical *Caritas in Veritate*: "A humanism which excludes Christ is an inhuman humanism."[38] Somehow the personal encounter with Christ must be fundamental to the Church's humanitarian work and not an optional extra. Cardinal Paul Cordes emphasized this principle in an address delivered to celebrate the release of *Caritas in Veritate*:

> Sometimes Church discussion gives the impression that we could construct a just world through the consensus of men and women of good will and through common sense. Doing so would make faith appear as a beautiful ornament, like an extension on a building—decorative, but superfluous. And when we look deeper, we discover that the assent of reason and good will is always dubious

---

[36] Joseph Ratzinger, *The Spirit of the Liturgy* (San Francisco: Ignatius Press, 2000), and *Theology of the Liturgy: Collected Works*, vol. 11 (San Francisco: Ignatius Press, 2014), 12.

[37] Robert Barron, *The Priority of Christ: Toward a Postliberal Catholicism* (Ada, MI: Baker Academic, 2018).

[38] Benedict XVI, *Caritas in Veritate* (2009), §78.

and obstructed by original sin—not only does faith tell us this, but experience, too. So we come to the realization that Revelation is needed also for the Church's social directives: the source of our understanding for "justice" thus becomes the LOGOS made flesh.[39]

The tendency to treat the Church as a philanthropic NGO is related to "moralism"—the Kantian tendency to reduce Christianity to the category of an ethical framework and to understand ethics within the boundaries of "reason alone." Such "reason," unhinged from revelation, fosters an understanding of the good as improving material conditions of living, eliminating poverty, opening access to health and educational institutions, and other forms of philanthropy. While there is nothing wrong with such projects per se, or with the Church's involvement in health, welfare, and education, Ratzinger would argue that the ethos of all such institutions governed by the Church must be Christocentric. The work of philanthropy should not be disengaged from the proclamation of the faith. In his essay "Faith, Reason and Culture," Ratzinger criticized the adoption of the biblical concept of the "kingdom" and its application to the "profane and utopian sphere" by people who no longer believe in truth:[40] "Ecclesiocentricity, christocentricity, theocentricity—all these now seem to be rendered obsolete by regnocentricity, the centering of things around the kingdom as the common task of all religions; and it is held that they [the world's religions] should meet only from this point of view and according to this standard."[41] In other words, Ratzinger is critical of the tendency to make Christianity popular by distilling from it the very things that form it—a religion based on a belief in the Holy Trinity, revealed to humanity by Christ, and sustained in the sacramental life of the Church. In these distillation processes one typically eliminates the importance of the Church (ecclesiocentricity), then Christ himself is marginalized as Christocentrism dissolves into a generic, no brand, theocentrism. Theocentrism is further refined to produce "values of the kingdom," free-floating concepts whose content is so insubstantial as to attract no social opposition.

---

[39] Paul Cordes, Address to Mark the Release of *Caritas in Veritate*, Australian Catholic University, Sydney, 2009.

[40] Joseph Ratzinger, *Truth and Tolerance: Christian Belief and World Religions* (San Francisco: Ignatius Press, 2004), 72–73.

[41] Ratzinger, *Truth and Tolerance*, 73.

CONCLUSION

In conclusion, we turn to the link between Mary and the *Ecclesia*. It is a theological commonplace that Mariology is intrinsically related to ecclesiology, such that anything said of the Church can also be said of Mary and vice versa. Regarding Ratzinger's false models of the Church, the Marian nature of the Church is altogether missing in the four deformed versions surveyed above. As Fr. Onuoha noted, "The link between Mary and the Church prevents a false model of 'renewal' of a quasi-political or corporatist kind such as Balthasar critically described above,"[42] and it "re-establishes the balance between male and female forms of being within the Church."[43] Quite simply, a Marian understanding of the Church as a bride and a mother is radically different from that of a corporation or other bureaucratic institution. Further, the Church as a complex network of sacramental relationships, encapsulated in the concept of *Communio*, in which the Marian disposition of availability to follow the will of the Holy Spirit is common to all the members of the Church, regardless of their place within the network, is radically different from that of a liberal democratic state, a debating society, a haberdashery shop, or yet another virtue-signaling philanthropic institution. The task of our time is, as Ratzinger and his *Communio* colleagues argued, to renew the sacramental nature of the Church with a Marian disposition of abiding availability for service—not to occlude the Trinity while feeding the hippopotamus!

---

[42] Onuoha, *Actio Divina*, xvii.

[43] Onuoha, *Actio Divina*, xxiii.

CHAPTER 7

Febronianism Revisited[1]

In a recent interview reported in the *Catholic World Report*, Cardinal Müller remarked,

> Since the eighteenth century, along with absolutism, we have even in Catholic France, Austria and Bavaria the unholy tradition of the official state church (Gallicanism, Febronianism, Josephinism).
>
> [As a result] the Church no longer defines herself in terms of her divine mission for the salvation of all people, but rather in terms of the service that she can perform for society within the parameters of the common good and dependence on the State. Only once, during the *Kulturkampf* [German Culture War] against Prussian state absolutism and against the totalitarian ideology, was there practical opposition in the name of her higher mission (Pius XI, Encyclical *Mit brennender Sorge*, 1937).
>
> Since then, [German-speaking] Catholics have obviously subordinated themselves to a great extent to secular governmental goals (so-called "system relevance") and have grappled with the aggressive de-Christianization of society only in the private sphere. A bishop in Central Europe today faces the choice of surviving through conformity or being branded a fundamentalist by ignorant people.[2]

---

[1] This short article was first published in the *Catholic World Report*, February 1, 2021. Used with permission.

[2] Gerhard Müller, "Cardinal Müller Discusses President Biden, Pro-Abortion Politicians, and the Bishops," interview by Cardinal Müller to kath.net, *Catholic World Report*, January 28, 2021, https://www.catholicworldreport.com/2021/01/28/cardinal-muller-discusses-president-biden-pro-abortion-politicians-and-the-bishops/.

The terms Gallicanism, Febronianism, and Josephinism do not often arise in Anglophone circles, though the Church of England is sometimes given as a concrete example of Febronianism in operation. The Church of England is a national church, deeply entangled with the state apparatus to such a degree that the British prime minister has a say in the appointment of the archbishop of Canterbury. Being C of E rather RC is often construed as a patriotic gesture. The mentality is that we do not want to be governed by foreigners. Catholicism is for the Italians and the Irish but not the British. Wanting one's church entirely governed by local officials is an archetypically Febronian mentality.

The original Febronian was Johann Nikolaus von Hontheim (1701–1790), a bishop of Trier who used the pseudonym Justinus Febronius for his book *De statu ecclesiae et legitima potestate Romani pontificis*—a treatise condemned by Clement XIII in 1764. Hontheim was influenced by the canonist Zeger Bernhard van Espen (1646–1728) while studying at the University of Leuven. Espen was regarded as a Gallicanist, someone who, in disputes about the authority of the papacy vis-à-vis French kings, agreed with the kings and affirmed their extensive list of canonical prerogatives.

The key hallmarks of Febronianism were that the powers of the keys were not given to Peter as an individual but to the whole Church, the Petrine office is primarily an administrative office and its occupant merely a symbol of Church unity, and appointing bishops, naming coadjutors with the right of succession, establishing dioceses, and condemning erroneous theological ideas should be a matter for local authorities. The pope cannot make judgments about issues of faith without the support of the entire episcopate, national synods are a highly recommended form of Church governance, and general councils of the Church have a higher authority than a pontiff whose ratification of conciliar documents is not required.

Karl von Dalberg (1744–1817), the Prince Primate of the Federation of the Rhine, was the most powerful promoter of Febronianism in his time. The realization of Dalberg's vision of a German national church largely independent of the Petrine office was thwarted by Pius VII (1742–1823) who signed concordats with individual German states rather than having a single concordant for all the Germanic territories. Dalberg and others who followed Hontheim hoped that by marginalizing the See of Peter they could effect a reconciliation of the German Catholics and Protestants who would all become members of one German national church. Many Protestants were, however, appalled by the suggestion that the only problem with Catholicism was the papacy and were keen to explain their other issues.

Historians indicate that ecumenism was not so much the major interest of the Febronians as their secular power. In the eighteenth century, many German bishops were also princes with a greater interest in their secular authority than their pastoral responsibilities. Febronian "theology" appealed to their secular priorities. The place where Febronianism was most extensively applied was Austria during the reign of Joseph II (1780–1790), hence the expression Josephinism in the trio of terms used by Cardinal Müller.

Although in theory Febronianism fosters greater power for bishops by diminishing papal control over the conduct of their office, in practice wherever national churches are established the major consequence for the bishops is that they become servants of state power. They can no longer hide behind the papacy, or take advantage of the diplomatic soft power of the papacy, or otherwise appeal to papal protection and support from local political powerbrokers. They are no longer in a position to say "No" to some demand of a local parliament or political leader on the grounds that such decisions cannot be made by them, only by the supreme pontiff.

One of Cardinal Newman's arguments in favor of Catholic Church superiority over the Church of England was that the Petrine office served to protect Catholics from being governed by local civil authorities:

> Our ears ring with the oft-told tale, how the temporal sovereign persecuted, or attempted, or gained, the local Episcopate, and how the many or the few faithful fell back on Rome. So it was with the Arians in the East and St. Athanasius; so with the Byzantine Empress and St. Chrysostom; so with the Vandal Hunneric and the Africans; so with the 130 Monophysite Bishops at Ephesus and St. Flavian; so was it in the instance of the 50 Bishops, who, by the influence of Basilicus, signed a declaration against the Tome of St. Leo; so in the instance of the Henoticon of Zeno; and so in the controversies both of the Monothelites and the Inconoclasts. . . . In later and modern times we see the same truth irresistibly brought out; not only, for instance, in St. Thomas's history, but in St. Anselm's, nay, in the whole course of English ecclesiastical affairs, from the Conquest to the sixteenth century, and, not with least significancy, in the primacy of Cranmer. Moreover, we see it in the tendency of the Gallicanism of Louis XIV, and the Josephism of Austria. Such, too, is the lesson taught us in the recent policy of the Czar towards the United Greeks, and in the present bearing of the English Government towards the Church of Ireland. In all of these instances, it is a struggle between the Holy See and some local, perhaps distant, government, the liberty and orthodoxy of its faithful people being

the matter in dispute; and while the temporal power is on the spot, and eager, and cogent, and persuasive, and dangerous, the strength of the assailed party lies in its fidelity to the rest of Christendom and to the Holy See.[3]

The recognition of this "service" that the Petrine office supplies to Catholics across the globe can be found in the decree *Christus Dominus*, on the pastoral office of bishops in the Church: "In order to safeguard the liberty of the Church and more effectively to promote the good of the faithful, it is the desire of the sacred Council that for the future no rights or privileges be conceded to the civil authorities in regard to the election, nomination, or presentation to bishoprics."[4] That conciliar desire was given legislative effect in the 1983 Code of Canon Law.

It has often been observed that Febronianism is quite a big issue in Germany because the Catholic Church receives so much money from the German government. In 2019 the figure was 6.76 billion euros. Whenever the Church becomes reliant upon governments for money, she loses a certain amount of her freedom. Bishops and other ecclesial leaders lose their capacity to be prophetic and counter-cultural, to speak truth to power. They become very compliant. It was precisely for this reason that Mother Teresa never accepted money from governments.

Those who think it would be good if the Petrine office was nothing more than a chairman of the board position, or a convenor of ecclesial managers without any special juridical authority should perhaps read a little more Church history. Similarly, those who think allowing totalitarian governments a role in ecclesial governance is a clever diplomatic move by, for example, allowing them a say in appointing bishops, should consider the martyrs who stood opposed to forms of Febronianism. Saints such as Thomas More continue to inspire generations of Catholics born centuries after their death, while the capitulation of ecclesial leaders to powerful psychopaths demoralizes the Catholic faithful. It is even sometimes a cause of despair following a loss of faith in both God and the Church.

---

[3] John Henry Newman, *Certain Difficulties Felt by Anglicans in Catholic Teaching Considered* (London: Longmans, Green & Co, 1894), 184–86.

[4] Second Vatican Council, *Christus Dominus* (1965), §20.

CHAPTER 8

Catholic Education and the Bureaucratic Usurpation of Grace[1]

There are striking similarities between the story of St. Marguerite Bourgeoys and St. Mary MacKillop, Australia's first saint. In both cases, a young woman struggled to educate children in a developing colony thousands of miles from the center of Christian civilization, while contending with authorities who were not always people of equal vision and imagination. As Joseph Ratzinger once observed, "The saints were all people of imagination, not functionaries of apparatuses."[2]

Writing earlier in the twentieth century, the French poet Paul Claudel spoke of the "tragedy of a starved imagination," and he blamed the Jansenist movement in France for holding the noble faculties of imagination and sensibility in contempt. He suggested certain lunatics would have added reason itself but for some sustained opposition from Jesuit quarters. Clearly St. Marguerite had not been infected with the Jansenist mentality although it was the most influential heresy of her time. On the contrary, her life's achievements exemplified the humanism of the Incarnation. This is a humanism founded on the idea that all human persons have been made in the image of God to grow into the likeness of Christ. As expressed in *Gaudium et Spes* §22, Jesus Christ, the redeemer of man, "fully reveals man to man himself and makes his supreme calling clear." This conciliar theme was reiterated by

---

[1] This paper was first delivered at McGill University in 2013 and later published in *Solidarity: The Journal of Catholic Social Thought and Secular Ethics* 4, no.1 (April 2014). Used with permission.

[2] Joseph Ratzinger, *Images of Hope*: *Meditations on Major Feasts* (San Francisco: Ignatius Press, 2006), 67.

Pope Benedict: he exhorted the leaders of Catholic universities to understand that "revelation must constitute the central point of teaching and research," because the human person "is incapable of fully understanding himself and the world without Jesus Christ."[3] Of all the paragraphs of the Second Vatican Council, *Gaudium et Spes* §22 was cited most often in the speeches and homilies of St. John Paul II.

In his first encyclical, *Redemptor Hominis*, the late pontiff echoed *Gaudium et Spes* §22 with his statement that the person who wishes to understand himself must appropriate "the whole of the reality of the Incarnation and Redemption in order to find himself."[4] Through grace, which comes from the Holy Spirit, the human person's social horizons are broadened and raised up to the supernatural level of divine life,[5] and people are able to free themselves from various forms of social conditioning.[6] As G. K. Chesterton expressed the idea, the Catholic Church is the only thing that stands between the human person and the indignity of being a child of one's time. Or, as Friedrich Nietzsche would have it, the indignity of being merely another member of the herd—someone who blindly follows social fashions without any evaluation of their meaning.

Early in the twentieth century, the Bolshevik theoretician Nikolai Bukharin famously argued that human beings are nothing more than collections of social influences united in a small unit, as the skin of a sausage is crammed with sausage meat. It is precisely from this kind of predicament that the Church strives to liberate people. As John Paul II remarked, "The human person must stave off a double temptation: the temptation to make the truth about himself subordinate to this freedom and the temptation to subordinate himself to the world of objects: he has to refuse to succumb to the temptation of both self-idolatry and of self-subjectification."[7]

More recently, another Russian writer called Alexander Boot, who is not a Bolshevik, wrote *How the West Was Lost*, claiming there are three types of people found in the Western world today: *Westman* (a generic term for Christians), *Modman Nihilist*, and *Modman Philistine*.[8] He probably could have added a fourth type, Islamic Man, but he did not, so I will confine my

---

[3] Benedict XVI, Address to the International Federation of Catholic Universities, Paul VI Audience Hall, November 19, 2009.

[4] John Paul II, *Redemptor Hominis* (1979), §10.

[5] John Paul II, *Dives in Misericordia* (1980), §58.

[6] *Dives in Misericordia*, §60.

[7] John Paul II, Apostolic Journey to Poland: Address to the World of Culture, *Aula Magna* of the Catholic University of Lublin, June 9, 1987.

[8] Alexander Boot, *How the West Was Lost* (London: I. B. Tauris, 2006).

remarks to what he said about the relationship of *Westman* to *Modman Nihilist* and *Modman Philistine*. His notion of *Modman Nihilist* would seem to equate with the person who succumbs to what John Paul II called "the temptation to self-idolatry." The nihilist idolizes himself and acknowledges very few limits, if any, to the exercise of his freedom. The typical academic nihilist believes that nature can be controlled and manipulated by science and thus scientific research becomes a holy grail which promises to free people from the burdens of genetics. The nihilist acknowledges no logic or order within nature worthy of human respect and giving rise to ethical obligations.

The philistine is different. In Nietzschean parlance, the philistine is a typical member of the herd who has no higher aspiration than to be a member of the herd. Unlike the nihilist, the philistine has no interest in asserting his individuality against social conventions. Instead, the nihilist succumbs to the second temptation identified by John Paul II, that of subordinating himself to the world of objects, allowing his life-style choices to be determined by the most immediate and easily available commodities presented to him in popular culture.

Boot argues that Christians are often defeated in social battles because the nihilist and philistine forces exist in a symbiotic relationship. Although they do not work together in any organizational sense, the arguments of the nihilist are buttressed by the behavior of the philistine. If Boot is correct in his sociological analysis, then Christian leaders need to fight on a double-front: against high-brow academic nihilism and low-brow anti-intellectual philistinism.

Therefore, at the heart of Catholic education at all levels, primary, secondary, and tertiary, there needs to be an objective to inoculate students against the worldviews of the nihilist and the philistine. Positively, students need to understand there are fundamental choices between the humanism of the Incarnation, as articulated by the great doctors of the Church, the Social Darwinism of Friedrich Nietzsche and his followers with its materialist cosmology, and the equally materialist cosmology of the philistine who is defined precisely by his lack of interest in projects of self-transcendence.

The first step toward this is to have a vision of Catholic education based on a Christocentric Trinitarian theological anthropology. One *cannot make any intellectual progress with students* unless they have some rudimentary understanding that they were created in the image of a tri-personal God and some understanding of how to relate to each person of the Trinity. In other words, students need to understand the role of the Holy Spirit in their lives, the role of Christ, and the role of God the Father.

One of my Dominican friends, the late Fr. Peter Knowles, would often complain that young men enter seminaries believing the Trinity is an old man, a young man, and a bird. This is exactly how the Trinity is presented above the altar of the Holy Trinity Church in Kraków, home to the world's largest Dominican priory. Perhaps for such reasons, John Paul II wrote a trilogy of encyclicals[9] explaining how the human person stands in relation to each particular person of the Trinity. The theological content of these encyclicals provides a summary of two millennia of theological reflection and is, arguably, the cement upon which the Catholic notion of education can be built. By linking theo-centrism with anthropocentrism, or we might say, by emphasizing the relationship between divinity and humanity rather than setting the two in opposition to each other, is "one of the basic principles, perhaps the most important one, of the teaching of the last Council."[10] While Immanuel Kant thought it made no difference whether people believe there are three persons in the Godhead or ten, two millennia of Catholic scholarship begs to differ.

Michael Hanby argued that the key issue in contemporary Catholic life is whether the meaning of human nature and human agency are understood to occur within Christ's mediation of the love and delight shared as a gift between the Father and the Son, or beyond it. One of the many errors of classical Pelagians was their attempt to create possibilities for human nature "outside" the Trinity and the mediation of Christ, and, in particular, their attempt to smuggle a Stoic account of human volition into the Christian tradition.[11]

In contrast to the Stoic tendency to suppress delight and desire in relation to the will, and the Kantian tendency to suppress delight and desire in relation to the intellect, in Catholic anthropology, love and reason stand together and work in tandem as the "twin pillars of all reality."[12]

Love, hope, and faith are theological virtues about which Benedict XVI offered a trilogy of encyclicals: *Deus Caritas Est* focused on love, *Spe Salvi* focused on hope, and *Lumen Fidei*, drafted by Benedict and promulgated by Francis, focused on faith.

Faith operates on the intellect to lead it to truth, and hope operates on the will to lead it to goodness, and it has a special association with memory and imagination, leading these faculties to presentiments of divine glory

---

[9] *Redemptor Hominis* (1979), *Dives in Misericordia* (1980), and *Dominum et Vivificantem* (1986).

[10] *Dives in Misericordia*, §14.

[11] Michael Hanby, *Augustine and Modernity* (London: Routledge, 2003).

[12] Joseph Ratzinger, *Truth and Tolerance: Christian Belief and World Religions* (San Francisco: Ignatius Press, 2004), 183.

and beauty. Therefore, spirituality is a kind of pathology report on how the theological virtues are operating or not operating within the soul. Different spiritual disorders arise when one or more of the theological virtues are weak.

Pope Benedict wrote that two common contemporary spiritual disorders are "bourgeois Pelagianism" and "pious Pelagianism." Here, "bourgeois" has little or nothing to do with being a member of the middle class, or at least not necessarily. He uses the adjective in the same sense as sociologists like Werner Sombart and the historian Christopher Dawson. Sociologists commonly assert that Protestant cultures are bourgeois, while Catholic cultures are aristocratic or sometimes the adjective "erotic" is used to convey the same idea of being based on a passionate quest for the most excellent. The bourgeois mentality concerns fitting in with contemporary social norms and being practical and efficient in one's use of resources. The bourgeois temperament is calculating, pragmatic, and focused on efficiency and predictable outcomes. It discourages moral heroism as unreasonable and gives priority to the goods of efficacy over the goods of excellence. Here "erotic" means passionate in the broadest sense, not in a narrow sexual sense, while aristocratic does not mean born with a title but the highest or most excellent. The movie *Babette's Feast* illustrates the aristocratic or erotic personality type. Babette spends her entire fortune on one party and invites the entire village. There is nothing left over, nothing held in reserve.

Transferred to the spiritual plane, the bourgeois Pelagian problem Pope Benedict identified is the attitude that God does not really expect people to be saints. Benedict diagnosed this mentality as evidence of the spiritual disease of acedia—an anxious vertigo that overcomes people when presented with the idea that they were made in the image of God to grow into the likeness of Christ.

The alternative spiritual pathology is the pious Pelagian who seeks a relationship with God modeled on contemporary professional practices, in particular the practice of enhancing one's curriculum vitae. The pious Pelagian performs certain works and says certain prayers and expects to get a return on his spiritual investment. While the bourgeois Pelagian despairs, regarding sanctity as an impossible pursuit, the pious Pelagian presumes, assuming he has a contractual relationship with God. The bourgeois Pelagian is particularly lacking in the theological virtue of hope, the pious Pelagian is quite anemic in relation to the theological virtue of love. Both have a warped understanding of faith.

Saints, like Marguerite, are not lacking in any of the theological virtues, though in many cases they need a particularly strong dose of hope to carry them through all manner of persecutions. No doubt St. Marguerite carried in her memory the beauty of the Catholic culture she found in her hometown of Troyes and used her imagination under the influence of the theological virtue of hope to envisage the wilds of seventeenth-century Quebec as valleys of pristine Catholic villages. She was not in any sense bourgeois apart from the sound of her name to Anglophone ears. When presented with the project of traveling to a colony thousands of miles from her home, indeed another continent, where the climactic conditions were harsh and European settlements were frequently attacked by members of the indigenous population, she did not make any calculations about the risk. She responded to the divine invitation to invest her life in the erotic project of bringing the faith to Quebec.

In the twentieth century, another French Catholic, the author Georges Bernanos, was also interested in the idea that there is something aristocratic and erotic about authentic Catholic spirituality. He was concerned about the problem which the young Karol Wojtyła called "servile conformism," or we might say, "herd-like" or philistine behavior. Bernanos wrote of a "flight to conformism"—"the blissful servitude that dispenses one from both willing and acting, that doles out a little task to each one and that, and in the near future, will have transformed man into the biggest and most ingenious of insects—a colossal ant."[13] He believed that modern man adores bureaucratic systems because it dispenses him from the daily risk of judging. His choices are made by the system for him. The analogue in Bernanos's writings between the bourgeois spiritual disposition and the aristocratic spiritual disposition is between the dispositions of the imbecile and the *honnête homme*, between a technocratic servility and an "aristocracy of the spirit." One might argue that for Bernanos, the imbecile embodies the worst elements of bourgeois Pelagianism and philistinism. In his work *We, the French*, Bernanos wrote,

> There exists a Christian order. This order is the order of Christ, and the Catholic tradition has preserved its essential principles. But the temporal realization of this order does not belong to the theologians, the casuists, or the doctors, but to us Christians. And it seems that the majority of Christians are forgetting this elementary truth. They believe that the Kingdom of God will happen all by itself, providing they obey the moral rules (which, in any event, are common to all decent people), abstain from working on Sunday (if, that is, their business doesn't suffer too much for it), attend a

---

[13] Hans Urs von Balthasar, *Bernanos: An Ecclesial Existence* (San Francisco: Ignatius Press, 1996), 588.

Low Mass on this same day, and above all have great respect for clerics. . . . This would be tantamount to saying that, in times of war, an army could quite fulfil the nation's expectations if its men were squeaky clean, if they marched in step behind the band, and saluted their officers correctly.[14]

These words were composed in 1939 and the examples today would be different. We rarely distinguish between high Masses and low Masses since most of our Masses are low Masses, and it has been a long time since people have thought of working on the Sabbath as something sinful, but Bernanos's point is still relevant—Christianity is not about following rules and regulations. These have their place, but they are very much ancillary to the personal relationship to the persons of the Trinity. Perhaps for this reason, Pope Benedict began *Deus Caritas Est* by emphasizing that Truth is a person.

Implicit in the bourgeois Pelagian mentality is a failure to critically analyze contemporary culture from a theological standpoint. This is not only a spiritual pathology of the individual but a prevalent pathology that adversely affects the Church's mission to be the light of the world.

In an essay on the Christocentrism of John Paul II, Cardinal Angelo Scola concluded with the rather chilling observation that "only Christians can make the antichrist possible since the anti-Christ is possible only if he maintains a Christianity without Christ as the point of reference."[15] In other words, an anti-Christ never arises without his anti-Christian culture or movement being in some sense parasitic on the Christian tradition. For example, Marxism was a system of thought that substituted a materialist cosmology for a Christian cosmology but otherwise sought to offer people many soteriological benefits of Christianity while Adolf Hitler's peculiar intellectual cocktail included a diabolical appropriation of Christian liturgical sensibility. One of the greatest dangers for Catholic educational institutions in our present time, when governments throughout the Western world actively promote secularism as a new social glue and civic virtue, is for Catholic educational leaders to package "Christian values" somehow distilled from Christ and his grace, thus avoiding friction with governments. To borrow an expression from William T. Cavanaugh, the temptation is for people to think that Christian symbols need to be "run through the sausage-grinder

---

[14] Balthasar, *Bernanos*, 555, quoting Bernanos, *We, the French*.

[15] Angelo Scola, "'Claim' of Christ, 'Claim' of the World: On the Trinitarian Encyclicals of John Paul II," *Communio: International Catholic Review* 18 (Fall 1991): 322–31, at 331.

of social ethics before coming out at the other end as publicly digestible policy."[16] In other words, since many people desire the social side-benefits of Christianity but do not want to buy the whole package, the best way forward is for some corporate governance "sausage grinder" to extract the Christian values form the Christian cosmology and anthropology before offering the sanitized values to the post-Christian world. Such practices have a self-secularizing effect on Catholic institutions.

John Henry Newman alluded to this problem when he wrote that "in every age of Christianity, since it was first preached, there has been what may be called a religion of the world, which so far imitates the one true religion, as to deceive the unstable and unwary." Different generations tend to fasten onto an aspect of Christianity, profess to embody this in its practice, while neglecting all other parts of the Church's teaching. He who cultivates "only one precept of the Gospel to the exclusion of the rest, in reality attends to no part at all."[17] The whole tendency he associated with the mind of the devil. As Ratzinger once remarked,

> A Christianity and a theology that reduce the core of Jesus' message, the "kingdom of God" to the "values of the kingdom" while identifying these values with the main watchwords of political moralism, and proclaiming them, at the same time, to be the synthesis of all religions . . . all the while forgetting about God, despite the fact that it is precisely he who is the subject and the cause of the "kingdom of God," does not open the way to regeneration, it actually blocks it.[18]

Ratzinger identified a slippery slope in this passage. First, the notion of the "kingdom of God," that is, of the reign of Christ over the entire world, his sovereignty one might say, is toned down to a package of values or dispositions. While such dispositions may include love of one's neighbor as a good thing, or mercy and compassion as good things, values tend to lose their specific Christian difference and become correlated to "the watchwords of political moralism" or the fashionable secular political projects. Most of these tend to be based on the master narrative of the eighteenth century,

---

[16] William T. Cavanaugh, *Theopolitical Imagination: Discovering the Liturgy as a Political Act in an Age of Global Consumerism* (London: T & T Clark, 2002), 81.

[17] John Henry Newman, *The Heart of Newman: A Synthesis*, ed. Erich Przywara (San Francisco: Ignatius Press, 1997), 371.

[18] Joseph Ratzinger, "Europe and the Crisis of Cultures," *Communio: International Catholic Review* 32 (Summer 2005): 345–56, at 346–47.

the idea that freedom and enlightenment flow from liberation from various traditions, especially liberation from Christianity.

The classic example is found in Catholic educational institutions, where employees are instructed not to make too much fuss about Christ and the Holy Trinity but to focus on social justice projects within the local community. This is especially true of Catholic universities, where a large percentage of the student body is not Christian, let alone Catholic. The idea is that no one can seriously have a problem with philanthropy and thus one can detach the socially acceptable Christian philanthropy from the socially contentious claims about the sovereignty of Christ or the kingdom of God. Ratzinger's point is when these practices take root in Catholic institutions as general policy orientations, they render those institutions impotent in proclaiming the Gospel.

As early as 1963, Balthasar was alert to this problem:

> The Gospel and the Church [may be] plundered like a fruit tree, but the fruits, once separated from the tree, go rotten and are no longer fruitful. The "ideas" of Christ cannot be separated from Him and so that they are of no use to the world unless they are fought for by Christians who believe in Christ, or at least by men who are inwardly, though unconsciously, open to Him and governed by Him.[19]

Radiance, Balthasar said, is only possible when the radiant center, that is Christ, is active and alive. In patristic times people spoke of the Christian practice of "plundering the spoils of the Egyptians," that is, assimilating the best of pagan thought into Christian theology. Over the past couple centuries, neo-pagans have plundered Christianity by detaching Christian concepts from the core principles of the creed and assimilating them to fashionable contemporary ideologies. Balthasar exhorted Christians not to be gulled into believing that neo-pagans mean the same things by the same concepts. Similarly, Georges Bernanos suggested that each time Christians dress up Christian ideas in secular dress and send them out into the world of ideas, like Little Red Riding Hood they "get raped at the next corner by some slogan in uniform."[20]

---

[19] Hans Urs von Balthasar, *Das Ganze im Fragment. Aspekte der Geschichtestheologie* (Einsiedeln: Johannes Verlag, 1963), as quoted in John Saward, "Chesterton and Balthasar: The Likeness is Greater," *The Chesterton Review* 22.3 (August 1996): 301–25, at 314.

[20] Georges Bernanos, *La liberté, pour quoi faire* (Paris: Gallimard, 1953), 208.

More recently, in a commentary on *Caritas in Veritate*, Pope Benedict's encyclical on charity, Cardinal Paul Cordes said,

> Sometimes Church discussion gives the impression that we could construct a just world through the consensus of men and women of good will and through common sense. Doing so would make faith appear as a beautiful ornament, like an extension on a building—decorative, but superfluous. And when we look deeper, we discover that the assent of reason and good will is always dubious and obstructed by original sin—not only does faith tell us this, but experience, too. So we come to the realization that Revelation is needed also for the Church's social directives: the source of our understanding for "justice" thus becomes the LOGOS made flesh.[21]

In *Caritas in Veritate* §78, Benedict XVI wrote that a "humanism that excludes Christ is an inhuman humanism." This is consistent with his previous statements that Christian charity is essentially different from other forms of social welfare.[22] While professional competence is fundamental for Christians in charitable institutions, it is not alone sufficient. Christian love should transform the very ethos, the fundamental practices, of Christian institutions. In practice, Catholic schools should not be just like government schools with an extra class called religious education, and Catholic hospitals should not be just like government-funded hospitals with the occasional crucifix, statue of a saint, or prayer room. Christian love, if authentic, changes everything. As Cordes rhetorically asked, what kind of person do we wish to promote? Do we desire development that limits the human person to a purely worldly horizon, consisting only in material well-being?

This raises a theological question: how is the grace of the Incarnation mediated through the Church's educational institutions and her social agencies? This, in turn, leads to institutional practices and the ethos of institutions. My particular interest is how contemporary bureaucratic practices operate to usurp the work of grace in our educational institutions and thus become a barrier to the humanism of the Incarnation. Just as Alasdair MacIntyre argued that there are at least three rival versions of justice and rationality operative in Western societies today,[23] there are also, I would argue, at least

---

[21] Paul Cordes, Address to Mark the Release of *Caritas in Veritate*, Australian Catholic University, Sydney, 2009.

[22] Benedict XVI, *Deus Caritas Est* (2005), §§25–42.

[23] Alasdair MacIntyre, *Three Rival Versions of Moral Enquiry* (London: Duckworth, 1990).

three rival tables of virtues and vices to govern institutional practices. One is associated with the Catholic tradition, one with the Liberal tradition, and one with the Postmodern tradition, though I think that in most institutions the practices are more liberal than postmodern. Fundamental to this framework is that institutional cultures are formed by different modes of participation in various social practices.

In his analysis of these issues, Alasdair MacIntyre famously draws upon the Thomistic observation that every human action has both a transitive and intransitive dimension, that is, that every human act has an impact upon the world at large and an internal impact on the soul of the person performing the action. John Paul II took up this theme in *Laborem Exercens* in which he argued that the intransitive dimension of human labor, that is, the internal effect of one's work, is much more important than the transitive dimension. The Catholic tradition is therefore keenly interested in the relationship between actions and character formation.

It is often said that authority within the Catholic Church is usually a mixture of traditional and charismatic authority rather than rational-legal or bureaucratic authority. The terms traditional, charismatic, and rational-legal are taken from sociology, particularly from Max Weber's classification. According to Weber, the legitimacy of traditional authority comes from an intellectual tradition; the legitimacy of charismatic authority comes from the personality and leadership qualities of the individual; and the legitimacy of rational-legal authority derives from powers that are bureaucratically and legally attached to certain positions. The Catholic intellectual tradition is the source of traditional authority within a Catholic context and ordination; forms of consecration, such as episcopal consecration and religious consecration, are forms of charismatic authority, while canon law is a form of rational-legal authority. The key difference between what Weber called charismatic authority and bureaucratic authority is that bureaucratic authority is based on policy regulations and the academic qualifications required to administer the policy regulations, not upon aspects of character such as a reputation for holiness or the ability to make sound prudential decisions. Bureaucratic authority operates in such a way that the personal judgments of the bureaucrat do not inform his decisions. With charismatic authority, however, personal judgments can and usually do inform decisions, and the basis of charismatic authority tends to be a combination of academic qualifications related to a tradition combined with character traits. When explaining the difference between charismatic and bureaucratic authority, Weber used the Catholic hierarchy and religious orders as his key example of institutions operating by reference to charismatic authority. Prior to the

1960s, the culture or ethos of most Catholic institutions was fostered by a mixture of traditional and charismatic authority where the tradition was the Catholic faith itself, understood both as a collection of beliefs and a collection of liturgical practices.

With the crisis in religious life that followed the cultural revolution of the 1960s, the governance of many Catholic institutions, including educational institutions, transferred from religious orders to professional laity. There is nothing in itself wrong with this, but the demise of the charismatic authority of the religious orders has coincided with the ascendency of rational-legal authority in other social institutions, such as courts, parliaments, and the public service—indeed almost every significant social institution, except, to some degree at least, the military. In this general social climate, Catholic institutions seem to take pains to mimic the bureaucratic practices of the corporate world without any awareness of the philosophical and theological principles in play and at stake. This danger appears to have two sources: one internal and one external.

The internal source is the desire of Catholic leaders to appear competent and professional in the eyes of the world. This is a laudable desire. There is nothing inherently virtuous about being a misfit, odd, or idiosyncratic. However, any conformity should not be uncritical. Catholic educational leaders need to be at least conscious of the character and limitations of rational-legal bureaucratic authority.

Quite an extensive analysis of the problems with rational-legal bureaucratic authority can be found in Alasdair MacIntyre's early publications. MacIntyre formed his judgments on this mode of authority during a period in his life when he was a Marxist. He now describes this period as "wrong-headed," but it gave him many insights into contemporary political theory and, in particular, to the power-games played through the exercise of bureaucratic authority. It taught him that materialists, that is, people who do not believe in things like souls, almost always end up in a love affair with policies, procedures, and bureaucracy in general. This was especially true of Marxist regimes because of their inherent distrust of the individual, and because they find it difficult to make distinctions between persons based on wisdom and prudence. The moment one walks into the territory of wisdom and prudence, one must acknowledge that some people are better at making judgments than others. Then one flounders about looking for some purely biological explanation, which leads into the dangerous territory of racism, or, eschewing a purely biological explanation, one is confronted with the terrible reality that there might be some value in the Christian anthropology. Thus, materialists of all species, including the Marxist and Liberal, tend to use bureaucracy as a means of controlling human behavior to achieve their social engineering objectives. It is an approach to governance that is designed to sidestep character judgments.

Against the background of his personal experience as a Trotskyite, the most intellectual species of the Marxist genus, MacIntyre argues that the appeal to "managerial skills or expertise" as the source of bureaucratic authority is often an attempt to blur the distinction between manipulative and non-manipulative conduct. Instead of the authority of institutions resting upon rational-legal authority, MacIntyre suggests that institutions should derive their authority from the tradition upon which they were founded, as was the case in premodern societies, including the society of the great universities established before the eighteenth century—Oxford, Cambridge, Bologna, the Sorbonne, Cologne, Salamanca, etcetera. Such societies had formal organizations, they had administration, but MacIntyre argues that those in authority always had to justify their decisions against appeals to the authority of the tradition upon which the organization was established.[24] Through the breakdown of traditions, bureaucratic modes of organization arise, and the nature of bureaucratic ideology is to conceal the features of the contestable concepts and situations that emerge from the breakdown. Where viable traditions exist, however, they shape the ethos of the organizations founded upon them, and the extent an organization flourishes can be determined by the extent it produces graduates who participate in the humanism of the Incarnation—or less poetically, people who are *practicing Catholics*!

David L. Schindler added to this basic Thomistic insight the idea that practices all have their own internal logic, distinguishing between practices and ways of thinking that have the form or *logos* of the machine and those with the form or *logos* of love. Bureaucratic practices typically take the form of the machine. Their rationality is a bureaucratic rationality that is not connected to the pursuit of any transcendental property such as truth, beauty, or goodness. Moreover, Schindler argued that the contest between the form of the machine and the form of love is also at the heart of the contemporary secularization of many Catholic educational institutions. As a matter of principle, "the order of knowledge itself is to be drawn first . . . from the order of love as revealed in the divine and indeed sacramental

---

[24] Alasdair MacIntyre, "Social Science Methodology as the Ideology of Bureaucratic Authority," in *Through the Looking Glass: Epistemology and the Conduct of Inquiry*, ed. Maria J. Falco (Seattle, WA: Washington University Press, 1979), 57–58.

realities of God, Christ and the Church, and not first from the order of physics, mechanistically conceived."[25]

> The basic flaw of the modern academy lies in the presumption that the order of the mind is primarily mechanistic and the life of the spirit primarily voluntaristic: in the presumption that contemplation and worship and love and service have nothing to do with the inner working of "critical" intelligence, with the very form and content of intelligence as such, as it operates down through all the disciplines, including the "natural-physical" sciences.[26]

A similar argument has been made by Adrian Walker:

> There exists an intimate relation between human knowing and Christ such that the decision for or against Christ that *in concreto* occurs in all knowing because of the universality of the offer of grace does not determine only one's openness or closure to Christ himself, but also the openness or closure of reason itself to reality as a whole (which, indeed, holds together in Christ)—and therefore, affects, either positively or negatively, but in any case, from top to bottom, the quality of one's every explicit cognitive engagement with particulars within that reality.[27]

The external source of the danger that Catholic educational institutions will unreflectively mimic rational-legal bureaucratic practices comes from the modern state. America's William T. Cavanaugh and, following Cavanaugh, Australia's Matthew Tan have both examined the modern state's attempt to offer itself as a parody of the Body of Christ. Cavanaugh argues that the modern state is best understood as a source of an alternative soteriology to that of the Church. It parodies the Body of Christ by offering itself as the source of salvation for humankind. It is based on alternative theories about human nature and the origins of human conflict contrary to those offered by revelation. According to this new political theory, religion is the source of conflict in the world. It therefore needs to be tamed and managed by the

---

[25] David L. Schindler, "The Catholic Academy and the Order of Intelligence: The Dying of the Light?" *Communio: International Catholic Review* 26 (Winter 1999): 722–45, at 736.

[26] Schindler, "Dying of the Light?," 741.

[27] Adrian Walker, "Christ and Cosmology: Methodological Considerations for Catholic Educators," *Communio: International Catholic Review* 28.3 (Fall 2001): 429–49, at 444.

post-Christian state. This state pretends to offer its citizens nothing other than efficiently run public utilities like airports, telephone and internet services, gas and electricity, and protection from the aggression (including all manner of negative "value" judgments) of other citizens. However, it also controls taxation and, to a large degree, regulates the education sector. Its taxation policies are rarely family friendly, and its educational institutions promote the post-Christian mythos.

Additionally, a general social trend toward mistrusting the judgment of professional people exists, which gained momentum in the late 1960s with the popularization of Antonio Gramsci's theory that professionalism is linked to the bourgeois mystification of knowledge. John Milbank observed that "professionals are no longer trusted, but instead must be endlessly spied upon, and measured against a spatial check-list of routinized procedure that is alien to all genuine inculcation of excellence."[28] Everyone from talented academics who would like to intellectually engage with their students to policemen who joined to catch criminals complain that by the time they finish their mountains of paperwork each day, the objective of which is to prove to some government department official that they have faithfully followed procedural protocols, there is no time left for intellectual conversations or catching criminals.

We see bureaucratic interference with professionals operating across all our institutions. Judges, for example, are routinely sent on "social awareness" camps to discourage them from embodying socially conservative values in their decisions. The great Lord Denning, who was given an honorary doctorate by McGill University in 1968, would not survive modern judiciary. In the famous case of *Miller v. Jackson*, where Lord Denning was called upon to make a judgment about the conflicting interests of a village cricket club and a property developer, he held in favor of the cricket club on these grounds: the game of cricket brings the old men and the young men of the village together, the old men would be lonely without the company of the young men, and the young men might get themselves into all manner of trouble if they were not focused on something wholesome like sport. Furthermore, Lord Denning noted that before the property developer moved into the village, the cricket field was surrounded by grazing cattle and "the animals did not mind the cricket."[29] The point is that this kind of professional exercise of prudent judgment is no longer tolerated. Bureaucratic policies exist to thwart this exercise of the virtue of prudence.

---

[28] John Milbank, *Being Reconciled: Ontology and Pardon* (London: Routledge, 2003), 185.
[29] *Miller v. Jackson* (1977), QB 966.

The problem for the Church is that she wants her institutions to foster some particular list of goods. The Church is not neutral in relation to the various ends to which human actions can tend. Perhaps for this reason, Ratzinger writes so many negative references to bureaucracy: "The saints were all people of imagination, not functionaries of apparatuses." They "reformed the Church in depth, not by working up plans for new structures, but by reforming themselves. What the Church needs in order to respond to the needs of man in every age is holiness, not management."[30] The Church, has "too much bureaucracy"—"everything should not take place by way of committees, there must even also be the personal encounter."[31]

A rather popular bureaucratic practice is the production of a mission statement. These are often constructed at staff weekend retreats where professional facilitators drawn for the world of psychology help the institution's employees to get in contact with their deepest dreams and desires for the said institution. The dreams and desires are then written on butcher paper in colored crayons and eventually converted into pithy statements that appear on the institution's marketing brochures. I have read many mission statements of Catholic schools and tertiary institutions, but I have rarely come across one that says, "We exist to promote the humanism of the Incarnation" or "to teach people to know, love, and serve God on earth so as to spend eternity in heaven"; or, even more simply, "to educate people with reference to the revelation of Jesus Christ." Rather, there tends to be references to a spirit of compassion and inclusivity, which gives the rather negative impression that the given institution is likely to be a sheltered workshop for people not welcome elsewhere. Unlike the enthusiasm for producing mission statements, Ratzinger observed that "St. Paul was effective, not because of brilliant rhetoric and sophisticated strategies, but rather because he exerted himself and left himself vulnerable in the service of the Gospel."[32]

This is not to suggest that Pope Benedict was some kind of anarchist, that he saw no value in administrative work at all. It is rather to say that leaders of Catholic educational institutions need to be conscious of how bureaucratic practices may act as a barrier to the work of grace. As members of the voting public, they should pay very close attention to the anthropological foundations of the policy objectives of politicians and public servants.

Paul Edward Gottfried focused on the issue of the acquiescence of voters

---

[30] Joseph Ratzinger, *The Ratzinger Report* (San Francisco: Ignatius Press, 1985), 53.

[31] Joseph Ratzinger, *Salt of the Earth: The Church at the End of the Millennium. Interview with Peter Seewald* (San Francisco: Ignatius Press, 1996), 266.

[32] Ratzinger, *Images of Hope*, 26.

in the expansion of the powers of public administrators,[33] observing that contrary to the spirit of nineteenth-century liberalism with its emphasis on individuality, the contemporary liberal state is more interested in promoting cultural uniformity. This task has provided employment within the state bureaucracy for psychiatrists, social psychologists, and even people with the job description "behavior economist," whose moral and political judgments are taken as "expert" opinions. Gottfried calls them "psychiatric theologians" since they are a modern secular analogue for a priesthood.

Following in the general direction of Alasdair MacIntyre's criticisms, Gottfried argues that much of the rhetoric of modern political life is designed to conceal both the power of these "psychiatric theologians" and the questionable legitimacy of their "expert" status. The contemporary liberal state is a classic example of a political culture, which seeks to hide the nature and exercise of its power behind technical jargon by down-playing political differences and claiming to be "neutral" in its treatment of contentious moral questions.

Gottfried describes himself as a "bourgeois-modernist"—which probably means that he is not looking to Christianity to provide a route out of this impasse. However, from an explicitly Christian perspective, the MacIntyrean solution is to foster the development of educational institutions in which the Catholic faith is not some optional extra for those who want to take it but something infrastructural, which determines the whole ethos of the institution from top to bottom, including, and above all, the curriculum. One might say that MacIntyre's recommendations are for Catholic educational institutions to be run on the "form of love" rather than the "form of the machine." At their heart, there will be priests and religious who provide the spiritual capital upon which the whole enterprise runs, and such institutions will typically be small and financially self-reliant—private rather than public.

To conclude, speaking of the spiritual life in general, Henri de Lubac remarked,

> You do not deliver yourself into the hands of authority like a man tired of using his initiative, abdicating; or like a sailor happy to find a quiet harbour at last after a stormy passage. On the contrary, you receive from authority the *Duc in altum*. You entrust yourself to it as to a ship leaving port for a glorious voyage and high adventure.[34]

---

[33] Paul Edward Gottfried, *After Liberalism: Mass Democracy in the Managerial State* (Princeton University Press, 2001).

[34] Henri de Lubac, *Paradoxes of Faith* (San Francisco: Ignatius Press, 1987), 25.

St. Marguerite did literally this. Transplanting the faith from Brittany to Quebec was her glorious and high adventure. She avoided the warped anthropology of the Jansenists, the tepidity of the bourgeois Pelagians, the pride of the pious Pelagians, and the anti-intellectualism of the philistines. She was no imbecile content to surrender her free will to the edicts of a bureaucratic machine. Positively, she established an order of religious women dedicated to the mission of Catholic education—dedicated, we might say, to fostering the humanism of the Incarnation. She laid the seeds of the faith in Quebec.

CHAPTER 9

The Wisdom of the Cross and the Challenges of Cultures
Theological Aspects[1]

Cultures may be understood as the social epiphenomena of theological anthropology, that is, the social consequences of various understandings of the meaning and purpose of human life. This includes attitudes toward death and eternal life, issues pertaining to the life of the mind and especially to the belief in the Trinitarian God of Christianity, or to the rejection of such a belief and preference for alternative systems of meaning, including alternative gods. Since different cultures are based upon different theological anthropologies, we speak of different humanisms.

In a monograph published in 1946 titled *Humanität und Christentum* (Humanity and Christianity), Gottlieb Söhngen offered a theological analysis of four different humanisms: (1) the noble humanism of the Greeks, (2) Christian humanism, (3) the "pure humanism" of the eighteenth century, and (4) the "*humanitas contra crucem*" (humanity opposed to the Cross).

Regarding the first, Söhngen noted that the Christian message of self-sacrificial love came into a world that spoke and thought in Greek, and that was filled with Greek education and its conceptions of a noble humanity. This Greek humanity survived the ancient Greeks and the ancient world. In Söhngen's analysis, the key concept distinguishing Greek noble humanism from the Christian humanism of St. Paul and other luminaries

---

[1] This paper was presented at the Wisdom of the Cross in a Pluralist World conference, Rome, September 2021. The conference was hosted by the Passionist Order celebrating the charism of its founder St. Paul of the Cross. Used with permission.

of the Catholic intellectual tradition is *agape*. In New Testament Greek, Christian love is not called *eros* but *agape*, and in the Latin bible it is called *caritas* or *dilectio*. From the very beginning of the Christian era, Christian *caritas* or *agape* "kept its distance" from Greek *eros*. Nonetheless, Söhngen rhetorically asked, "Can Greek *Eros* and Christian *Agape* not join hands like a youth and a virgin who both come from noble families and have received a noble education? Could it not be the case that in Christian *Agape* the divine revelation with divine wisdom and power has accomplished what human wisdom and power only incompletely knew and created in Greek *Eros*?"[2]

Söhngen answered his own question in the affirmative but with the caveat that it is not appropriate to speak of the Holy Spirit, the bond of love between God the Father and God the Son, using the language of *eros*. The platonic language of *eros* and the Christian language of *agape* sound together in counterpoint—the "Holy Spirit of a new love has not displaced the beautiful spirit of *Eros*; but Christian longing for eternal life borrows wings and delirious enthusiasm from *Eros*."[3]

The Christian and the noble Greek both reach for the most excellent and most beautiful, and their union brings about the *Humanitas Christiana*. This union, so to speak, is blessed by St. Paul in his First Letter to the Corinthians. Here the contrast between the wisdom of the Cross and the wisdom of the Greeks is directly addressed. St. Paul offers a conception of a *Dei humanitas in mysterio crucis*—a divine humanity within the mystery of the Cross. In Söhngen's terms, for St. Paul there can be a union between the noble Greek and a Christian virgin but only under the sign of the Cross.[4]

Numerous accounts of this union are in the patristic authors, but in St. Thomas Aquinas we arrive at what Söhngen described as a conception of human moral formation that takes the form of a "triptych": "On the central panel there are the theological virtues of faith, hope and love, while on one side panel there are the platonic cardinal virtues (wisdom, courage, temperance and justice) and on the other side panel the Aristotelian virtues with their heart-piece, the virtue of *Megalopsychia*."[5] Moreover, the *Humanitas Christiana*—the union of the erotic Greek quest for the most beautiful and excellent with the Christian quest for the most beautiful and most

---

[2] Gottlieb Söhngen, *Humanität und Christentum* (Essen: Augustin Wibbelt Verlagsgesellschaft, 1946), 37.

[3] Söhngen, *Humanität und Christentum*, 29.

[4] As was recognised in *Gaudium et Spes* §37, all human activity, constantly imperiled by man's pride and deranged self-love, must be purified and perfected by the power of Christ's Cross and Resurrection.

[5] Söhngen, *Humanität und Christentum*, 37.

excellent—is not only manifest in the lives of the Christian saints but also in Christian music, art, and architecture. In Christian literature, the contribution of Dante Alighieri is the most obvious, and possibly, highest example.

Furthermore, a Roman element fed into the *Humanitas Christiana*. The adjectives Theodor Haecker, author of *Virgil: Father of the West*, used to describe Aeneas, the hero of Virgil's epic poem, are pious, paternal, and magnanimous. Ernst A. Schmidt added loyalty, faith, sacrifice, renunciation, and self-abnegation[6] to this list. Haecker compared Virgilian noble humanism with Christian humanism in the following paragraph:

> In the last hour before the fullness of time [Virgil] fulfilled the measure of what was good in the ancient paganism, as others fulfilled the measure of its evil. This he did on the very threshold of the Advent, after which it was granted to man, a mere creature, to exceed his own limitations, and that without doing violence to his status as a creature. Thereafter it was given to man to be limitless, though in one direction only, namely in the love of God, which is the supernatural excess. The loftiest ideal and reality of the ancient world was the hero, the ultimate motive of whose being was his own glory, achieved, whether in life or in death, through two things— fate, and the heroic deed accomplished through freedom of the will. After the Incarnation the loftiest ideal and reality is the saint, the ultimate motive of whose being is the glory of God, also achieved whether in life or in death, through two things—first grace, which implies Providence, the greater name of fate, more full of light; and secondly, a boundless love of God, which also implies a heroic quality of mind and heroic action achieved through the mystery of freedom. The essential nature of the two ideals remains the same: each is achieved through the agency of one divine and one human actor; but between them lies the Incarnation and the Revelation.[7]

Haecker could also have written, but between them lies the Incarnation and the crucifixion.

Examining these hallmarks of Greek and Roman noble humanism and their synthesis with Christian humanism that flows from the Incarnation and the crucifixion, we can conclude that they share an interest in heroism,

---

6 Ernst A. Schmidt, "The German Recovery of Vergil in the Early Years of the 20th Century (1900–1938)," *Vergilius* 54 (2008): 124–49, at 142–43.

7 Theodor Haecker, *Virgil: Father of the West* (London: Sheed and Ward, 1934), 38.

in sacrifice, in piety, loyalty, renunciation, self-abnegation, and, above all, the virtue of *Megalopsychia*, or magnanimity. The stand-out difference between the two is, however, what Söhngen identified as the new Christian conception of love or *agape* in Greek, *caritas* in Latin. *Agape* is a form of love directed to the good of the other, exemplified most powerfully in the crucifixion of Christ, which is the greatest and unsurpassable act of self-sacrificial love in history. As Söhngen declared, "There is only one way to the glory of that humanity that shines in the light of clarification through the Christian trinity of faith, hope and love, and that way is through the suffering and cross of Christ, that is, the way of suffering and dying with Christ."[8] The *caritas* of the Cross is the yardstick by which the *Humanitas Christiana* is judged.

There is, however, another way, the reverse way, of examining the meeting of noble humanity with Christian love. Here noble humanity becomes the universal standard by which the Christian message of faith is to be judged, and here Söhngen observes, "The cross is a real nuisance because the cross appears as the absence of any kind of humanity."[9] When this reverse way is adopted, as it was by numerous philosophers in the eighteenth century, the *Humanitas Christiana* is challenged by a new form of humanism that attempts to free the Christian message of God's fatherly love—and the Christian commandment of our brotherly love—from what were deemed to be mere historical accidents: the formation of the Church and the enunciation of her creeds and dogmas. Instead of noble humanity under the law and spirit of the Christian faith, Christian love is subjected to the limits of a pure nature without grace and a pure reason without revelation.

A doctoral dissertation could be written on the place of the Cross in the pure humanism of German idealism, or what the contemporary philosopher Rémi Brague calls the "exclusive humanism," exclusive because it excludes the Trinitarian God of Christianity. Suffice to say, a humanism that champions a conception of brotherly love unhinged from any relationship to the Trinity does not have much need for the Cross. When Immanuel Kant argued that it does not matter whether there are three persons in the Godhead or ten, he showed his profound ignorance of the bonds of love within the Trinity and their part in the passion of Christ.

While the pure humanism of the eighteenth century occluded the Cross, there arises in the late nineteenth century a new humanism that wages war on the Cross—the *humanitas contra crucem*, associated with the anti-Christian polemics of Friedrich Nietzsche, especially Nietzsche's

---

8 Söhngen, *Humanität und Christentum*, 39.
9 Söhngen, *Humanität und Christentum*, 40.

declaration that Christianity is a crime against life itself. In a monograph on Friedrich Nietzsche, Theodor Steinbüchel developed the argument that Nietzsche is a highly powerful opponent of Christianity not primarily because of his attacks on Christian morality but because of his attempt to offer an alternative theological anthropology. The fundamental question posed to Christianity by Nietzsche is this: Is the transcendence of God the danger for the immanent becoming of the human person, or is the relation of the human person to the transcendent God the guarantee for the real and full development of the personality of the human being?[10] In other words, does a relationship to the Holy Trinity and all that this entails, including the theology of the Cross, diminish our humanity or ennoble our humanity? Nietzsche thought the former and fostered the morality of the herd. For Nietzsche, Christianity was something like a malignant growth in the culture of classical Greece.

Numerous books and articles have been written about Nietzsche's hostility to Christianity, and most agree that he had some issues with German pietism, especially the pietism of his maiden aunts. Against this German-Protestant cultural background, Steinbüchel argued that Nietzsche failed to appreciate "the meta-cosmic depth of sin, the tragedy of the demonic uprising against the Lord of the world and the drama of the demons wrestling with the redeemed world, the degradation or self-emptying (*Kenosis*) of the Son of God to the status of a servant, the satanic robbery of divinity and equation of the creature with God."[11] Nietzsche never appreciated the cosmic drama of the Incarnation and the Cross, "the battle between the *mysterium caritatis* and the *mysterium iniquitatis*."[12] He failed to understand that on the Cross all the demonic realities of world history were trumped by the power of *agape*, the power of a divine love that elevates the human being to God.

One of the most poetically powerful expositions of this theme is in the "Cosmic Tree" homily of a fifth century author:

> When this cosmic combat came to an end . . . the heavens shook; almost, the stars fell from the skies; the light of the sun was extinguished for a time; rocks were split asunder; the entire world was all but shattered. . . . But the great Jesus breathed forth his divine Soul, saying: "Father, into Thy hands I commend my spirit." And

---

[10] Theodore Steinbüchel, *Friedrich Nietzsche. Eine christliche Besinnung* (Stuttgart: Deutsche Verlags-Anstalt, 1946), 7.

[11] Steinbüchel, *Friedrich Nietzsche*, 25.

[12] Steinbüchel, *Friedrich Nietzsche*, 25.

lo, even while all things shuddered and heaved in earthquake, reeling for fear, his divine Soul ascended, giving life and strength to all; and again creation was still, as if this divine Crucifixion and Extension had everywhere unfolded and spread, penetrating all things, through all, and in all.[13]

The typology of the Cosmic Tree can be traced back at least as far as the prophecy of Ezekiel (17:22–24), where he spoke of the Lord placing a tree on a mountain in Israel that would put forth branches and bear much fruit. In the medieval period, this theme reappears in *The Tree of Life*, St. Bonaventure's reflection on the spiritual fruits of the Cross using the metaphor of a tree with twelve branches. On the first branch, the soul devoted to Christ perceives the flavor of sweetness by recalling the distinguished origin and sweet birth of the Savior; on the second branch, the soul meditates upon the humble mode of life which Christ condescended to adopt; on the third, the loftiness of Christ's perfect power; on the fourth, the plenitude of Christ's most abundant piety; on the fifth, the confident dignified demeanor with which Christ comported himself during his trial; on the sixth, the patience exhibited by Christ in bearing great insults and injuries; on the seventh, the constancy maintained by Christ during the experience of torture; on the eighth, the victory achieved by Christ's endurance; on the ninth, the novelty of Christ's resurrection embellished with remarkable gifts; on the tenth, the sublimity of his ascension, pouring forth spiritual charisms; on the eleventh, the equity of Christ's future judgment; and on the twelfth, the eternity of Christ's kingdom.[14]

The Cosmic Tree homily and St. Bonaventure's meditations highlight the meta-cosmic nature of the Cross, and our present time needs this amplification of such a theology. As Steinbüchel concluded,

You have to bring up this depth of the Christian mystery as a salvation event if you really want to counter the seriousness of Nietzsche's attack on Christianity and not insist on the much easier criticism of Nietzsche's ethical misappropriation of Christianity. Anyone

---

[13] Pseudo-Chrysostom, Homily VI for Holy Week (PG, 9:743–46).

[14] St. Bonaventure, *The Soul's Journey into God, the Tree of Life, the Life of St. Francis* (London: Paulist Press, 2020). For a summary, see Christopher Benson's webpage *Bensonian*, https://bensonian.wordpress.com/author/bensonian/.

who, like Nietzsche, condemns the mythology of Christianity can only be answered with reference to the mystery of Christianity.[15]

In other words, to deal with the Nietzschean *humanitas contra crucem*, one should not occlude the Cross with talk of all the good social services that Christianity has brought the world—hospitals, orphanages, nursing homes, homes for the poor—the whole raft of social security institutions that arrived in the world with the rise of religious orders and lay movements. These elements of a Christian culture are certainly praiseworthy, and when operating well, they too are built upon divine love, upon *agape*, but they are cultural epiphenomena. They only exist because of the magnanimity of the Second Person of the Trinity becoming united to humanity first in the womb of the Virgin and then on the wood of the Cross. Christian institutions become secularized when they shy away from the Cross, and Christianity without the Cross becomes what Ratzinger called "a new political moralism,"[16] a mere philanthropic project, no different from other philanthropic projects currently on offer from billionaire celebrities. Steinbüchel's point is that if we want Christianity to be more attractive to people than the pure or exclusive humanism of the eighteenth century that occludes the Trinity, or the explicitly anti-Christian *humanitas contra crucem* of Nietzsche and his followers, then we should not fight them on their ground but force them to fight on ours, and our ground, so to speak, is Golgotha.

Balthasar also made this point: "Whoever removes the Cross and its interpretation by the New Testament from the center, in order to replace it, for example, with the social commitment of Jesus to the oppressed as a new center, no longer stands in continuity with the apostolic faith. He does not see that God's commitment to the world is most absolute precisely at this point across a chasm,"[17] that is, at the point of the Cross. Balthasar reads the crucifixion as an event that transvalues human suffering. With it, "light has for the first time penetrated into the closed dungeons of human and cosmic suffering and dying," and thus, for the first time in human history, "pain and death receive meaning."[18] Of all the transvaluations that Christianity brought about, this was perhaps the greatest:

---

[15] Steinbüchel, *Friedrich Nietzsche*, 26.

[16] Joseph Ratzinger, "Europe and the Crisis of Cultures," *Communio: International Catholic Review* 32 (Summer 2005): 345–56, at 346.

[17] Hans Urs von Balthasar, *A Short Primer for Unsettled Laymen* (San Francisco: Ignatius Press, 1985), 91.

[18] Balthasar, *Short Primer*, 91.

The great religions had mostly been ingenious methods of escaping suffering or of making it ineffective. The highest that was reached was voluntary death for the sake of justice: Socrates and his spiritualized heroism.... But what Christ did on the Cross was in no way intended to spare us death but rather to revalue death completely. In place of the "going down into the pit" of the Old Testament, it became "being in paradise tomorrow." Instead of fearing death as the final evil and begging God for a few more years of life, as the weeping king Hezekiah does, Paul would like most of all to die immediately in order "to be with the Lord" (Phil 1:23). Together with death, life is also revalued: "If we live, we live in the Lord; if we die, we die in the Lord" (Rom 14:8).[19]

One conclusion of this paper is that to meet the challenges posed to the Church in contemporary Western culture—a Western cocktail heavily infused with eighteenth-century pure humanism and nineteenth-century *humanism contra crucem*, where Christian elements are internally quite diffused and even contradictory (e.g., Calvinism and Catholicism)—we need to return to Golgotha and amplify the theology of the Cross. We need to explain that the crucifixion is not about some dreamer getting himself into political trouble with powerful people and ultimately finding himself nailed to a cross and defeated, but rather that the Cross is the highest fusion of the Virgilian values of piety, paternity, and magnanimity with divine love, with *agape*. Further, this fusion offers us the prospect of a new humanism, transvalues human pain and suffering, and defeats the demonic quest to destroy humanity, since it (the Cross) confers the gift of redeeming grace. To rouse Western culture out of is materialist torpor fostered by pure humanism and to turn around the *humanism contra crucem* to embrace the Cross as the most noble, most magnanimous standard, the cosmic dimension of the Cross needs to be amplified, not muted.

This amplification also entails explaining the links between the Cross and sacramentality. Here again, Pope Benedict's *Doktorvater*, Gottlieb Söhngen, has something to contribute:

Baptism is the inner simulacrum of the death of Christ upon the cross and his internment in the grave as our rebirth to new life through the death of the old Adam; Confirmation is the inner simulacrum of the sufferings of Christ as our consecration in the Holy Spirit

---

[19] Balthasar, *Short Primer*, 92–93.

for heroic witness; the Eucharist is the inner simulacrum of the sacrificial death of Christ as a self-offering of the Lord for his bride the Church; reconciliation is the inner simulacrum of the atoning death of Christ as a gracious judgment of our sins and we sinners; extreme unction is the inner simulacrum of Christ's combat unto death as our strengthening in the final combat; ordination is the inner simulacrum of the bloody sacrifice of Christ as the particular qualification for service in the new cultic sanctuary of the eternal High Priest that was inaugurated by the death of Christ; marriage is the inner simulacrum of the betrothal of Christ in his death with the Church as the indissoluble bond between a man and wife in Christ and in his Church.[20]

Without the theology of the Cross and, in particular, the understanding of Christ as the Paschal lamb, there can be no proper understanding of the Eucharist; and without a proper understanding of the Eucharist, there can be no proper understanding of the priesthood, or the Church, or the nobility and indissolubility of a sacramental marriage. The theology of the Cross holds the whole sacramental economy together. Benedict XVI highlighted the cosmic quality of these relationships in *Sacramentum Caritatis*, §11:

> The Eucharist draws us into Jesus' act of self-oblation. More than just statically receiving the incarnate *Logos*, we enter into the very dynamic of his self-giving. Jesus "draws us into himself." The substantial conversion of bread and wine into his body and blood introduces within creation the principle of a radical change, a sort of "nuclear fission," to use an image familiar to us today, which penetrates to the heart of all being, a change meant to set off a process which transforms reality, a process leading ultimately to the transfiguration of the entire world, to the point where God will be all in all (cf. 1 Cor 15:28).

In the era of Soviet Communism, the Venerable Fulton Sheen remarked that the countries caught behind the Communist Iron Curtain had the Cross without Christ, while the countries on the Western side of the curtain had Christ without the Cross. Christ has become detached from the Cross as a prime cause of the contemporary crisis within Western Christianity. At this

---

[20] Gottlieb Söhngen, *Symbol und Wirklichkeit im Kultmysterium* (Bonn: Peter Hanstein Verlagsbuchhandlung, 1937), 93.

moment in world history, described by St. John Paul II as a battle between the culture of death and the civilization of love, the wisdom of the Cross is both the antidote to the culture of death and the tonic needed by the civilization of love.

However, the world is much wider than that of the Occident, wider than the Anglosphere and the countries of the old Christendom. In this context, Jean Daniélou remarked that "an essential and often overlooked aspect of the mystery of the Cross is its universal character."[21] After speaking of the brazen serpent raised on a wooden pole, Christ says, "When I will be exalted, then I will draw all men to myself" (cf. John 12:32). With this statement, he showed the relationship between the mystery of the Cross and the union of all things in him, a theme taken up by St. Paul when he speaks of the New Covenant uniting Jews and pagans. Daniélou suggested that everything St. Paul said about the relationship between the Jews and the pagans can be said about the relationship between Christians and non-Christians. The great mystery of the unity of the Cross requires all peoples of all races and nations to set aside notions of being the recipients of some form of enlightenment only available to them. Daniélou further observed,

> This universalistic aspect of the cross appears to be symbolized during the Mass at that moment when the priest makes a large sign of the cross over the corporal after making the offering with the host and speaks the words: "*Pro totius mundi salute*—for the salvation of the whole world." By this gesture he somehow takes possession of the whole world in the name of the cross, which is in the "*oblata*," the offerings, in order to consecrate them to the Father through the sign of Christ. And what is signified by this sign of the cross, *pro totius mundi salute*, is the cosmic character of salvation; it means the four cardinal points, thus embracing all nations, those from north and south, from east and west; for the salvation *totius mundi* the sacrifice of the Mass, the sacrifice on the cross, is offered.[22]

Daniélou concluded that the image of the Cross as the Cosmic Tree has great value as a missionary symbol, especially in India where there is a concept of a universal axis planted in the center of the world which reaches

---

[21] Jean Daniélou, *Das Geheimnis vom Kommen des Herrn* (Frankfurt am Main: Verlag Josef Knecht, 1951), 139.

[22] Daniélou, *Kommen des Herrn*, 141.

down into the depths of the earth and somehow unites the world. Indeed, this concept of a cosmic or world tree connecting every aspect of the universe is not only found in India. Carl Jung argued that it appears as a universal archetype in the symbolism and mythologies of numerous world religions, including pre-Christian Indo-European, Hungarian, Turkish, Mongol, Norse, German, Chinese, and Siberian mythologies to name only a few.

The difference, of course, between all these mythologies and the wood of the Cross is that the wood of the Cross was real. It was not merely a metaphor or symbol. To paraphrase the words of the poet Geoffrey Hill, the crucifixion of Christ was not another "bloodless myth."[23] The Church affirms this principle in *Dominus Iesus*: "Jesus Christ has a significance and value for the human race and its history, which are unique and singular, proper to him alone, exclusive, universal and absolute."[24]

In an address given in Jerusalem in 1994 at the invitation of Rabbi Rosen, Ratzinger described Christ's crucifixion as an "act endured in innermost solidarity with the Law and with Israel"; it was the perfect realization of what the signs of the Jewish Day of Atonement signify.[25] All sacrifices are acts of representation, which, from being typological symbols in the Old Testament, become reality in the life of Christ, so that the symbols can be dropped without one iota being lost.

> The universalising of the Torah by Jesus, as the New Testament understands it, is not the extraction of some universal moral prescriptions from the living whole of God's revelation. It preserves the unity of cult and ethos. The ethos remains grounded and anchored in the cult, in the worship of God, in such a way that the entire cult is bound together in the Cross, indeed, for the first time it has become fully real.[26]

Moreover, "Christ, who makes an offering of himself on the Cross, is therefore the true and eternal high priest anticipated symbolically by the Aaronic priesthood."[27]

It is beyond the scope of this paper to examine in depth how the Cross may be best presented to the very large number of wisdom traditions that exist

---

[23] We are indebted to Fr. Aidan Nichols for this reference to the poetry of Geoffrey Hill.

[24] Congregation for the Doctrine of the Faith, *Dominus Iesus* (2000), §15.

[25] Joseph Ratzinger, *Many Religions, One Covenant: Israel, the Church and the World* (San Francisco: Ignatius Press, 1992), 32.

[26] Ratzinger, *Many Religions*, 41.

[27] Ratzinger, *Many Religions*, 41.

in the Orient. As a generalization, however, a common theme across Eastern religions is their interest in self-transcendence. Therefore, it would seem important for Christian missionaries to not only explain the meta-cosmic and universal meaning of the Cross but also the very personal spirituality of the Cross that is central to any Christian conception of spiritual development and thus self-transcendence. In this context, there is a whole honor board of names of saintly mystics who penetrated the depths of the wisdom of the Cross to a much greater degree than their peers. Some of them fostered the practice of meditating on the five wounds of Christ, others on his sacred heart, and others, more recently, on his divine mercy. These include Sts. Mechtilde (1240/1–1298) and Gertrude von Helfta (ca. 1256–1302), Sts. Margaret Mary Alacoque (1647–1690) and Claude de la Columbière (1641–1682), Sts. John of the Cross (1542–1591) and Teresa of Ávila (1515–1582), Sts. Louis de Montfort (1673–1716) and Alphonsus Liguori (1696–1787), the Servant of God Jules Chevalier (1824–1907) and the Venerable Alain de Boismenu (1870–1953), Sts. Thérèse of Lisieux (1873–1897) and Teresa-Benedicta of the Cross (1891–1942), Sts. Maximilian Kolbe (1894–1941) and Faustina Kowalska (1905–1938), and last but far from least, St. Paul of the Cross (1694–1775), whose Passionist order is the subject of our celebration today.

Many of these saints fostered devotions that led to artistic depictions of the passion of Christ and of his sacred heart, some of which have greater aesthetic appeal than others. Romano Guardini alluded to this in a homily delivered at the University of Munich in 1955. He nonetheless argued that whatever one makes of the sentimentality associated with devotion to the sacred heart of Jesus, beneath all the sentimentality and behind all the artistic depictions lies the never to be exhausted truth that in Christ, God's love took responsibility for our guilt and atoned for it. When we meditate on this, Christ's disposition of self-sacrificial love takes hold of us.

> If you succeed in gaining this awareness and keeping it awake, a feeling of honour arises out of faith, which slowly but consistently changes our lives. . . . [W]hat bears this form of piety is a sacred nobility. The Lord of the world stands up for man so that his guilt may be atoned for and so that he may live in freedom, but the person who understands receives from this the command to be vigilant so that one's own actions do not increase the infinite burden that lies on Christ.[28]

---

[28] Romano Guardini, "Herz Jesu," *Wahrheit und Ordnung* 22 (Herbst, 1955): 527.

These words were written just one decade after the end of the Second World War that was both a Gethsemane and Golgotha experience for a multitude of people. From the list of spiritual masters listed above, both Kolbe and Teresa-Benedicta of the Cross died martyrs' deaths in Auschwitz. It is hard to imagine a more magnanimous human act than Kolbe's offer of his own life in return for that of a fellow prisoner. It is also recorded that when the Gestapo came to arrest Teresa-Benedicta and her sister Rosa, she remarked, "Come, let us go for our people."[29] Again, magnanimity, driven by *agape*, was the order of the day.

Furthermore, Blessed Vilmos Apor (1892–1945), the bishop of Győr, was martyred defending a group of women from being violated by soldiers of the Red Army. His episcopal motto was "The Cross strengthens the weak and makes the strong gentle." In this motto and his martyrdom there is a combination of piety (devotion to the Cross), paternity (fatherly care for the weak and vulnerable), and magnanimity (placing his own life at risk to protect others). Apor, Kolbe, and Teresa-Benedicta of the Cross are merely three of many Catholic martyrs of the Second World War whose biographies are rent through with the spirituality of the Cross.

Another suite of saints who are even more closely associated with the particular spirituality of St. Paul of the Cross are Blessed Dominic Barberi, the Venerable George Spencer, and the greatest of Barberi's converts St. John Henry Newman. Everyone has heard of Newman's *Apologia Pro Vita Sua*, the story of his conversion, his *Grammar of Assent*, and his *Essay on the Development of Doctrine*, but he also wrote meditations on the stations of the Cross linking individual human sins to each station. The reader of Newman's meditations does not simply imagine the pain of the Cross for Christ but considers the relationship between personal sin and Christ's passion.

This trio of Barberi, Spencer, and Newman each dedicated their lives to the conversion of England. It is testimony to the magnanimous character of St. Paul of the Cross that he spent some five decades of his life praying for the faith in a country that was not his own. Such prayers for the conversion of England continue today in the Tyburn monasteries in England, Scotland, Ireland, New Zealand, Peru, Ecuador, Colombia, Italy, France, and Australia.

What Romano Guardini described as the sacred nobility that flows from the spirituality of the Cross is a direct answer to Nietzsche's statement that if Christians wished for him to believe in their "god," then they should at least look as though they have been redeemed. As St. John Paul II noted,

---

[29] Romanus Cessario, "Edith Stein's Last Words," *National Catholic Register*, November 8, 1998, https://www.ncregister.com/commentaries/edith-steins-last-words.

"Suffering in the light of Christ becomes an invitation to manifest the moral greatness of man, his spiritual maturity."[30] The saints and martyrs are those who do this to a high degree. They are exemplars par excellence of the Christian form of self-transcendence. It was precisely such moral greatness and spiritual maturity that first led St. Teresa-Benedicta of the Cross to the Christian faith. She began her journey to the Church having witnessed the courage of a Christian friend when confronted by the news that her husband had been killed in the First World War. Teresa-Benedicta wrote, "It was my first encounter with the cross and the divine power that it bestows on those who carry it. . . . For the first time, I was seeing with my very eyes the church, born from its Redeemer's sufferings, triumphant over the sting of death. That was the moment my unbelief collapsed and Christ shone forth—in the mystery of the cross."[31]

In *Dives in Misericordia*, St. John Paul II described the Cross as "the most profound condescension of God to man" and as "a touch of eternal love upon the most painful wounds of man's earthly existence."[32] When presented in these terms and *agape*'s concrete embodiment in the lives of the saints, the Cross is not some ancient Semitic or contemporary Western cultural icon imposed on the world in a battle of the nations for cultural supremacy. Rather the Cross completely transcends all national and class divisions and draws all nations together in a noble humanity open to integrating the best intuitions of the great wisdom traditions, seeing them represented by the Magi at the birth of Christ in Bethlehem. It can do this because, at its heart, there is *agape*. There is also piety, paternity and magnanimity.

---

[30] John Paul II, *Salvifici Doloris* (1984), §22.
[31] Waltraud Herbstrith, *Edith Stein: A Biography* (San Francisco: Harper & Row, 1985), 25.
[32] John Paul II, *Dives in Misericordia* (1980), §8.

Excerpts from the International Theological Commission Documents on the Dispositions Required for a Possession of the *Sensus Fidei*[1]

Sensus Fidei in the Life of the Church Document of the International Theological Commission (2014)

87. The *sensus fidei* is essential to the life of the Church, and it is necessary now to consider how to discern and identify authentic manifestations of the *sensus fidei*. Such a discernment is particularly required in situations of tension when the authentic *sensus fidei* needs to be distinguished from expressions simply of popular opinion, particular interests or the spirit of the age. Recognising that the *sensus fidei* is an ecclesial reality in which individual believers participate, the first part of this chapter seeks to identify those characteristics which are required of the baptised if they are truly to be subjects of the *sensus fidei*, in other words, the dispositions necessary for believers to participate authentically in the *sensus fidelium*. The criteriology offered in the first part is then supplemented by consideration of the practical application of criteria with regard to the *sensus fidei* in the second part of the chapter. Part two considers three important topics: first, the close relationship between the *sensus fidei* and popular religiosity; then, the necessary distinction between the *sensus fidei* and public opinion inside or outside the Church; and, finally, the question of how to consult the faithful in matters of faith and morals.

---

1. Dispositions needed for authentic participation in the *sensus fidei*

88. There is not one simple disposition, but rather a set of dispositions, influenced by ecclesial, spiritual, and ethical factors. No single one can be discussed in an isolated manner; its relationship to each and all of the others has to be taken into account. Only the most important dispositions for authentic participation in the *sensus fidei* are indicated below, drawn from biblical, historical and systematic investigation, and formulated so as to be useful in practical situations of discernment.

a) Participation in the life of the Church

89. The first and most fundamental disposition is active participation in the life of the Church. Formal membership of the Church is not enough. Participation in the life of the Church means constant prayer (cf. 1 Thess 5:17), active participation in the liturgy, especially the Eucharist, regular reception of the sacrament of reconciliation, discernment and exercise of gifts and charisms received from the Holy Spirit, and active engagement in the Church's mission and in her *diakonia*. It presumes an acceptance of the Church's teaching on matters of faith and morals, a willingness to follow the commands of God, and courage both to correct one's brothers and sisters, and also to accept correction oneself.

90. There are countless ways in which such participation may occur, but what is common in all cases is an active solidarity with the Church, coming from the heart, a feeling of fellowship with other members of the faithful and with the Church as a whole, and an instinct thereby for what the needs of and dangers to the Church are. The necessary attitude is conveyed by the expression, *sentire cum ecclesia*, to feel, sense and perceive in harmony with the Church. This is required not just of theologians, but of all the faithful; it unites all the members of the people of God as they make their pilgrim journey. It is the key to their "walking together."

91. The subjects of the *sensus fidei* are members of the Church who participate in the life of the Church, knowing that "we, who are many, are one body in Christ, and individually we are members one of another" (Rom 12:5).

b) Listening to the word of God

92. Authentic participation in the *sensus fidei* relies necessarily on a profound and attentive listening to the word of God. Because the Bible is the original testimony of the word of God, which is handed down from generation to generation in the community of faith, coherence to Scripture and Tradition is the main indicator of such listening. The *sensus fidei* is the appreciation of the faith by which the people of God "receives not the mere word of men, but truly the word of God."

93. It is not at all required that all members of the people of God should study the Bible and the witnesses of Tradition in a scientific way. Rather, what is required is an attentive and receptive listening to the Scriptures in the liturgy, and a heartfelt response, "Thanks be to God" and "Glory to you, Lord Jesus Christ," an eager confession of the mystery of faith, and an "Amen" which responds to the "Yes" God has said to his people in Jesus Christ (2 Cor 1:20). Participation in the liturgy is the key to participation in the living Tradition of the Church, and solidarity with the poor and needy opens the heart to recognise the presence and the voice of Christ (cf. Mt 25:31–46).

94. The subjects of the *sensus fidei* are members of the Church who have "received the word with joy inspired by the Holy Spirit" (1 Thess 1:6).

c) Openness to reason

95. A fundamental disposition required for authentic participation in the *sensus fidei* is acceptance of the proper role of reason in relation to faith. Faith and reason belong together. Jesus taught that God is to be loved not only "with all your heart, and with all your soul, . . . and with all your strength," but also "with all your mind [*nous*]" (Mk 12:30). Because there is only one God, there is only one truth, recognised from different points of view and in different ways by faith and by reason, respectively. Faith purifies reason and widens its scope, and reason purifies faith and clarifies its coherence.

96. The subjects of the *sensus fidei* are members of the Church who celebrate "reasonable worship" and accept the proper role of reason illuminated by faith in their beliefs and practices. All the faithful are called to be "transformed by the renewing of your minds, so that you may discern what is the will of God—what is good and acceptable and perfect" (Rom 12:1–2).

d) Adherence to the magisterium

97. A further disposition necessary for authentic participation in the *sensus fidei* is attentiveness to the magisterium of the Church, and a willingness to listen to the teaching of the pastors of the Church, as an act of freedom and deeply held conviction. The magisterium is rooted in the mission of Jesus, and especially in his own teaching authority (cf. Mt 7:29). It is intrinsically related both to Scripture and Tradition; none of these three can "stand without the others."

98. The subjects of the *sensus fidei* are members of the Church who heed the words of Jesus to the envoys he sends: "Whoever listens to you listens to me, and whoever rejects you rejects me, and whoever rejects me rejects the one who sent me" (Lk 10:16).

e) Holiness—humility, freedom and joy

99. Authentic participation in the *sensus fidei* requires holiness. Holiness is the vocation of the whole Church and of every believer. To be holy fundamentally means to belong to God in Jesus Christ and in his Church, to be baptised and to live the faith in the power of the Holy Spirit. Holiness is, indeed, participation in the life of God, Father, Son and Holy Spirit, and it holds together love of God and love of neighbour, obedience to the will of God and engagement in favor of one's fellow human beings. Such a life is sustained by the Holy Spirit, who is repeatedly invoked and received by Christians (cf. Rom 1:7–8, 11), particularly in the liturgy.

100. In the history of the Church, the saints are the light-bearers of the *sensus fidei*. Mary, Mother of God, the All-Holy (*Panaghia*), in her total acceptance of the word of God is the very model of faith and Mother of the Church. Treasuring the words of Christ in her heart (Lk 2:51) and singing the praises of God's work of salvation (Lk 1:46–55), she perfectly exemplifies the delight in God's word and eagerness to proclaim the good news that the *sensus fidei* produces in the hearts of believers. In all succeeding generations, the gift of the Spirit to the Church has produced a rich harvest of holiness, and the full number of the saints is known only to God. Those who are beatified and canonised stand as visible models of Christian faith and life. For the Church, Mary and all holy persons, with their prayer and their passion, are outstanding witnesses of the *sensus fidei* in their own time and for all times, in their own place and for all places.

101. Because it fundamentally requires an *imitatio Christi* (cf. Phil 2:5–8), holiness essentially involves humility. Such humility is the very opposite of uncertainty or timidity; it is an act of spiritual freedom. Therefore openness (*parrhesia*) after the pattern of Christ himself (cf. Jn 18:20) is connected with humility and a characteristic of the *sensus fidei* as well. The first place to practice humility is within the Church itself. It is not only a virtue of lay people in relation to their pastors, but also a duty of pastors themselves in the exercise of their ministry for the Church. Jesus taught the twelve: "Whoever wants to be first must be last of all and servant of all" (Mk 9:35). Humility is lived by habitually acknowledging the truth of faith, the ministry of pastors, and the needs of the faithful, especially the weakest.

102. A true indicator of holiness is "peace and joy in the Holy Spirit" (Rom 14:17; cf. 1 Thess 1:6). These are gifts manifested primarily on a spiritual, not a psychological or emotional, level, namely, the peace of heart and quiet joy of the person who has found the treasure of salvation, the pearl of great price (cf. Mt 13:44–46). Peace and joy are, indeed, two of the most characteristic fruits of the Holy Spirit (cf. Gal 5:22). It is the Holy Spirit who moves the heart and turns it to God, "opening the eyes of the mind and giving 'joy and ease to everyone in assenting to the truth and believing it [*omnibus suavitatem in consentiendo et credendo veritati*].'" Joy is the opposite of the bitterness and wrath that grieve the Holy Spirit (cf. Eph 4:31), and is the hallmark of salvation. St. Peter urges Christians to rejoice in sharing Christ's sufferings, "so that you may also be glad and shout for joy when his glory is revealed" (1 Pet 4:13).

103. The subjects of the *sensus fidei* are members of the Church who hear and respond to the urging of St. Paul: "make my joy complete: be of the same mind, having the same love, being in full accord and of one mind." "Do nothing from selfish ambition or conceit, but in humility regard others as better than yourselves" (Phil 2:2–3).

f) Seeking the edification of the Church

104. An authentic manifestation of the *sensus fidei* contributes to the edification of the Church as one body, and does not foster division and particularism within her. In the First Letter to the Corinthians, the very essence of participation in the life and mission of the Church is such edification (cf. 1 Cor 14). Edification means building up the Church both in the inner consciousness

of its faith and in terms of new members, who want to be baptised into the faith of the Church. The Church is the house of God, a holy temple, made up of the faithful who have received the Holy Spirit (cf. 1 Cor 3:10–17). To build the Church means seeking to discover and develop one's own gifts and helping others to discover and develop their charisms, too, correcting their failures, and accepting correction oneself, in a spirit of Christian charity, working with others and praying with them, sharing their joys and sorrows (cf. 1 Cor 12:12, 26).

105. The subjects of the *sensus fidei* are members of the Church who reflect what St. Paul says to the Corinthians: "To each is given the manifestation of the Spirit for the common good" (1 Cor 12:7).

Synodality in the Life and Mission of the Church Document of the International Theological Commission (2018)

108. The same dispositions that are required to live and bring to maturity the *sensus fidei*, with which all believers are endowed, are also required to put it to use on the synodal path. This is an essential point in forming people in a synodal spirit, since we live in a culture where the demands of the Gospel and even human virtues are not often the object of appreciation or sufficient preparation. It is worth remembering these dispositions: participation in the life of the Church centered on the Eucharist and the Sacrament of Reconciliation; listening to the Word of God in order to enter into a dialogue with it and put it into practice; following the Magisterium in its teachings on faith and morals; the awareness of being members of each other as the Body of Christ and of being sent to our brothers and sisters, first and foremost to the poorest and the most excluded. It is about attitudes summed up in the formula *sentire cum Ecclesia*: "to feel, sense and perceive in harmony with the Church" which "unites all the members of the People of God as they make their pilgrim journey" and is "the key to their 'walking together.'" In reality, it is about revealing the spirituality of communion as "the guiding principle of education wherever individuals and Christians are formed, wherever ministers of the altar, consecrated persons and pastoral workers are trained, wherever families and communities are being built up."

Excerpts from the Catechism of the Catholic Church on the Nature of the Sacred Hierarchy[1]

I. THE HIERARCHICAL CONSTITUTION OF THE CHURCH

Why the ecclesial ministry?

874. Christ is himself the source of ministry in the Church. He instituted the Church. He gave her authority and mission, orientation and goal:

> In order to shepherd the People of God and to increase its numbers without cease, Christ the Lord set up in his Church a variety of offices which aim at the good of the whole body. The holders of office, who are invested with a sacred power, are, in fact, dedicated to promoting the interests of their brethren, so that all who belong to the People of God . . . may attain to salvation.[2]

875. "How are they to believe in him of whom they have never heard? And how are they to hear without a preacher? And how can men preach unless they are sent?"[3] No one—no individual and no community—can proclaim the Gospel to himself: "Faith comes from what is heard." No one can give himself the mandate and the mission to proclaim the Gospel. The one sent by the Lord does not speak and act on his own authority, but by virtue of Christ's authority; not as a member of the community, but speaking to it in the name of Christ. No one can bestow grace on himself; it must be given and offered. This fact presupposes ministers of grace, authorized and empowered by Christ. From him, they receive the mission and faculty ("the sacred power") to act *in persona Christi Capitis*. . . . The ministry in which Christ's

---

[1] ©Dicastery for Communication-Libereia Editrice Vaticana. Used with permission.

[2] *LG* 18

[3] Rom 10:14–15.

emissaries do and give by God's grace what they cannot do and give by their own powers, is called a "sacrament" by the Church's tradition. Indeed, the ministry of the Church is conferred by a special sacrament.

876. Intrinsically linked to the sacramental nature of ecclesial ministry is its character as service. Entirely dependent on Christ who gives mission and authority, ministers are truly "slaves of Christ,"[4] in the image of him who freely took "the form of a slave" for us.[5] Because the word and grace of which they are ministers are not their own, but are given to them by Christ for the sake of others, they must freely become the slaves of all.[6]

877. Likewise, it belongs to the sacramental nature of ecclesial ministry that it have a collegial character. In fact, from the beginning of his ministry, the Lord Jesus instituted the Twelve as "the seeds of the new Israel and the beginning of the sacred hierarchy."[7] Chosen together, they were also sent out together, and their fraternal unity would be at the service of the fraternal communion of all the faithful: they would reflect and witness to the communion of the divine persons.[8] For this reason every bishop exercises his ministry from within the episcopal college, in communion with the bishop of Rome, the successor of St. Peter and head of the college. So also priests exercise their ministry from within the presbyterium of the diocese, under the direction of their bishop.

878. Finally, it belongs to the sacramental nature of ecclesial ministry that it have a personal character. Although Christ's ministers act in communion with one another, they also always act in a personal way. Each one is called personally: "You, follow me"[9] in order to be a personal witness within the common mission, to bear personal responsibility before him who gives the mission, acting "in his person" and for other persons: "I baptize you in the name of the Father and of the Son and of the Holy Spirit . . . "; "I absolve you. . . ."

879. Sacramental ministry in the Church, then, is at once a collegial and a personal service, exercised in the name of Christ. This is evidenced by the

---

[4] Rom 10:17.
[5] Cf. Rom 1:1.
[6] Cf. 1 Cor 9:19.
[7] *AG* 5.
[8] Cf. Jn 17:21-23.
[9] Jn 21:22; Cf. Mt 4:19–21; Jn 1:4

bonds between the episcopal college and its head, the successor of St. Peter, and in the relationship between the bishop's pastoral responsibility for his particular church and the common solicitude of the episcopal college for the universal Church.

Excerpts from the Post-Synodal Apostolic Exhortation of St. John Paul II *Pastores Dabo Vobis* (1992)[1]

THE NATURE AND MISSION OF THE MINISTERIAL PRIESTHOOD

A Look at the Priest

11. "The eyes of all in the synagogue were fixed on him" (Lk. 4:20). What the evangelist Luke says about the people in the synagogue at Nazareth that Sabbath, listening to Jesus' commentary on the words of the prophet Isaiah which he had just read, can be applied to all Christians. They are always called to recognize in Jesus of Nazareth the definitive fulfillment of the message of the prophets: "And he began to say to them, 'Today this Scripture has been fulfilled in your hearing'" (Lk. 4:21). The "Scripture" he had read was this: "The Spirit of the Lord is upon me, because he has anointed me to preach good news to the poor. He has sent me to proclaim release to the captives and recovery of sight to the blind, to set at liberty those who are oppressed, to proclaim the acceptable year of the Lord" (Lk. 4:18–19; cf. Is. 61:1–2). Jesus thus presents himself as filled with the Spirit, "consecrated with an anointing," "sent to preach good news to the poor." He is the Messiah, the Messiah who is priest, prophet and king.

These are the features of Christ upon which the eyes of faith and love of Christians should be fixed. Using this "contemplation" as a starting point and making continual reference to it, the synod fathers reflected on the problem of priestly formation in present-day circumstances. This problem cannot be solved without previous reflection upon the goal of formation, that is, the ministerial priesthood, or more precisely, the ministerial priesthood as a participation—in the Church—in the very priesthood of Jesus Christ. Knowledge of the nature and mission of the ministerial priesthood

---

[1] ©Dicastery for Communication-Libereia Editrice Vaticana. Used with permission.

is an essential presupposition, and at the same time the surest guide and incentive toward the development of pastoral activities in the Church for fostering and discerning vocations to the priesthood and training those called to the ordained ministry.

A correct and in-depth awareness of the nature and mission of the ministerial priesthood is the path which must be taken—and in fact the synod did take it—in order to emerge from the crisis of priestly identity. In the final address to the synod I stated: "This crisis arose in the years immediately following the Council. It was based on an erroneous understanding of—and sometimes even a conscious bias against—the doctrine of the conciliar magisterium. Undoubtedly, herein lies one of the reasons for the great number of defections experienced then by the Church, losses which did serious harm to pastoral ministry and priestly vocations, especially missionary vocations. It is as though the 1990 synod—rediscovering, by means of the many statements which we heard in this hall, the full depth of priestly identity—has striven to instill hope in the wake of these sad losses. These statements showed an awareness of the specific ontological bond which unites the priesthood to Christ the high priest and good shepherd. This identity is built upon the type of formation which must be provided for priesthood and then endure throughout the priest's whole life. This was the precise purpose of the synod."

For this reason the synod considered it necessary to summarize the nature and mission of the ministerial priesthood, as the Church's faith has acknowledged them down the centuries of its history and as the Second Vatican Council has presented them anew to the people of our day.

In the Church as Mystery, Communion and Mission

12. "The priest's identity," as the synod fathers wrote, "like every Christian identity, has its source in the Blessed Trinity," which is revealed and is communicated to people in Christ, establishing, in him and through the Spirit, the Church as "the seed and the beginning of the kingdom." The apostolic exhortation *Christifideles Laici*, summarizing the Council's teaching, presents the Church as mystery, communion and mission: "She is mystery because the very life and love of the Father, Son and Holy Spirit are the gift gratuitously offered to all those who are born of water and the Spirit (cf. Jn. 3:5) and called to relive the very communion of God and to manifest it and communicate it in history [mission]."

It is within the Church's mystery, as a mystery of Trinitarian communion in missionary tension, that every Christian identity is revealed, and likewise the specific identity of the priest and his ministry. Indeed, the priest, by virtue of the consecration which he receives in the sacrament of orders, is sent forth by the Father through the mediatorship of Jesus Christ, to whom he is configured in a special way as head and shepherd of his people, in order to live and work by the power of the Holy Spirit in service of the Church and for the salvation of the world.

In this way the fundamentally "relational" dimension of priestly identity can be understood. Through the priesthood which arises from the depths of the ineffable mystery of God, that is, from the love of the Father, the grace of Jesus Christ and the Holy Spirit's gift of unity, the priest sacramentally enters into communion with the bishop and with other priests in order to serve the People of God who are the Church and to draw all mankind to Christ in accordance with the Lord's prayer: "Holy Father, keep them in your name, which you have given me, that they may be one, even as we are one . . . even as you, Father, are in me, and I in you, that they also may be in us, so that the world may believe that you have sent me" (Jn. 17:11, 21).

Consequently, the nature and mission of the ministerial priesthood cannot be defined except through this multiple and rich interconnection of relationships which arise from the Blessed Trinity and are prolonged in the communion of the Church, as a sign and instrument of Christ, of communion with God and of the unity of all humanity. In this context the ecclesiology of communion becomes decisive for understanding the identity of the priest, his essential dignity, and his vocation and mission among the People of God and in the world. Reference to the Church is therefore necessary, even if not primary, in defining the identity of the priest. As a mystery, the Church is essentially related to Jesus Christ. She is his fullness, his body, his spouse. She is the "sign" and living "memorial" of his permanent presence and activity in our midst and on our behalf. The priest finds the full truth of his identity in being a derivation, a specific participation in and continuation of Christ himself, the one high priest of the new and eternal covenant. The priest is a living and transparent image of Christ the priest. The priesthood of Christ, the expression of his absolute "newness" in salvation history, constitutes the one source and essential model of the priesthood shared by all Christians and the priest in particular. Reference to Christ is thus the absolutely necessary key for understanding the reality of priesthood.

Bibliography

Augustine. *De Trinitate*.

Balogh, Margit. *"Victim of History": Cardinal Mindszenty, a Biography*. Washington, DC: Catholic University of America Press, 2021.

von Balthasar, Hans Urs. *Bernanos: An Ecclesial Existence*. San Francisco: Ignatius Press, 1996.

———. "Current Trends in Catholic Theology and the Responsibility of the Christian." *Communio* 5, no. 1 (Spring 1978): 77–85.

———. *Das Ganze im Fragment. Aspekte der Geschichtestheologie*. Einsiedeln: Johannes Verlag, 1963.

———. *Elucidations*. San Francisco: Ignatius Press, 1998.

———. *Explorations in Theology*. Vol. 2, *Spouse of the Word*. San Francisco: Ignatius Press, 1991.

———. *Explorations in Theology*. Vol. 3, *Creator Spirit*. San Francisco: Ignatius Press, 1993.

———. *The Office of Peter and the Structure of the Church*. San Francisco: Ignatius Press, 1986.

———. *A Short Primer for Unsettled Laymen*. San Francisco: Ignatius Press, 1985.

———. *Theology of Karl Barth*. San Francisco: Ignatius Press, 1992.

Barron, Robert. *The Priority of Christ: Toward a Postliberal Catholicism*. Ada, MI: Baker Academic, 2018.

Benedict XVI. Address to the International Federation of Catholic Universities. Paul VI Audience Hall. November 19, 2009.

———. Address to the International Theological Commission. Hall of the Popes. December 7, 2012.

———. Address to the Representatives of British Society. Westminster Hall. Westminster. September 17, 2010.

———. *Anglicanorum Coetibus*. 2009.

———. *Caritas in Veritate*. 2009.

———. *Deus Caritas Est*. 2005.

———. "General Audience." St. Peter's Square. November 5, 2008.

———. *Images of Hope: Meditations on Major Feasts*. San Francisco: Ignatius Press, 2006.

———. *Jesus of Nazareth: From the Baptism in the Jordan to the Transfiguration*. New York: Doubleday, 2007.

———. *Light of the World: The Pope, the Church and the Signs of the Times*. San Francisco: Ignatius Press, 2010.

———. *What is Christianity? The Last Writings*. San Francisco: Ignatius Press, 2023.

———. "With Cardinal Sarah, the Liturgy is in Good Hands." *First Things*. May 17, 2017. https://www.firstthings.com/web-exclusives/2017/05/with-cardinal-sarah-the-liturgy-is-in-good-hands.

Bernanos, Georges. *La liberté, pour quoi faire*. Paris: Gallimard, 1953.

Biffi, Giacomo. *Casta Meretrix, "The Chaste Whore": An Essay on the Ecclesiology of St. Ambrose*. Farnborough, England: St. Austin Press, 2000.

Boeve, Lieven. "The Enduring Significance and Relevance of Edward Schillebeeckx: Introducing the State of the Question in Medias Res." In *Edward Schillebeeckx and Contemporary Theology*, ed. Lieven Boeve, Frederiek Depoortere, and Stephan van Erp. London: T & T Clark, 2010.

———. *Interrupting Tradition: An Essay on Christian Faith in a Postmodern Context*. Louvain Theological and Pastoral Monographs, vol. 30. Leuven, Belgium: Peeters Press, 2003.

———. *Lyotard and Theology*. London: Bloomsbury, 2014

———. *Theology at the Crossroads of University, Church and Society: Dialogue, Difference and Catholic Identity*. London: Bloomsbury, 2017.

———. Frederiek Depoortere, and Stephan van Erp, eds. *Edward Schillebeeckx and Contemporary Theology*. London: Bloomsbury, 2012.

Boot, Alexander. *How the West Was Lost*. London: I. B. Tauris, 2006.

Borgman, Erik. *Edward Schillebeeckx: A Theologian in his History*. Vol. 1, *A Catholic Theology of Culture (1914–1965)*. London: Continuum, 2004.

———. "*Gaudium et spes*: The Forgotten Future of a Revolutionary Document." *Concilium* 4 (2005): 54.

Bouyer, Louis. *The Church of God: Body of Christ and Temple of the Spirit*. San Francisco: Ignatius Press, 2011.

Brague, Rémi. *The Kingdom of Man: Genesis and Failure of the Modern Project*. Notre Dame, IN: University of Notre Dame Press, 2018.

Cavanaugh, William. "The City Beyond Secular Parodies." In *Radical Orthodoxy*, 182–201. Edited by John Milbank, Catherine Pickstock, and Graham Ward. Oxford: Blackwell, 1999.

———. *Field Hospital: The Church's Engagement with a Wounded World*. Grand Rapids, MI: Eerdmans, 2016.

———. *Theopolitical Imagination: Discovering the Liturgy as a Political Act in an Age of Global Consumerism*. London: T & T Clark, 2002.

Cessario, Romanus. "Edith Stein's Last Words." *National Catholic Register*. November 8, 1998. https://www.ncregister.com/commentaries/edith-steins-last-words.

Chaput, Charles. "Only Worthy Agenda for Synod Is One Given to Us by Jesus in the Gospels." Interview by Kelsey Wicks. *Catholic News Agency*. February 10, 2023. https://www.catholicnewsagency.com/news/253604/synod-on-synodality-archbishop-chaput-asks-bishops-only-to-use-jesus-agenda.

Congar, Yves. "Actualité de la Pneumatologie." In *Credo in Spiritum Sanctum. Atti del Congresso teologico internazionale pneumatologia*, vol. I, 15–28. Edited by J. Saraiva Martins. Roma, 22–26 marzo 1982. Libreria Editrice Vaticana, Città del Vaticano, 1983.

———. *I Believe in the Holy Spirit*. Vol. I, *The Experience of the Spirit*. London: Geoffrey Chapman, 1983.

———. *I Believe in the Holy Spirit*. Vol. II, *Lord and Giver of Life*. London: Geoffrey Chapman, 1983.

———. *Lay People in the Church*. London: Geoffrey Chapman, 1965.

Congregation for the Doctrine of the Faith. *Dominus Iesus*. On the Unicity and Salvific Universality of Jesus Christ and the Church. 2000.

———. *Inter Insigniores*. On the Question of the Admission of Women to the Ministerial Priesthood. 1976.

———. *Instruction on Certain Aspects of the "Theology of Liberation."* 1984.

———. *Letter to the Bishops of the Catholic Church on Some Aspects of the Church Understood as Communion*. 1992.

———. *The Primacy of the Successor of Peter in the Mystery of the Church*. 1998.

Cooper, Adam. "History as an Ontological Experience." Paper presented at the Transcending Dualisms Conference, John Paul II Institute for Marriage and Family, Melbourne, May 10, 2014.

Cordes, Paul. Address to Mark the Release of *Caritas in Veritate*. Australian Catholic University, Sydney. 2009.

Cyril of Alexandria. *Commentary on the Gospel of St. John* (Lib. 12,1: PG, 74:707–10).

Daniélou, Jean. *Das Geheimnis vom Kommen des Herrn*. Frankfurt am Main: Verlag Josef Knecht, 1951.

———. "Missionary Nature of the Church." In *The Word in the Third World*, edited by James P. Cotter, 11–43. Washington, DC: Corpus Books, 1968.

Davis, Charles. "Theology and Praxis." *Cross Currents* 23, no. 2 (Summer 1973): 154–68.

Day, Dorothy. "In Peace Is My Bitterness Most Bitter." *Catholic Worker* 33, no. 4 (January 1967): 1–2.

Doumit, Monica. "The Day I became a 'Crumb Maiden.'" *The Catholic Weekly.* Archdiocese of Sydney. July 14, 2022. https://www.catholicweekly.com.au/monica-doumit-the-day-i-became-a-crumb-maiden/.

Dulles, Avery. *Models of the Church.* New York: Doubleday, 1978.

Felluga, Dino Franco. *Critical Theory: The Key Concepts.* London: Routledge, 2002.

Francis. Address to the International Theological Commission. Hall of Popes. December 6, 2013.

———. *Amoris Laetitia.* 2016.

———. *Evangelii Gaudium.* 2013.

———. *Lumen Fidei.* 2013.

Fulkerson, Mary McClintock, and Sheila Briggs, eds. *The Oxford Handbook of Feminist Theology.* Oxford: Oxford University Press, 2014.

Geuss, Raymond. *The Idea of a Critical Theory: Habermas and the Frankfurt School.* Cambridge University Press, 1981.

Görres, Albert. "Glaubensgewissheit in einer pluralistischen Welt." *IKaZ* 12 (1983): 117–32.

Gottfried, Paul Edward. *After Liberalism: Mass Democracy in the Managerial State.* Princeton University Press, 2001.

Grillmeier, Aloys. "The Mystery of the Church." In Vorgrimler, *Commentary on the Documents of Vatican II.*

Groppe, Elizabeth Teresa. *Yves Congar's Theology of the Holy Spirit.* Oxford University Press, 2004.

Guardini, Romano. "Herz Jesu." *Wahrheit und Ordnung* 22 (Herbst, 1955): 527.

Guarino, Thomas. "Postmodernity and Five Fundamental Theological Issues." *Theological Studies* 57, no. 4, (December 1996): 654–90.

Haecker, Theodor. *Virgil: Father of the West.* London: Sheed and Ward, 1934.

Hanby, Michael. *Augustine and Modernity.* London: Routledge, 2003.

Henry, Paul. "Christian Philosophy of History." *Theological Studies* 13, no. 1 (March 1952): 419–32.

Herbstrith, Waltraud. *Edith Stein: A Biography.* San Francisco: Harper & Row, 1985.

Hilkert, Mary Catherine. "The Threatened *Humanus* as *Imago Dei*: Anthropology and Christian Ethics." In Boeve, Depoortere, and van Erp, *Edward Schillebeeckx,* 127–142.

Hoskins, Gregory. "Interview with Lieven Boeve." *Journal of Philosophy and Scripture* 3, no. 2 (Spring 2006): 31–37.

von Hildebrand, Dietrich. *Celibacy and the Crisis of Faith*. Chicago: Franciscan Herald, 1971.

International Theological Commission. *Sensus Fidei*. In the Life of the Church. 2014.

———. *Synodality in the Life and Mission of the Church*. 2018.

Jaki, Stanley. *Theology of Priestly Celibacy*. West Chester, PA: Christendom, 1997.

John Paul II. Apostolic Journey to Poland: Address to the World of Culture, *Aula Magna* of the Catholic University of Lublin, June 9, 1987.

———. *Apostolos Suos*. 1988.

———. *Christifideles Laici*. 1988.

———. *Dives in Misericordia*. 1980.

———. *Pastores Dabo Vobis*. 1992.

———. *Redemptor Hominis*. 1979.

———. *Salvifici Doloris*. 1984.

Kasper, Walter. "On the Church: A Friendly Reply to Cardinal Ratzinger." *The Tablet* 255 (June 23, 2001): 927–30.

Kołakowski, Leszek. *Main Currents of Marxism*. Vol. 3, *The Breakdown*. Oxford: Clarendon Press, 1978.

Koster, Mannes D. *Ekklesiologie im Werden*. Paderborn: Bonifatius-Druckerei, 1940.

Kress, Robert. "Praxis and Liberation." *Communio* 6, no. 1 (Spring 1979): 113–34.

Küng, Hans. *Reforming the Church Today: Keeping Hope Alive*. New York: Crossroad, 1990.

———. *Structures of the Church*. London: Burns & Oates, 1965.

La Potterie, Ignace de. "L'Esprit Saint et l'Église." In *Credo in Spiritum Sanctum. Atti del Congresso teologico internazionale pneumatologia*, vol. I, 791–808. Edited by J. Saraiva Martins. Roma, 22–26 marzo 1982. Libreria Editrice Vaticana, Città del Vaticano, 1983.

La Soujeole, Benoît-Dominique de. *Introduction to the Mystery of the Church*. Washington, DC: Catholic University of America Press, 2014.

Lefsrud, Sigurd. *Kenosis in Theosis: An Exploration of Balthasar's Theology of Deification*. Eugene, OR: Pickwick Publications, 2020.

Le Guillou, Marie-Joseph. "Le développement de la doctrine sur l'Esprit Saint dans les écrits du Nouveau Testament." In *Credo in Spiritum Sanctum. Atti del Congresso teologico internazionale pneumatologia*, vol. I, 729–39. Edited by J. Saraiva Martins. Roma, 22–26 marzo 1982. Libreria Editrice Vaticana, Città del Vaticano, 1983.

———. *Les Témoins sont parmi nous. L'expérience de Dieu dans l'Esprit Saint*. Paris: Fayard, 1976.

———. *L'expérience de l'Esprit-Saint en Orient et en Occident*. Saint-Maur, France: Parole et Silence, 2000.

Lee, James Ambrose, II. "Shaping Reception: Yves Congar's Reception of Johann Adam Möhler." *New Blackfriars* 92 (2016): 693–72.

Leo XIII. *Divinum Illud Munus*. 1897.

Lobkowicz, Nikolas. *Theory and Practice: History of a Concept from Aristotle to Marx*. Notre Dame, IN: University of Notre Dame Press, 1967.

de Lubac, Henri. *Catholicism: Christ and the Common Destiny of Man*. San Francisco: Ignatius Press, 1988.

———. *The Motherhood of the Church*. San Francisco: Ignatius Press, 1982.

———. *Paradoxes of Faith*. San Francisco: Ignatius Press, 1987.

———. *La révélation divine*. Paris: Cerf, 1968.

———. *The Splendor of the Church*. San Francisco: Ignatius Press, 1999.

MacIntyre, Alasdair. *Three Rival Versions of Moral Enquiry*. London: Duckworth, 1990.

———. "Social Science Methodology as the Ideology of Bureaucratic Authority." In *Through the Looking Glass: Epistemology and the Conduct of Inquiry*, edited by Maria J. Falco, 42–58. Seattle, WA: Washington University Press, 1979.

Maier, Hans. "Vom Getto der Emanzipation. Kritik der 'demokratisierten' Kirche." *Hochland* 62 (1970): 385–99.

Marcuse, Herbert. *One Dimensional Man: Studies in the Ideology of Advanced Industrial Society*. London: Taylor and Francis, 2013.

McGregor, Peter. *Heart to Heart: The Spiritual Christology of Joseph Ratzinger*. Eugene, OR: Pickwick Publications, 2016.

McInerny, Brendan. *The Trinitarian Theology of Hans Urs von Balthasar*. Notre Dame, IN: University of Notre Dame Press, 2020.

McManus, Kathleen. "Suffering, Resistance and Hope: Women's Experience of Negative Contrast and Christology." In Boeve, Depoortere, and van Erp, *Edward Schillebeeckx*, 111–26.

Melina, Livio. *Sharing in Christ's Virtues: For the Renewal of Moral Theology in the Light of Veritatis Splendor*. Translated by William E. May. Washington, DC: Catholic University of America Press, 2001.

Meszaros, Andrew. *The Prophetic Church: History and Doctrinal Development in John Henry Newman and Yves Congar*. Oxford: Oxford University Press, 2016.

Milbank, John. *Being Reconciled: Ontology and Pardon*. London: Routledge, 2003.

Möhler, Johann Adam. *Unity in the Church, or, The Principles of Catholicism: Presented in the Spirit of the Church Fathers of the First Three Centuries*. Translated by Peter C. Erb. Washington, DC: Catholic University of America Press, 2016.

Müller, Gerhard. "Cardinal Müller Discusses President Biden, Pro-Abortion Politicians, and the Bishops." Interview by Cardinal Müller to kath.net. *Catholic World Report*. January 28, 2021. https://www.catholicworldreport.com/

2021/01/28/cardinal-muller-discusses-president-biden-pro-abortion-politicians-and-the-bishops/.

———. "Development, or Corruption?" *First Things*. February 20, 2018. https://www.firstthings.com/web-exclusives/2018/02/development-or-corruption.

Nachef, Antoine E. *The Mystery of the Trinity in the Theological Thought of Pope John Paul II*. New York: Peter Lang, 1999.

Newman, John Henry. *Certain Difficulties Felt by Anglicans in Catholic Teaching Considered*. London: Longmans, Green & Co, 1894.

———. "On Consulting the Faithful in Matters of Doctrine." *The Rambler* (July 1859).

———. *The Heart of Newman: A Synthesis*. Edited by Erich Przywara. San Francisco: Ignatius Press, 1997.

———. "The Orthodoxy of the Body of the Faithful during the Supremacy of Arianism." *Newman Reader*. https://www.newmanreader.org/works/arians/note5.html.

Nicholas, Marc. *Jean Daniélou's Doxological Humanism: Trinitarian Contemplation and Humanity's True Vocation*. Eugene, OR: Pickwick Publications, 2012.

Nichols, Aidan. *Figuring out the Church: Her Marks, and Her Masters*. San Francisco: Ignatius Press, 2013.

———. *Holy Order: Apostolic Priesthood from the New Testament to the Second Vatican Council*. Dublin: Veritas, 1990.

del Noce, Augusto. *The Age of Secularization*. Montreal: McGill-Queen's University Press, 2017.

O'Grady, Desmond. *The Turned Card: Christianity Before and After the Wall*. Chicago: Loyola, 1997.

Onuoha, Martin. Actio Divina: *The Marian Mystery of the Church in the Theology of Joseph*. New York: Peter Lang, 2021.

Parsons, Susan Frank, ed. *The Cambridge Companion to Feminist Theology*. Cambridge: Cambridge University Press, 2002.

Paul VI. *Ecclesiae Sanctae*. Roma: Libreria Editrice Vaticana, 1966.

———. *Sacerdotalis Caelibatus*. Roma: Libreria Editrice Vaticana, 1967.

Pieper, Josef. *Tradition: Concept and Claim*. Wilmington, DE: ISI Books, 2008.

Pius XII. *Mystici Corporis Christi*. Roma: Libreria Editrice Vaticana, 1943.

Pole, Reginald. *De summo pontifice Christi in terris vicario eiusque officio potestate liber vere*. Gregg Press International, 1969.

Pseudo-Chrysostom. Homily VI for Holy Week. PG, 9:743–46.

Rahner, Karl. *The Shape of the Church to Come*. London: SPCK, 1974.

———. *The Trinity*. New York: Herder & Herder, 1970.

———. "Zur scholastiischen Begrifflichkeit der ungeschaffenen Gnade." *Zeitschrift für katholische Theologie* 63 (1939): 137–57.

Ratzinger, Joseph. *Called to Communion: Understanding the Church Today*. San Francisco: Ignatius Press, 1996.

―――. *Church, Ecumenism, and Politics: New Essays in Ecclesiology*. New York: St. Paul Publications, 1988.

―――. *Church, Ecumenism, and Politics: New Endeavors in Ecclesiology*. San Francisco: Ignatius Press, 2008.

―――. "Demokratische Auslegung der Grundelement des Kirchen-Begriffs." In Ratzinger and Maier, *Demokratie in der Kirche*.

―――. "Demokratisierung der Kirche—Dreissig Jahre Danach." In Ratzinger and Maier, *Demokratie in der Kirche*, 78–92.

―――. "Der Ausgangspunkt vom Begriff der Demokratie." Chapter 1 in Ratzinger and Maier, *Demokratie in der Kirche*.

―――. *The Divine Project: Reflections on Creation and the Church*. San Francisco: Ignatius Press, 2023.

―――. *Dogma and Preaching: Applying Christian Doctrine to Daily Life*. San Francisco: Ignatius Press, 2011.

―――. "The Ecclesiology of the Second Vatican Council." *Communio: International Catholic Review* 13, no. 3 (Fall 1986): 239–52.

―――. "The Ecclesiology of the Second Vatican Council." In *Joseph Ratzinger in Communio*. Vol. 1, *The Unity of the Church*. Grand Rapids, MI: Eerdmans, 2010.

―――. "Europe and the Crisis of Cultures." *Communio: International Catholic Review* 32 (Summer 2005): 345–56.

―――. Foreword to *The Organic Development of the Liturgy: The Principles of Liturgical Reform and their Relation to the Twentieth-Century Liturgical Movement Prior to the Second Vatican Council*, by Alcuin Reid. San Francisco: Ignatius Press, 2005.

―――. "General Audience." Saint Irenaeus of Lyons. Vatican. March 28, 2007.

―――. "Glaube, Geschichte und Philosophie Zum Echo auf meine 'Einführung in das Christentum.'" In *Gesammelte Schriften*, vol. 4, 323–39. Freiburg: Herder & Herder, 2014.

―――. *Gesammelte Schriften*. Vol. 9. Freiburg: Herder & Herder, 2016.

―――. *Images of Hope: Meditations of Major Feasts*. San Francisco: Ignatius Press, 2006.

―――. *Introduction to Christianity*. San Francisco: Ignatius Press, 1990.

―――. "The Local Church and the Universal Church: A Response to Walter Kasper." *America: The Jesuit Review* 185, no. 16 (November 19, 2001): 7–11.

―――. *Many Religions, One Covenant: Israel, the Church and the World*. San Francisco: Ignatius Press, 1992.

―――. *The Nature and Mission of Theology: Approaches to Understanding Its Role in the Light of Present Controversy*. San Francisco: Ignatius Press, 1995.

——. Preface to *The Organic Development of the Liturgy*, by Alcuin Reid. Farnborough: St. Michael's Abbey Press, 2004.

——. "Presentation on the Occasion of the First Centenary of the Death of Cardinal John Henry Newman." April 28, 1990. Rome.

——. *Principles of Catholic Theology: Building Stones for a Fundamental Theology*. San Francisco: Ignatius Press, 1987.

——. *The Ratzinger Report*. San Francisco: Ignatius Press, 1985.

——. *Salt of the Earth: The Church at the End of the Millennium. Interview with Peter Seewald*. San Francisco: Ignatius Press, 1997.

——. *The Spirit of the Liturgy*. San Francisco: Ignatius Press, 2000.

——. *Theology of the Liturgy: Collected Works*. Vol. 11. San Francisco: Ignatius Press, 2014.

——. "The Transmission of Divine Revelation." In Vorgrimler, *Commentary on the Documents of Vatican II*.

——. *Truth and Tolerance: Christian Belief and World Religions*. San Francisco: Ignatius Press, 2004.

——. *Why I Am Still in the Church*. In *Two Say Why*, by Joseph Ratzinger and Hans Urs von Balthasar. Chicago: Franciscan Herald Press, 1973.

——, and Hans Maier. *Demokratie in der Kirche: Möglichkeiten und Grenzen*. Limburg: Lahn-Verlag, 2000.

Rowland, Tracey. "Between the Theory and the Praxis of the Synodal Process." *The Thomist* 87, no. 2 (April 2023): 233–54.

——. *Catholic Theology*. London: Bloomsbury, 2017.

——. "On the Development of Doctrine: A Via Media between Intellectualism and Historicism." In *A Guide to John Henry Newman: His Life and Thought*, edited by Juan R. Vélez, 352–72. Washington, DC: Catholic University of America Press, 2022.

Ruddy, Christopher. *The Local Church: Tillard and the Future of Catholic Ecclesiology*. New York: Herder and Herder, 2006.

Salatino, Kevin. "The Frescoes of Fra Angelico for the Chapel of Nicholas V: Art and Ideology in Renaissance Rome." PhD diss., University of Pennsylvania, 1992.

Sarah, Robert. *He Gave Us So Much*. San Francisco: Ignatius Press, 2023.

Saward, John. "Chesterton and Balthasar: The Likeness is Greater." *The Chesterton Review* 22.3 (August 1996): 301–25.

Scannone, Juan Carlos. "El papa Francisco y la teologia del pueblo." *Razón y Fe* 217 (2015): 31–50.

Schillebeeckx, Edward. *Clerical Celibacy Under Fire*. London: Macmillan, 1895. First published, London: Sheed and Ward, 1968.

———. *The Understanding of Faith: Interpretation and Criticism*. London: Sheed & Ward, 1974.

Schindler, David L. "David Schindler on Cardinal Ratzinger's Ecclesiology." Interview with editor of *Communio*. *Zenit*. May 1, 2005. https://zenit.org/2005/05/01/david-schindler-on-cardinal-ratzinger-s-ecclesiology/.

———. "The Catholic Academy and the Order of Intelligence: The Dying of the Light?" *Communio: International Catholic Review* 26 (Winter 1999): 722–45.

Schmidt, Ernst A. "The German Recovery of Vergil in the Early Years of the 20th Century (1900–1938)." *Vergilius* 54 (2008): 124–49.

Schumacher, Michele M. *A Trinitarian Anthropology: Adrienne von Speyr and Hans Urs von Balthasar in Dialogue with Thomas Aquinas*. Washington, DC: Catholic University of America Press, 2014.

Scola, Angelo. "'Claim' of Christ, 'Claim' of the World: On the Trinitarian Encyclicals of John Paul II." *Communio: International Catholic Review* 18 (Fall 1991): 322–31.

Second Vatican Council. Decree Concerning the Pastoral Office of Bishops in the Church *Christus Dominus*. October 28, 1965. *Vatican*.

———. Dogmatic Constitution on the Church *Lumen Gentium*. November 21, 1964. *Vatican*.

———. Decree on the Ministry and Life of Priests *Presbyterorum Ordinis*. December 7, 1965. *Vatican*.

Shakespeare, Lyndon. *Being the Body of Christ in the Age of Management*. Eugene, OR: Cascade, 2016.

Söhngen, Gottlieb. *Humanität und Christentum*. Essen: Augustin Wibbelt Verlagsgesellschaft, 1946.

———. *Symbol und Wirklichkeit im Kultmysterium*. Bonn: Peter Hanstein Verlagsbuchhandlung, 1937.

Spaemann, Robert. "Weltethos als 'Projekt.'" *Merkur* 50 (1996): 893–904.

Steinbüchel, Theodore. *Friedrich Nietzsche. Eine christliche Besinnung*. Stuttgart: Deutsche Verlags-Anstalt, 1946.

Stickler, Alfons. *The Case for Clerical Celibacy: Its Historical Development and Theological Foundations*. San Francisco: Ignatius Press, 1995.

Sullivan, Francis A. "The Teaching Authority of Episcopal Offices." *Theological Studies* 63 (2002): 472–93.

Talbot, George. Letter to the Archbishop of Westminster. April 25, 1867. Cited in *Life of Cardinal Manning: Archbishop of Westminster*, vol. 2, by Edmund Sheridan Purcell. London: Forgotten Books, 2018.

van Vliet, Cornelis Th. M. *Communio sacramentalis: Das Kirchenverständnis von Yves Congar—genetisch und systematisch betrachtet*. Mainz: Matthias-Grünewald, 1995.

Voderholzer, Rudolf. "Joseph Ratzinger's Martyrological Understanding of Papal Primacy: A Key for Unresolved Ecumenical Problems." In *Joseph Ratzinger and the Healing of the Reformation-Era Divisions*, 1–17. Edited by Emery de Gaál and Matthew Levering. Steubenville, OH: Emmaus Academic, 2019.

Vorgrimler, Herbert, ed. *Commentary on the Documents of Vatican II*. Vol. 1. New York: Herder & Herder, 1969.

Walker, Adrian. "Christ and Cosmology: Methodological Considerations for Catholic Educators." *Communio: International Catholic Review* 28.3 (Fall 2001): 429–49.

Weigel, George. "Pope Francis is Playacting Realpolitik." *Foreign Policy*. February 15, 2018. https://foreignpolicy.com/2018/02/15/pope-francis-is-playacting-realpolitik/.

Wojtyła, Karol. *In God's Hands*: *The Spiritual Diaries of Pope St. John Paul II*. New York: Harper Collins, 2017.

Wu, Venus. "Cardinal Says Vatican-China Deal Would Put Catholics in Communist Cage." *Reuters World News*. February 10, 2018. https://www.reuters.com/article/idUSKBN1FT283/.

Zen, Joseph. *For Love of My People I Will Not Remain Silent: On the Situation of the Church in China*. San Francisco: Ignatius Press, 2019.

Zizioulas, John D. "The Teaching of the Second Ecumenical Council on the Holy Spirit in Historical and Ecumenical Perspective." In *Credo in Spiritum Sanctum. Atti del Congresso teologico internazionale pneumatologia*, 29–53. Edited by J. Saraiva Martins. Roma, 22–26 marzo 1982. Libreria Editrice Vaticana, Città del Vaticano, 1983.

Index of Names

Index of Subjects